CW00983952

Theory and Practice in Heritage and Sustainability

This book views heritage as a process that contributes through cultural sustainability to human well-being and socially- and culturally-sensitive policy. By examining the interactions between people and communities in the places where they live it exemplifies from a broad interdisciplinary perspective the diverse ways in which a people-centred heritage builds identities and supports individual and collective memories.

With theoretically-informed case studies from leading researchers, the book addresses both concepts and practice, in a range of places and contexts including landscape, townscape, museums, industrial sites, everyday heritage, 'ordinary' places and the local scene, and even UNESCO-designated sites. The contributors, most of whom, like the editors, were members of the COST Action 'Investigating Cultural Sustainability', demonstrate in a cohesive way how the cultural values that people attach to place are enmeshed with issues of memory, identity and aspiration and how they therefore stand at the centre of sustainability discourse and practice. The cases are drawn from many parts of Europe, but notably from the Baltic, and central and south-eastern Europe, regions with distinctive recent histories and cultural approaches, and heritage discourses that offer less well-known but transferable insights. They all illustrate the contribution that dealing with the inheritance of the past can make to a full cultural engagement with sustainable development.

An introductory framework to guide readers opens the book, and a concluding section draws on the case studies to emphasise their transferability and specificity, and outlines their potential contribution to future research, practice and policy in cultural sustainability. This is a unique offering for postgraduate students, researchers and professionals interested in heritage management, governance and community participation and cultural sustainability.

Elizabeth Auclair is Assistant Professor in the geography department at Cergy-Pontoise University, France, where she is director of a master's degree on cultural development and heritage valorisation. **Graham Fairclough** is a Principal Research Associate in the McCord Centre for Historic and Cultural Landscape in Newcastle University, UK, having previously worked for English Heritage (one of the UK's national heritage agencies) and its predecessors until 2012.

Routledge Studies in Culture and Sustainable Development

Series Editors:

Katriina Soini

University of Jyväskylä, Finland, and Natural Resources Institute Finland

Joost Dessein

Institute for Agricultural and Fisheries Research (ILVO) and Ghent University, Belgium

Culture as an aspect of sustainability is a relatively new phenomenon but is beginning to attract attention among scholars and policy makers. This series opens up a forum for debate about the role of culture in sustainable development, treating culture and sustainability as a meta-narrative that will bring together diverse disciplines. Key questions explored in this series will include: how should culture be applied in sustainability policies; what should be sustained in culture; what should culture sustain; and what is the relationship of culture to other dimensions of sustainability?

Books in the series will have a variety of geographical foci and reflect different disciplinary approaches (for example geography, sociology, sustainability science, environmental and political sciences, anthropology, history, archaeology and planning). The series will be addressed in particular to postgraduate students and researchers from a wide cross-section of disciplines.

Cultural Sustainability in European Cities

Imagining Europolis

Edited by Svetlana Hristova, Milena Dragićević Šešić, and Nancy Duxbury

Theory and Practice in Heritage and Sustainability

Between past and future

Edited by Elizabeth Auclair and Graham Fairclough

Cultural Sustainability and Regional Development

Theories and practices of territorialisation

Edited by Joost Dessein, Elena Battaglini and Lummina Horlings

Theory and Practice in Heritage and Sustainability

Between past and future

**Edited by Elizabeth Auclair
and Graham Fairclough**

Routledge
Taylor & Francis Group

LONDON AND NEW YORK

publishing for a sustainable future

First published 2015
by Routledge
2 Park Square, Milton Park, Abingdon, Oxon OX14 4RN

and by Routledge
711 Third Avenue, New York, NY 10017

Routledge is an imprint of the Taylor & Francis Group, an informa business

© 2015 Elizabeth Auclair and Graham Fairclough

The right of the editors to be identified as the authors of the editorial material, and of the authors for their individual chapters, has been asserted in accordance with sections 77 and 78 of the Copyright, Designs and Patents Act 1988.

All rights reserved. No part of this book may be reprinted or reproduced or utilised in any form or by any electronic, mechanical, or other means, now known or hereafter invented, including photocopying and recording, or in any information storage or retrieval system, without permission in writing from the publishers.

Trademark notice: Product or corporate names may be trademarks or registered trademarks, and are used only for identification and explanation without intent to infringe.

British Library Cataloguing-in-Publication Data
A catalogue record for this book is available from the British Library

Library of Congress Cataloging-in-Publication Data
A catalog record for this book has been requested

ISBN: 978-1-138-77890-0 (hbk)
ISBN: 978-1-315-77161-8 (ebk)

Typeset in Times New Roman
by Saxon Graphics Ltd, Derby

MIX
Paper from
responsible sources
FSC
www.fsc.org   FSC® C013056

Printed and bound in Great Britain by
TJ International Ltd, Padstow, Cornwall

Contents

Figures and tables

Tables

Contributors

Elizabeth Auclair, M.A. in Regional Planning, Ph.D. in Geography, is an Assistant Professor at Cergy-Pontoise University (France). She is head of the 'Cultural development and heritage valorisation' Master's Studies programme, a Researcher in the geography research institute MRTE (Mobility, Networks, Territories and Environment) and coordinator of the research programme 'Social, cultural and political dynamics'. Her principal work focuses on cultural policies, sustainability and local development.

Inger Birkeland has a Ph.D. in Human Geography from the University of Oslo (2002) and is Associate Professor in cultural analysis at Telemark University College, Norway. Her research interests span cultural geography, nature–society relations, culturally sustainable development, and human place-making. Her current research focus is the sustainable use and re-use of industrial heritage. Her latest book is *Kulturelle Hjørnesteiner* (Cappelen Damm Akademisk, 2014) on social learning for sustainability and cultural regeneration of a post-industrial region in southern Norway.

Nikolaos Boukas holds a Ph.D. in Management Studies from the University of Exeter, UK. He is an Assistant Professor of Hospitality and Tourism Management, the Coordinator of the BBA in Hotel, Tourism and Event Management at the European University Cyprus in Nicosia, and the Director of the Center for Sustainable Management of Tourism, Sport and Events (CESMATSE). His research interests are related to cultural tourism, tourist behaviour, destination planning policy and island tourism.

Alexandra Bounia, Ph.D., is an Associate Professor of Museology at the University of the Aegean, Greece, Department of Cultural Technology and Communication. She studied archaeology and history of art at the University of Athens and museum studies at the University of Leicester, UK. Her research interests are on the history, theory and management of collections and museums, the interpretation of material culture, and the use of new media in museums. She has published in Greek and international journals and participates in research projects in Greece and abroad.

Mariusz Czepczyński is a Cultural Geographer working as Professor at the Department of Spatial Management at the University of Gdańsk, Poland. His research focuses on cultural landscapes, post-socialist cities, quality of life, and local and regional development. Major publications include *Cultural Landscape of Post-Socialist Cities: Representation of Powers and Needs* (Ashgate, 2008); *The City during the Times of Transformation: Experiencing 20 Years of Self-Governance in Gdansk* (ed., 2011, in Polish); *Spaces of the Post-Socialist Cities: Social Transformations of Urban Areas* (ed., 2006, in Polish); *Featuring the Quality of Urban Life in Contemporary Cities of Eastern and Western Europe* (co-ed. with I. Sagan, 2004).

Michał Czepczyński is a Political Scientist and Cultural Anthropologist, a graduate in Political Science and Ethnology at the University of Szczecin, Poland. His research interests are focused on symbolic and mythical dimension of politics, identity and ethnic minorities in post-socialist states and historic policy. His publications include *A Tale of Two (and a half) Cities: Historic Narration in the Urban Landscape of Koszalin* (ed., 2010, in Polish); *Opportunities and Threats for Ethnic Parties in the Post Socialism Era: The Example of the Crimean Tatar Organization Milli Firka* (ed. 2010, in Polish).

Nevena Daković, Ph.D., is Head of Art and Media Interdisciplinary Ph.D. Studies and Professor of Film Studies at the University of Arts in Belgrade and is a visiting professor at several universities (Oxford, Nottingham, Ankara, Ljubljana, Istanbul, etc.), and a member of several research groups in Serbia, the UK, Bulgaria, Sweden and Norway. She is author and co-author of several books (*Balkan as (Film) Genre: Text, Nation, Representation*, 2008), editor and co-editor of international publications (*Media(ted) Identities*, 2001) and author of over fifty articles.

Graham Fairclough is a Principal Research Associate in the McCord Centre of Historic and Cultural Landscape in Newcastle University (UK). An archaeologist by initial training, he worked for many years in practice and policy at the UK Heritage Board 'English Heritage' and increasingly since 1990 in the realms of interdisciplinary landscape research, and is co-editor of the journal *Landscapes*. He has worked with the Council of Europe on the European Landscape and the Faro Conventions, and is currently co-ordinator of the EC JPI Cultural Heritage-funded network 'CHeriScape'.

Anne Hertzog is Assistant Professor in Geography at Cergy-Pontoise University, France. She works on uses of the past in socio-spatial organisations. Her recent research and publication are focused on heritage processes and cultural tourism politics and practices in relation to war heritage in contemporary Europe, and the territorialisation of urban heritage through museums. She also works in memory studies in a post-colonial perspective.

Henry Johnson is Professor of Music at the University of Otago, New Zealand. His research interests are in island studies, Asian studies and ethnomusicology, and he has carried out field research in a number of island cultures in Europe, Asia and Australasia. His books include *The Koto* (2004), *Asia in the Making of New Zealand* (2006, co-edited), *Performing Japan* (2008, co-edited), *The Shamisen* (2010), and *The Shakuhachi* (2014). His publications in the field of island studies have appeared in *Shima, Journal of Marine and Island Cultures*, and *Island Studies Journal*. He is from Jersey.

Linda Kaljundi is a research fellow at the Institute of History, Tallinn University, Estonia. Her research interests include medieval and early modern historiography on the colonisation and 'otherness' of the Baltic and Nordic regions, and cultural memory studies with a focus on young nationalisms and intermediality.

Rachael Kiddey has just finished her Ph.D. at the University of York. She works part-time as an Editorial Assistant for Outreach and P.R. for the Independent Social Research Foundation (www.isrf.org) and is currently applying for post-doctoral funding to continue her research into the social relevance and usefulness of collaborative heritage work.

Leen Kosatka obtained the degree of Art Science in 2003 at the University of Ghent. After a year's internship at the East Flanders provincial service for monuments and landscapes service, and a scholarship in Italian art history and urban design at the University of Siena, she gained an interdisciplinary M.Sc. in 2013 from the Artesis Hogeschool in Antwerp in the revalorisation of monuments and landscapes with a thesis under the supervision of Maria Leus on 'Sustainable heritage management as an engine for social revaluation of a historic site'.

Maria Leus has been Professor at the Faculty of Architecture at Hasselt University, Belgium, since 1989. Over the years she has supervised several master's and doctoral theses in cultural heritage and has acted on the committee of numerous other postgraduate programmes. Her current scientific research focuses on projects relating to the re-use and revalorisation of monuments and sites. This activity has translated into publications and lectures at international congresses.

Anka Mišetić, Ph.D., is an academic and research expert who has twenty years of professional experience in the field of urban sociology. She is Professor at the Faculty of Architecture, University of Zagreb. Her research interest is mainly in the development of the social sustainability concept and re-examination of the role of different social actors in post-modern processes of urban transformation. She has participated in a number of projects, as well as research related to quality of life and town planning, as project leader or researcher.

Mirjana Nikolić, Ph.D., is Director of the Research Institute and Professor at the Department for Management and Production of Theatre, Radio and Culture at the

Faculty of Dramatic Arts in Belgrade. She is a member of the editorial board and co-editor of a number of publications, and has published three books and over thirty articles in scientific and professional publications.

Hannes Palang is Professor of Human Geography and Head of the Centre of Landscape and Culture at Tallinn University, Estonia, where he runs the research programme entitled 'Culturescapes in transition'. His research focuses on landscape and culture.

Anna Laura Palazzo is a Civil Engineer, Associate Professor in Urban Planning at Roma Tre University of Rome, and Vice-coordinator of the Ph.D. programme 'Landscapes of the contemporary city – policies, techniques and visual studies'. She holds a Ph.D. in Urban and Territorial Planning and an M.Sc. in Investigation and Restoration of Monuments. She is involved in national and international research networks concerning regional development, urban regeneration, heritage and landscape planning, and has published several books, peer-reviewed articles and international research reports.

Anu Printsmann, M.Sc., is a researcher in landscape studies at the Centre for Landscape and Culture, Estonian Institute of Humanities, Tallinn University. Trained in geo-informatics, cartography and human geography, her current specialisations are in historical geography, heritage studies, landscape perception and values, collaborative landscape planning, cognitive modelling, moral geography, and life stories.

Antonio Pugliano, Architect, is Associate Professor in Restoration at Roma Tre University of Rome, is a member of the MiBAC-ICCD Scientific Committee, and is involved in scientific activities at the universities of Malaga, Cordoba, Caceres-Extremadura, and Politecnica de Madrid. He is an expert in philological restoration, and has planned the restoration of ancient, medieval and modern monuments and the enhancement of historical and archaeological urban sites. He is the author of numerous publications, including a major thesaurus of architectural terms, and is a member of several international journal scientific committees.

Ljiljana Rogač Mijatović, Ph.D., is a research fellow and lecturer in cultural policy and theory of arts and media at the University of Arts in Belgrade and is coordinator of the research project on memory and identity discourses at the Faculty of Dramatic Arts. She has published several papers in academic reviews and journals.

John Schofield is Head of the Department of Archaeology at the University of York. He was previously an archaeologist with English Heritage, an organisation he joined following his Ph.D. in 1989 and where he remained until 2010. John is a Fellow of the Society of Antiquaries of London, a member of the Institute for Archaeologists and a Docent in Cultural Heritage, Landscape and Contemporary

Archaeology at the University of Turku (Finland). He has published extensively in the fields of cultural heritage, archaeology of the recent and contemporary pasts, and the archaeology of conflict.

Theopisti Stylianou-Lambert, Ph.D., is an Assistant Professor at the Cyprus University of Technology and the Visual Sociology and Museum Studies Lab (ww.vsmslab.com). She has published widely on museums, photography and tourism. She is the co-editor of *Re-envisioning Cyprus* (2010) and *Photography and Cyprus: Time, Place and Identity* (2014). She earned her Ph.D. in Museum Studies from the University of Leicester and has received several awards and scholarships including a Smithsonian Institute Fellowship (USA), an Arts and Humanities Research Council Award (UK) and a Fulbright Scholarship (USA).

Sara Ursić, Ph.D., is a junior researcher in the Ivo Pilar Institute of Social Sciences in Croatia. She obtained her M.A. in Sociology and Anthropology at the Faculty of Humanities and Social Sciences, Zagreb, and in 2014 a Ph.D. in Sociology. Her scientific interest is in the field of urban sociology and urban planning, with emphasis on suburban and edge spaces. She has published several scientific papers and one book. As part of the scientific team in the Institute of Social Sciences Ivo Pilar, she has worked on projects in the field of urban sociology as well as on projects related to urban planning and quality of life.

Tõnu Viik is a Professor of Philosophy at Tallinn University, Estonia, and previous and currently acting director of the Estonian Institute of Humanities. He graduated from Moscow State University and received his Ph.D. from Emory University, Atlanta, USA. His present research is devoted to cultural phenomenology, focusing on socially conditioned meaning-formation processes.

COST – European Cooperation in Science and Technology

This publication is supported by COST.

COST – European Cooperation in Science and Technology is an inter-governmental framework aimed at facilitating the collaboration and networking of scientists and researchers at European level. It was established in 1971 by 19 member countries and currently includes 35 member countries across Europe, and Israel as a cooperating state.

COST funds pan-European, bottom-up networks of scientists and researchers across all science and technology fields. These networks, called 'COST Actions', promote international coordination of nationally-funded research. By fostering the networking of researchers at an international level, COST enables breakthrough scientific developments leading to new concepts and products, thereby contributing to strengthening Europe's research and innovation capacities.

COST's mission focuses in particular on:

- *Building capacity by connecting high quality scientific communities throughout Europe and worldwide;*
- *Providing networking opportunities for early career investigators;*
- *Increasing the impact of research on policy makers, regulatory bodies and national decision makers as well as the private sector.*

Through its inclusiveness policy, COST supports the integration of research communities in less research-intensive countries across Europe, leverages national research investments and addresses societal issues.

Over 45,000 European scientists benefit from their involvement in COST Actions on a yearly basis. This allows the pooling of national research funding and helps countries research communities achieve common goals.

As a precursor of advanced multidisciplinary research, COST anticipates and complements the activities of EU Framework Programmes, constituting a "bridge" towards the scientific communities of emerging countries.

Traditionally, COST draws its budget for networking activities from successive EU RTD Framework Programmes.

COST is supported by the EU Framework Programme Horizon 2020.

Series introduction

Katriina Soini and Joost Dessein

Achieving a more sustainable level of development is the biggest global challenge of the 21st century, and new approaches are urgently needed to ensure that development is much better aligned with the environmental, societal, and economic problems we are facing. Scholars and policymakers have recognized the contribution of culture in sustainable development. The issue of culture in sustainable development is also being increasingly discussed in debates in various international, national, and local arenas, and there are ample local actor-driven initiatives. Yet despite this growing attention there have been only a very few attempts to consider culture in a more analytical and explicit way within the frames of sustainability. The challenge of incorporating culture in sustainable development discourse, both scientifically and politically, is derived from the complex, normative, and multidisciplinary character of both culture and sustainable development. This difficulty should not, however, be any excuse for ignoring the cultural dimension within sustainable development.

The series "Routledge Studies in Culture and Sustainable Development" aims to analyse the diverse and multiple roles that culture plays in sustainable development. It takes as one of its starting points the idea that culture in sustainability serves as a "meta-narrative" which will bring together ideas and standpoints from an extensive body of academic research currently scattered among different disciplines and thematic fields. Moreover, the series responds to the strengthening call for inter- and transdisciplinary approaches, which is being heard in many quarters, but in few fields more strongly than that of sustainability and sustainable development, with its complex and systemic problems. By combining and confronting the various approaches, in both the sciences and the humanities and in dealing with social, cultural, environmental, political, and aesthetic disciplines, the series offers a comprehensive contribution to the present-day sustainability sciences as well as related policies.

The books in the series will take a broad approach to culture, giving space to all the possible understandings of culture from art-based definitions to way-of-life based approaches, and beyond. Furthermore, culture is not seen only as an additional aspect of sustainable development – as a "fourth pillar" – but, rather, as a mediator, a cross-cutting transversal framework, or even as new set of guiding principles for sustainable development research, policies, and practices.

The essence of culture in, for, and as sustainable development will be explored through the series in various thematic contexts, representing a wide range of practices and processes (e.g., everyday life, livelihoods and lifestyles, landscape, artistic practices, aesthetic experiences, heritage, tourism). These contexts may concern urban, peri-urban, or rural contexts, and regions with different trajectories of socio-economic development. The perspectives of the books will stretch from local to global and cover different temporal scales from past to present and future. These issues are valorized by theoretical or empirical analysis; their relationship to the ecological, social, and economic dimensions of sustainability will be explored, when appropriate.

The idea for the series is derived from the European COST Action IS1007 "Investigating Cultural Sustainability," running between 2011 and 2015. This network is comprised of a group of around one hundred researchers from 26 European countries, and representing many different disciplines. They have brought together their expertise, knowledge, and experience, and based on that they have built up new inter- and transdisciplinary understanding and approaches that can enhance and enrich research into culture in sustainable development, and support the work of the policymakers and practitioners in this field.

Urbanization is one of the major trends guiding and affecting development both in cities as well as in surrounding regions and rural areas. Therefore, finding sustainable strategies for cities of all sizes is a fundamental challenge globally, but the focus on small and medium-sized cities allows to better understand the changing relationship between urban and rural realities. There is ample research on cities and sustainability, but unlike most of the other contributions, this book brings culture in sustainable urban development to the core: It investigates, in particular, how participatory culture and artistic expression contribute to the sustainable future(s) of the cities. By focusing on various strategies, policies, and bottom-up practices of small and medium-sized cities in Europe, the book offers a perspective to imagine sustainable future(s) for smaller European cities as well as others worldwide.

Ultimately, the book seeks to explore different models of local sustainability that incorporate emotions and attachment to one's living place and move beyond profit-driven approaches, which tend to use culture and cultural policies only as a means for embellishment of the urban environment and propelling economic viability. The book also implicitly reveals path-dependencies of the development of European cities; each city has its history, which affects its future development. At the same time, cities are not "trapped" in their past and, as the cases in this book show, the human agency, imagination, and cooperative efforts of residents can alter local development trajectories. Therefore, as the editors of the book wisely note, there are no copy-paste strategies. Rather, each city should find its own path to sustainability through innovative re-imagination of its own cultural assets and traditions and creatively applying the lessons learned elsewhere.

Living between past and future
An introduction to heritage and cultural sustainability

Elizabeth Auclair and Graham Fairclough

Heritage and sustainable development: key issues for the twenty-first century

Over a quarter of a century after coming to full public visibility, notably through the Brundtland Report of 1987, the concept of sustainable development is scarcely a new idea. Moreover, it is roughly half a century since two other milestones responsible for changing the way many people saw the future of the planet: first the publication in 1962 of Rachel Carson's prophetic and anticipatory book *Silent Spring*, and second the release of the iconic photograph, sometimes called 'Earthrise', or 'Fragile Earth', taken from an Apollo spacecraft showing our planet in all its vulnerability, and, as many have said, kick-starting the populist environmental movement.

But all these years later, how widely or fully understood is 'sustainability'? The Brundtland Report took discussion towards 'sustainable development', and led academic, scientific and political attention to concentrate on questions of environmental implementation. Is greater attention still required to its conceptual aspects, notably in the relationship between sustainability and culture, which might be argued to be root causes and central solutions? Though culture seems nowadays to be acknowledged in the discourse as a key factor of sustainability, numerous actors at international, national and local levels are still battling to integrate culture and heritage issues into agendas, and to fix them into tangible policies. A number of debates, seminars and publications – including the European network 'Investigating Cultural Sustainability' of which this book (and book series) is a product – have been addressing the growing relationship between the two concepts of culture, on the one hand, and sustainable development on the other. Definitive answers and consensus still seem slightly out of reach, however.

It appears quite crucial therefore to continue to look for ways to give a greater place to culture and heritage in sustainability. Since 2008, the particularly severe social, economic and environmental worldwide crisis raises many questions concerning the present and future of our societies; and cultural attitudes and solutions, and cultural needs and aspirations, are at the centre of most of them. What kind of development do we wish to see? For what type of progress are we aiming? Even more significantly – and in the very much longer term, the sort of *longue durée* that we learn from heritage – what will be the character and nature of the planet that we are going to provide for the next generations? What resources and materials (including the cultural products and adaptations of previous generations as well as 'natural' resources) that we have inherited from our past will we be able to transmit onwards, and in what condition, distribution and context? Questions such as this show that this global crisis can be considered as a 'cultural' crisis, but they also illustrate another crisis addressing the concept of sustainable development itself (Auclair 2010; 2011; 2014a). Indeed, the increasing social inequalities inside as well as between countries, the deterioration of the environmental and climatic situation, and the incapacity of nations to take collectively urgent decisions (i.e. the Copenhagen and Cancun conferences in 2009 and 2010, and the Rio+20 UN Summit in 2012, and as we write this, Lima 2014), raise many doubts about a concept that is supposed to solve these problems. This remains true in spite of recent declarations such as the G20 Summit in November 2014, or the China–USA agreement concerning climate issues. Against this fragile background, a strengthened cultural dimension for sustainability and for sustainable societies seems essential.

Although the value of culture for development is stated in a few recent international texts, at the start the cultural dimension of sustainability was not well indicated, and perhaps was not well recognised or accepted. The World Conference on Cultural Policies in 1982 concluded with a declaration emphasising for the first time the importance of culture for a harmonious development. In the formal documents most commonly regarded as the founding texts of the sustainable development agenda, however – the 'Brundtland' Report of 1987, and the Rio Summit Declaration and Agenda 21 of 1992 – the concept of sustainable development rested almost exclusively on ecological, social and economic dimensions, and only the protection of cultural minorities was mentioned in any significant way. Even the limited ways in which past and potential future cultural attitudes and behaviours had been factored into earlier research – for example by the Club of Rome's *Limits to Growth* of 1972 (Meadows et al. 1972) – were scarcely reflected in these documents. In 1996, however, Perez de Cuellar's report *Our Creative Diversity* for the World Commission on Culture and Development insisted on the importance of preserving the diversity of cultures and populations (UNESCO 1996). At the UN 2002 Summit in Johannesburg, the necessity to protect cultural as well as biological diversity was expressed in the introduction of the action plan (UN 2002). Even so, in spite of such discussions and statements, culture remained weakly considered in political frameworks, and was even largely invisible in the United Nations' Millennium Development Goals of 2000 (with their deadline of 2015).

Changes in attitudes at this political level only began to appear in the first decade of the twenty-first century, when the cultural dimensions of sustainability began to be more greatly acknowledged in several UNESCO and European conventions (see below). At the same time Agenda 21 for Culture began to be taken up by a number of major cities in the policy frame designed and promoted from 2004 by the umbrella association United Cities and Local Governments

(UCLG). Furthermore, UCLG through its Committee on Culture, has recently published in conjunction with three other global networks the manifesto *Culture as a Goal in the post-2015 Development Agenda* (Agenda 21 et al. 2014) and will in 2015 present an updated version of Agenda 21 for Culture to further establish the necessary link between culture and sustainable development for local policies. Perhaps as a consequence of these developments, UNESCO devoted its 2013 Congress to the theme 'Culture: Key to Sustainable Development' and the Congress's concluding statement, the 'Hangzhou Declaration', formally and strongly acknowledged culture as a central element of sustainability, indeed as being 'at the heart' of sustainable development policy (UNESCO 2013).

Within culture sits heritage of course, and the relationship between heritage and sustainable development policy has followed a similarly slow and tortuous route towards a level of recognition, from the earliest – usually at national level – reflective attitudes such as the discussion paper 'Sustaining the Historic Environment', calling for a more people-centred and participative and integrated approach to heritage (English Heritage 1997) to very much more recent global recognition of the role that heritage can play in culture and sustainability, such as the ideas embedded in the Faro Convention (Council of Europe 2005) or in UCLG's recent policy briefing 'Cultural Heritage as a Driver of Sustainability' (UCLG 2014). This is the context for the present book, part of the dialogue generated by the European network organised through the COST Action 'Investigating Cultural Sustainability' (COST 2011; Fairclough et al. 2014).

Heritage, often perceived simplistically as 'protecting the past', or even 'saving' or 'rescuing' it, is in fact as complex and elusive to define as are the words 'culture' and 'sustainability'. Within the covers of a single book such as this one there can be great diversity, fluidity and contingency in the concept, which demonstrates how both culture and 'heritage' are less any particular set of outcomes than continual processes of remaking, firmly rooted in social construction, in individual and collective perception and in their specificities of time and place. Heritage is a part of culture, as the case studies in the following pages demonstrate very well, but it also supports and transmits culture, and at the same time is culturally (and socially) defined and constructed. This cultural construction raises the somewhat problematic or at least often unresolved relationship between cultural sustainability and social sustainability. Heritage is a central thread of sustainability, not only as an issue of preservation but of creation, adaptation and resilience to change. Indeed, it is widely claimed, but not always accepted, that preserving historic buildings is inherently sustainable because it retains embodied energies and minimises the consumption of new energy and raw materials. That is, however, the least important aspect of the relationship of heritage to sustainability. More important is the cultural and social contribution that heritage makes every day to how lives are lived, and to the ways in which identities and relationships are formed.

Individuals and communities unavoidably live amidst the legacy of their predecessors, whether it is architecturally special or more mundane, whether physically significant or emotionally and symbolically important. Heritage, in this wide sense often called 'everyday heritage', is the heritage of 'home' not of 'holidays', not merely a tool for the tourist industry. It affects at a fundamental level who we think we are, how we live and how we make the future. Its key contribution to sustainability comes from the process of 'doing heritage', a cultural and social engagement with the past in order to survive the present and make the future. Thus, the concept of heritage is seen here not as a collection (whether national, European or worldwide) of special sites and objects, but as the process by which those objects – and the various associations they have for us, the memories they embody and the narratives they support – make us who we are, colour how we interact, and shape the futures that we can envisage and might create.

In planning this book, we sought case studies from many parts of Europe that could illuminate the connections and interactions between people and communities in the places where they live, and the ways in which these contribute through cultural modes and behaviours to sustainability at several levels. We expected the chapters in the book to lead us, as they have done, from heritage 'pure and simple' to the concept of 'place', and onwards towards 'landscape' more widely (landscape in the sense of areas perceived by people and of areas shared collectively by people through experience, performance and lifeways, cf. ESF/COST 2010). In this way, we hoped to exemplify the many and diverse ways in which heritage is used to forge identities and to support and create memory, individually and collectively. The extremely broad span (both potential and real) of current understandings of heritage, in both tangible and intangible manifestations, required us to focus the collection on particular dimensions of heritage. The key area of concern that emerged is the so-called 'everyday' lived heritage, the heritage of place and of political and community interactions, which affects everyone and in that sense is more truly 'cultural' than a distant World Heritage Site (WHS) visited as a 'lifetime leisure experience'. This focus largely explains the book's preoccupation with urban, city or post-industrial contexts, where the majority of the population (at least in many parts of Europe) live out their lives.

This fundamental aspect of the book – the basic and all-encompassing importance of the everyday, the collectively shared, and the age-old concept of 'commons' – also reflects a trend in heritage that has been running in parallel with, and which regularly intertwines with, the growth of the sustainability discourse. It has some roots in the early discourse of sustainable development (e.g. English Heritage 1997), and is simultaneously entangled with evolving notions of landscape as *cadre de vie*, a way of seeing and interacting with each other that can help to respond to major societal and environmental challenges (ESF/COST 2010; Council of Europe 2000). This dimension of heritage theory – often termed 'critical heritage' or 'new heritage' – is still emerging but already has a substantial academic literature and growing case evidence (see, for example, Harrison 2013; Smith 2006; Fairclough 2008; 2009; Fairclough et al. 2008; Schofield and Szymanski 2010; Holtorf and Fairclough 2013) and of course, is promoted by work surrounding the Faro Convention (e.g. Council of Europe 2009). The labels attached to these 'new' ways of thinking about and practising and, more importantly, contextualising heritage in broader societal, political and cultural frames denote an intention to re-imagine heritage for the twenty-first century, an aim that can be followed through the chapters in the present book.

Cultural sustainability: a relevant outline for theory and practice

All the contributors to this book, not least in almost every case through participating in and contributing to the COST network 'Investigating Cultural Sustainability', are very conscious of the great conceptual breadth of both 'culture' and 'sustainability'. Many definitions exist, but few are widely shared. In this Introduction, for example, the term 'sustainability' is used as being more useful, and closer to what we see as the goals or context of heritage and culture, than 'sustainable development'. The lack of interpretative closure surrounding these concepts, and the lack of certainty that attaches to them could, of course, be argued to be a virtue of sorts. In general, our contributors, whether explicitly and theoretically or more indirectly through case studies that speak for themselves, have allowed their case studies to make their own contribution to defining cultural sustainability as a meaningful concept, usually based on new ways of thinking the relationship between culture and sustainable development that sets people at the core of policies and projects. The chapters highlight many aspects of cultural sustainability that help to support human well-being through socially and culturally sensitive policy and practice.

The relationship between culture and sustainable development is, of course, strongly marked by the changes that affect both sectors. The culture sector in many countries is today facing ideological as well as financial questioning. Some questions are related to the widening of culture towards a more anthropological meaning, others to the rising concepts of cultural diversity and cultural rights. Some changes are notably linked to recent UNESCO conventions. In particular, UNESCO's 2005 Convention on the Protection and Promotion of the Diversity of Cultural Expressions (UNESCO 2005) encourages a shift in the institutional representations of culture by 'taking into account that culture takes diverse forms across time and space'. In addition, many voices have been promoting culture rights during the last decade, notably through the 'Fribourg Declaration on cultural rights', which argues that the 1948 Universal Declaration of Human Rights lays insufficient emphasis on cultural rights (IIEDH 2007). However, these notions of cultural diversity and cultural rights raise difficult questions of whether all cultural traditions and behaviours deserve defence, and if not, of who decides which are not to be safeguarded, or which 'ought' to be modified. If applied without awareness, such issues risk aggravating tensions between communities (Auclair 2014b).

Culture is now generally considered as a holistic concept encapsulating the various dimensions of life, and not only through a more traditional way of viewing arts and heritage. Promoting culture is regarded as a means to support human dignity and human rights. However, these representations induce significant changes of practice for actors in institutional sectors. In addition, globalisation has also become an important matter, with fears of standardisation of culture and domination by mass culture owing to the rapid growth of cultural industries and of cultural tourism. Moreover, the financial problems linked to the progressive withdrawal of public support in favour of culture, observed in many European countries, make the cultural sector more fragile.

Besides, despite the worldwide spread of the concept of sustainable development, a number of criticisms have questioned or challenged the economic dimension that seems over-dominant in the way that the term is used, with its predominant emphasis on economic growth and consumerism, to the detriment of other types and forms of human development. Some of these criticisms are recent (Abraham et al. 2011), but the unease about defining sustainability as 'development that is durable or sustainable' – rather than as 'ways of life that are sustainable' (and of course 'ways of life' is by some definitions another way of saying 'culture' more generally) – goes back at least as far as Brundtland. The governments of 'western' countries – of whatever political inflection – turn their faces against using the word sustainability, however, insisting that growth and economic development simply need a little mitigation. In more recent years, the objectives of sustainable development have become tightly embedded in neoliberal ideology, and in the economic systems it creates, systems commonly rejected by many researchers, politicians and civil society movements.

A number of works are currently exploring alternative models of development without growth (Latouche 2007; Jackson 2009), and investigating new indicators of wealth (Méda 2008; Caillé 2012; Cobb and Venetoulis 2004; Brown 2001) as well as innovative governance tools using the rediscovered concept of commons (Bollier and Helfrich 2012). The aim is to identify values for the well-being of present and future generations and to establish new models of sustainability based on people-centred approaches and qualitative criteria, notably by using cultural indicators. Moreover, it can be argued that the concept of sustainable development, which relates to the 'essential needs' of the present and future generations, does not cover all the needs, and that cultural needs in particular are not sufficiently taken into account in public policy. One result of these critical works is – finally – the increasing use in anglophone contexts, of the term sustainability, or equity, and in francophone contexts of words such as *équilibré*, *équitable*, or *sobriété*, instead of sustainable development or *developpement durable*. We can also see that the term 'ecological and social transition' has been spreading since the 2012 Rio+20 Summit.

Consequently, cultural sustainability can be considered as a renewed theoretical structure for the relationship between culture and sustainable development. What is the aim of this relationship? Does this relationship aim at promoting sustainable development (or at 'saving its soul'), or is it viewed as a way to support culture and heritage policies? In recent years many research works have investigated this relation and highlighted different models. The suggestion of culture as the fourth pillar of sustainability, as found for example, in the work of Jon Hawkes (2001), was taken up by many researchers and actors, such as UCLG, who officially adopted this idea as a political position in 2010. Other schemes for the relationship of culture with sustainability have been studied and proposed, and are in use in various disciplines or policy contexts. A recent discourse review of cultural sustainability, carried out by members of the COST 'Investigating Cultural Sustainability' network mentioned earlier, concluded that

> a number of story lines are at play through which cultural sustainability is articulated in the scientific literature, indicating that it is at an early stage in its conceptual evolution. ... under the umbrella of cultural sustainability, there is a range of representations of political ideologies, from conservatism to liberalism to communitarianism and environmentalism that express solutions ...
>
> (Soini and Birkeland 2014, 221)

Simply adding culture as a fourth pillar to the existing model, therefore, as we hope the chapters in this book begin to show, is unlikely to do full justice to the complexity of cultural sustainability as a concept or, even more so, to its multiple and diverse relationships to the three pillars. After all, 'culture' in its broadest sense shapes society, governs our economic models and ambitions, and through those shapes our environment and dictates to a large degree human responses to environmental change and potential future collapse. Culture surely must be seen and used as a transversal force that informs, influences, guides and shapes or determines the economic, social and environmental dimensions of sustainability. In this view, cultural issues are naturally fundamental to all policy formation, their role merely needing to be more explicit. Put in another way, culture needs to be placed at the heart of sustainability, being the fundamental element of sustainable policies. Employing cultural sustainability as the theoretical outline for the book implicitly means focusing on this latter, embedded, approach, that is to say seeing culture as the fundamental element of sustainability which supports, interconnects and overarches the traditional three pillars, all of which, of course, exist in a cultural context, and all of which can be seen as cultural constructs.

A framework of international texts and conventions for heritage and sustainability

This book presents a number of case studies where the heritage issues are more or less directly related to the important and influential framework provided by international texts: the European Landscape Convention (the 'Florence Convention', Council of Europe 2000) and the Faro Convention on the Value of Cultural Heritage for Society (Council of Europe 2005), the ideas embedded in the UNESCO 2005 Convention on the Protection and Promotion of the Diversity of Cultural Expressions (UNESCO 2005), as well as the UNESCO 1972 and 2003 conventions relating to tangible and intangible heritage, and the UNESCO 2011 Recommendation on Historical Urban Landscapes (UNESCO 2011). However, the case studies also reflect less institutionally-founded models of heritage such as participative heritage, critical heritage and the idea of active, everyday, experiential heritage.

Practically all these international texts insist on broadening the concepts of heritage and developing people-centred approaches. According to the UNESCO 2005 Convention on the Protection and Promotion of the Diversity of Cultural Expressions, member states are expected to recognise cultural diversity and consequently the diversity of heritage and landscapes. This means acknowledging the plurality of individual and collective identities, and encouraging dialogue and exchange between generations, between neighbourhoods, and between communities both established and newly formed. This leads to an enhancement of social, economic and cultural resources that in turn can contribute to shaping territories and identities. While one of the aims of this Convention is also to withdraw culture and arts from market oriented activities within the WTO debates, Article 13 explicitly encourages member states to integrate culture into sustainable development policies.

With 'HUL' – the UNESCO 2011 Recommendation on Historical Urban Landscapes – the member states are also invited to widen the range of heritage elements to be protected, to make more use of the notion of landscape, and to promote local participation. Interestingly, this document is beginning to face criticism from within ICOMOS on exactly the same defensive if not alarmist objections that previous attempts to introduce new heritage ideas have met. This fear is that a wider canvas, more participation and a more welcoming breadth of uses/reuses for heritage will somehow undermine the gains made by historic conservation in the past half century (or less in some parts of the world). HUL has even been called 'a developer's charter' in some heated debates. But HUL of course stands on the shoulders of two Council of Europe conventions which have transformed heritage and landscape thinking and practice in the 'wide Europe' of the Council of Europe (which stretches from Russia to Ireland – and Canada, with observer status). The European Landscape Convention (ELC) considers landscapes as the result and interaction of natural and human factors, and therefore views landscapes as processes more than as products, with big implications for how landscape can be better protected, managed and planned/improved. The states party to the ELC are invited to take into consideration ordinary landscapes and not exclusively the exceptional ones, which means according greater attention to the landscapes lived in and experienced by people. The Faro Convention on the Value of Cultural Heritage for Society, the ELC sister convention, takes up the argument from that point, encouraging states to increase the role of citizens in defining, deciding and managing their cultural environment. It explicitly mentions ordinary heritage as a noteworthy category and recommends the use of specific criteria capable of placing people in the core of heritage policies and projects (Fairclough 2009; 2011). One aim is to highlight elements that support sense and identity for local populations (Wolferstan and Fairclough 2013).

All these texts aim at changing and improving heritage approaches and policies. The objective is no longer to rely only on experts for identifying and defining the aesthetic and historical values of heritage and landscape, but to analyse and inventory the elements recognised as heritage by the inhabitants themselves, what elements are meaningful for the population, and what elements reinforce the sense of place. The texts encourage a view of heritage as not simply protected 'artefacts' but more importantly as a people-centred process.

Memory, identity, place: heritage as people-centred process

This book explores new issues of heritage in the twenty-first century and demonstrates how heritage and sustainability share the broadest common ground when both are perceived first as being ongoing processes rather than immediate end-products, and second as being people-centred (culturally as well as socially) rather than object-oriented. Seeing heritage as a people-centred process, as the Faro Convention does, is crucial to articulating and encouraging cultural sustainability. Our case studies show heritage as ultimately being about intergenerational transfer and about the present-day as a bridge from past to future. Many ways in which this fusion and transmission happens are discussed, but the main focus is on how heritage functions through the concepts of place and landscape. Both these are defined as intangible constructs – perceived and occupied by people – that are drawn from a combination or amalgam of both inherited and created objects. Heritage, like cultural action, is rooted in space as well as time, and is consequently more often than not place-based, site-specific, locality-sensitive and community-contextualised. It is this everyday aspect and 'use' that makes heritage – buildings, places, townscapes, landscapes – a key component of social and cultural sustainability.

Our book's examples also analyse and reveal that distinctive but shared identities can be constructed on the basis of place as well as parenthood, of predecessors instead of ancestors, and of landscape rather than land. So heritage is seen as the interaction between people and their world, between people and communities; not primarily a set of objects 'worthy of protection' but a continuing, complex and iterative cultural and social process of definition and use, that includes the creation as well as the preservation of heritage, i.e. the cultural aspects of inheritance and change. Instead of being valued for its intrinsic worth, heritage in Europe (and particularly in central, eastern and southeastern parts of Europe) has been discovered to be valuable for conflict resolution, economic regeneration, and education for citizenship and sustainable development. This gives heritage a much greater power and influence in contemporary society. The Faro Convention suggests that rather than heritage being served by society, now heritage must serve society. This standpoint helps to ground cultural sustainability in common human experience.

The contributors to this book in several different ways reflect on the notion of place and people's various responses to it, as constructed through the interaction of heritage and culture in order to contribute to social sustainability. They highlight the cultural role of memory, especially when it is tied to the material traces of the past which help to create 'place'. More generally they underline the ways in which the heritage process contributes to the social and cultural aspects of sustainability, particularly through use of heritage as an instrument of identity and social cohesion, economic viability and good governance. So the book's principal focus is placed on the 'why' and the 'how' (but not the mere techniques) of heritage management, that is to say on the ways in which heritage is made and seen to matter to society on a wide range of fronts, from the economic to the political. It contributes ideas to the implementation of public policy and practice for sustainability supported by heritage at all levels. Doing so is a matter of some urgency at a time when in most countries the role of heritage and culture within sustainability doctrines and practice is insufficiently evident.

International and interdisciplinary ideas for practice: the structure of the book

Our book's analysis of the contribution of heritage to cultural sustainability is made through the lens of theoretically informed case studies. These all address both concepts and practical applications, in a range of places, contexts and forms. Taken as a whole, they show how the cultural values that people attach to place – and particularly in the present volume urban places and cities, for reasons mentioned earlier – are enmeshed with issues of memory, identity and place, and how they therefore stand at the centre of sustainability discourse and practice. The examples are drawn from Europe, but they all offer more universal and we hope transferable lessons that might have value to other regions of the world. They have been chosen to illustrate the particular contribution that the inheritance of the past can make to cultural engagement with sustainability.

A particular point has been made of including several chapters from Baltic, central, eastern and southeastern Europe, and from little-heard voices elsewhere. These are regions with distinctive cultural approaches, discourse and social challenges, which in recent decades have undergone difficult times, which adds value to the examination of how their heritage has been used (and abused) to forge identities and frame political action. Voices from these regions have been heard relatively rarely in global academic literature, yet they act as key laboratories for research in heritage, memory and identity, offering many lessons and ideas for other parts of the world. The book also offers an interesting interdisciplinary approach – still quite rare in academic research – as the different analyses come from the fields of sociology, philosophy, various forms of geography, musicology, heritage studies, arts and media, archaeology, and city planning.

The twelve chapters are organised in two parts, entitled 'Equity, Inclusion, Citizenship' and 'Construction, Recovery, Resilience'. The two groupings overlap, of course, not least because heritage, culture and sustainability all aim at being holistic concepts. Chapters in one part of the book also speak to issues covered in the other.

The six chapters in Part I, 'Equity, Inclusion, Citizenship', mostly connect with the themes surrounding cultural and social issues of fairness, democracy and participation (and their opposites). This first part of the book looks at various types of heritage that both embody history and support or even create memory. It explores why and how heritage can contribute to social and cultural sustainability through the development, enhancement and valorisation of a sense of place, with all that entails for a sense of belonging, ownership, community and familiarity through the creation of local identities. They show examples of the means by which social cohesion might be promoted, and how culturally sustainable heritage can be an instrument for improving quality of life. Several fundamental issues relating to 'managing' heritage (not the techniques and the tools, but the policies, objectives and strategies) are also raised in this section.

The six chapters in Part II of the book, 'Construction, Recovery, Resilience', reflect principally on ideas and valuations of heritage, and on how these are made, remade and renegotiated through complex cultural, social and political situations. They consider the role of narrative, taking into account particularly dissonant or alternative heritage, recognised or everyday heritage. They also introduce a greater time dimension – the idea of heritage is not all that young – by presenting examples of the modification or reinvention of heritage values in the long-term trajectory of history and memory. This second part also examines different attitudes to identity and community, and explores the strategies, interests and motivations that exist behind narratives and discourses.

Important and recurring themes cut across this two-part division of the book, however, and readers will encounter them in either part. In the remainder of this Introduction, therefore, to reveal some of the book's overall cohesion, we draw attention to some of the cross-cutting themes that will accompany readers as they progress, in whatever order, through the collection of chapters. Thereafter we suggest a few specific threads that might guide readers through the various case studies to our conclusions at the end of the book.

Cross-cutting themes within the case studies

Past and present political contexts for heritage theory and practice

Several chapters explore how the way that heritage is seen and how heritage is practised are dependent and contingent on specific historical, cultural and political contexts that are often specific to and distinctive of particular countries. They cover issues concerning the link between heritage and political situations, specifically the different political contexts and assumptions prevailing at different times in different countries, and analyse the evolutions due to political changes. They emphasise the importance of embedded political representations (and the stresses and tensions they cause) on the 'construction' of heritage, and examine ways of handling a past that is marked by turbulent history through overcoming conflicts, escaping nationalism and promoting local and supranational values (most obviously perhaps in places such as the Baltic, Cyprus and Belgrade – chapters 8, 9, 11 and 12 – but very similar or at least parallel issues arise or are hidden in several other contributions, such as chapters 1, 2 and 5). Some of the chapters approach this theme through analysis of the attitudes to heritage as being 'ours' or 'theirs', such oppositions being problematical and sometimes difficult to overcome; they do, however, show how change can occur over time, as in the Baltic examples (chapters 8 and 9). This theme also surfaces in those chapters that address heritage management related to pain and trauma (wars and conflicts), and tells us how cities and territories such as Cyprus and Belgrade deal with difficult memory – what parts of the past must be preserved and for whom – whilst at the same time living everyday lives.

Living heritage: taking into account the needs of present-day life

A major theme of the book is indeed the way the remains and memories of the past – heritage – not only represent the past, but live – or should live – in the present. They are the backdrop of everyday life, the landscape of people's lives, and several chapters focus on how history and heritage need to be viewed as essential components of the daily life of the population. Dealing with heritage does not mean only focusing on the past: heritage must be articulated with the needs and aspirations of modern life, most particularly perhaps in heavily populated and ever-changing wor.d heritage cities such as Rome or Brussels where the influx of temporary populations of tourists and workers brings additional complexity. Heritage of recognised high status, such as World Heritage Sites, as represented in this book by Rome, Dubrovnik, Brussels and Cyprus (an application has been made to inscribe Rjukan as well) is obviously considered as a resource for cities for a good living environment. In some cases, however, heritage preservation is also in some ways a 'burden' in the sense of being an inherited responsibility that cannot be put down. It is necessary to make sure the burden can be carried without damaging or limiting other aspects of life, such as contemporary arts and creativity, without inducing negative socio-demographic and economic changes such as deterioration, urban shrinkage or gentrification, and within a strongly cohesive social context.

The social dimensions of heritage

The idea that revealing and enhancing ordinary heritage, and at the same time pursuing people-centred rather than object-centred approaches for heritage preservation, can help community building and contribute to social cohesion and understanding, is explored in many chapters, whether in Parisian suburbs or in Rome (chapters 1 and 3), through the eyes of homeless city-dwellers (chapter 2) or in dealing with the aftermath of de-industrialisation (chapter 10), through the re-balancing of established museum policies in local museums in France or national museums in Cyprus (chapters 5 and 11) and in the 'open-air' museum that Rome sometimes appears to be (chapter 3), or to counter the slow decline of minority languages (chapter 7). In all these examples and others, we are shown ways in which sharing heritage strengthens relations between communities, between neighbourhoods and between generations. Enhancing local heritage and making people aware of and concerned about the existing heritage is viewed as a resource for the well-being of the inhabitants (most dramatically perhaps in the therapeutic results of the homeless project described in chapter 2), but equally in other cases, as the slow coming to terms with the past history of the Belgrade fairground (chapter 12); conversely, failure to do so can exclude and devalue heritage, whether in Estonia prior to recent shifts in meaning and appreciation (chapter 9) or even in Rome (chapter 3). Developing participation processes, educational activities and collaborative work creates place-identity and reinforces sense of place (e.g. Fairclough 2011). This is evidenced by all our chapters to one degree or another.

Heritage 'ownership' rather than legal ownership

Sustainability means including the living community in the heritage process and taking into account the cultural vitality of the population: it supposes selecting from the past (and perhaps modifying present-day behaviour) and finding ways to ensure (not merely physically but also symbolically) that the past contributes to quality of life, as shown in Paris suburbs, Rome, Dubrovnik, Brussels or Norway. This involves, as we see in several of the case studies (chapters 3, 4, 6, 10 and 11), some recognition that heritage can be owned by everyone; commonly this leads to suggestions of privileging local inhabitants, although there are other forms of community and of 'ownership', as the Faro Convention recognises, such as communities of interest, or national and ethnic communities (which raises issues of balancing rights, responsibilities and respect of the 'other') and of course 'communities' (or perhaps, better, the 'interests') of tourism. Several chapters dealing notably with WHSs explore the complex balance between heritage preservation for tourism and heritage management in favour of inhabitants. The issue raised is how to preserve heritage and at the same time avoid the traps of 'museification' and 'petrification', particularly in WH places. The risk for a city or place with excessive levels of tourism is of becoming a 'destination' and not a 'place', and of becoming a 'frozen city' marked by the dissolution of the social fabric.

The values of participation for increasing citizenship and peace building

This book raises many governance issues related to heritage management, and (e.g. in chapters 1 and 2) underlines the need for participation in developing a sense of place and social inclusion. Many chapters show that heritage can be controversial: various narratives of history exist, various groups claim their own heritage by excluding others, and official narratives can dominate community expressions, such as in Noyon, the Baltic cities, Estonia and Cyprus (chapters 5, 8, 9 and 11). Most of the case studies (but notably in chapters 3, 4, 6, 11 and 12) also demonstrate that cultural sustainability means reconsidering the interconnected roles of politicians, experts and inhabitants (linking the set of values and judgements of specialists and the set of common knowledge), and increasing the participation of the population in defining heritage and heritage policies, in order to improve community life and promote values of tolerance and peace.

Respect for and promotion of diversity

Almost everything written in this book underlines the balance between different cultural models and identities that is presupposed by the idea of cultural sustainability, whether that between global and local influences, between and within communities, or between inhabitants and visitors, or inhabitants and experts. The chapters analyse models of heritage management that enable wider and more diverse groups of people to explore their perspectives, in order that dominant narratives are countered by an array of alternative or changing points of view. There seems agreement that the aim is to increase the representation of plural and multiple experiences, through increased tolerance for difference and wider appreciation of the palimpsestic identity of towns and cities, and through ensuring that more people feel that they belong where they live. The book shows that there is a need to promote social sustainability by cultural and democratic means, and not only (as often seems to be the assumption) by economic ones.

The power and function of narratives

The power and function of heritage and memory and other narratives is a strong thread through the book, in which a wide range of discourses are studied (open ended narratives, subversive narrative, multiple narratives). All the chapters, in one way or another, study the impact of 'official' narratives on creating and interpreting heritage. They also highlight the resilience of other narratives (some subordinate, some subversive and some conforming to other norms) and in some cases the way that museums, for example, may be seduced into encapsulating official but not necessarily (the only) valid cultural narratives. We can find examples of this in a wide range of contexts and circumstances, for example in small city museums (chapter 5), World Heritage cities (chapter 6) – and in regions undergoing the aftermath of traumatic and far reaching change, whether de-industrialisation (e.g. chapter 10), political and demographic change (chapters 8 and 9), 'frozen' community and national conflict (chapter 11) or, of course, the continued fallout from the 1940s Holocaust and ethnic 'cleansings' (chapter 12). Narratives are dynamic as well, and can be transformed over time, sometimes very quickly, for various social, economic or political reasons.

The present day as the interface between past and future

This book shows how heritage fosters the ongoing relationship between past, present and future. All the chapters underline the importance of intergenerational approaches which articulate both inheritance (that which we inherit from the past) and bequest (that which we will pass on); they tell us there is a responsibility to pass on heritage unchanged, but also a right to pass it on transformed and changed, and a responsibility to create potential for new heritage. The chapters show that cultural sustainability supposes a necessary balance between heritage and modernity, between the old and the new, between cultural heritage and modern cultural and artistic production. It is demonstrated that a city does not – and must not – stop producing history; cities create culture and culture produces history. Revitalisation of local heritage by creative interventions can be a way to join the past and the future, heritage and modernity.

Conscious bequests to the future, or newly made or newly valued heritage?

All heritage carries in it the seeds, often indeed the imperative, of transmission as well as of inheritance. Several case studies offer insights into the processes related to creating future individual or collective future identities by virtue of what is retained, looked after and left for those who follow us (e.g. chapters 1, 3 and 4); this necessarily involves processes of recovering, creating and transmitting memory – which also relates to transmitting principles and values through broad societal mechanisms. Some chapters such as those on Jersey and on the Baltic regions, examine how new culture and new heritage can be created, and how in the process heritage can be transformed, reanimated and preserved (chapters 7, 8 and 9). Questions of the authenticity of heritage (what is real?) and the destination of cultural and heritage policies (is the purpose to satisfy visitors or the local population?) are raised too, especially in contexts where 'official' 'authoritative' views are imposed, such as in the Dubrovnik and Noyon cases (chapters 4 and 5) and within the past practice of museums in Cyprus (chapter 11), or simply by virtue of external perspectives, sometimes long-established, coming under challenge from the inside (chapters 10 and 12).

Threading a way through the book

Our set of twelve chapters is begun by one of the editors, with 'Ordinary Heritage, Participation and Social Cohesion: The Suburbs of Paris'. The suburbs around Paris, although towns in their own right, like the extensive, heavily populated surroundings of many cities, are not only continually impacted by physical change such as massive 'regeneration' operations, loss of public spaces and infrastructure issues, but suffer from both insider and external perceptual problems and image issues. The narratives that surround the suburbs – the stereotype of the excluded *banlieue* – are very often almost wholly negative, damaging to social cohesion and likely to promote cultural un-sustainability. This opening chapter looks at how the use of new models of 'museum' that are rooted in participation and sense of place are being used to work towards more culturally sustainable futures. 'Everyday' heritage (interpreted positively and broadly as the urban fabric but also as including histories, traditions and values and reflecting the aspirations of the inhabitants) can enrich citizens' recognition and valuation of sense of place, develop social cohesion, increase links between the town's districts, between generations, and between different communities living in suburban towns.

Very similar cultural uses of the heritage process form part of the case study in chapter 2, '"Keeping it Real": Social Sustainability in the Homeless Heritage Project in Bristol and York'. This account of working collaboratively with homeless people living in two major British cities, both in different ways significant heritage and tourist places, investigate the completely separate and very different townscapes constructed and experienced by those literally living on the street – the sense of place of those who do not, conventionally, 'have' a place. In the Homeless Heritage project, archaeologists, and others, helped to make room for homeless people to engage – and to do so, most importantly, on their own terms (because this is the expert as facilitator and colleague not as teacher or leader) – with their landscapes and heritages. The project confirms that heritage as a collaborative social process can counter dominant narratives, and it can materialise multiple, even conflicting, perspectives. Its results also suggest – perhaps even more importantly – that active participation in collaborative heritage work can aid recovery from traumatic or distressing experiences and situations, and that it can actively contribute to cultural and social sustainability through increasing equality and tolerance, and by enhancing understanding about and between communities. There are few clearer demonstrations of the maxims of 'new heritage' (or of the precepts of the Florence and Faro conventions) that everyone has a heritage (or multiple heritages) with which they identify, and which deserves the respect of others.

The rich, deep and all-pervasive, indeed dominating, heritage of the city and environs of Rome seems very distant from the Paris *banlieue* or the streets of Bristol, but the same themes run through the third chapter, 'The Burden of History: Living Heritage and Everyday Life in Rome'. In Rome, life is lived amidst the remains and ruins of a distant past, which indeed has moulded the very shape of the present city. Apart from the major monuments, many of which have been torn from the urban fabric which once accreted around them, there are more or less minor remains of the antique and medieval world throughout the city's present-day suburbs. History and heritage are an integral element of daily life, and the treatment of archaeological remains over a very extensive area is a primary concern of planning and architecture. This chapter examines the effect of such an all-pervasive heritage on everyday life and on the planning of the future urban fabric. A lesson to learn, but not yet learnt widely, is that to be effective and socially sustainable, practices of recovery, reuse and recycling of heritage must be embedded in a place-based and people-sensitive approach, and must be able to cope with the real commonsense experience of places where modern life is lived. As in Parisian suburbs, this requires that citizens recover and value their own heritage; as on the streets of Bristol, it requires that space be made to allow them to do this.

There are forms of exclusion other than those implied in the first three chapters. In smaller cities with a very rich architectural heritage, such as Dubrovnik, a UNESCO 'World Heritage City', discussed in our fourth chapter, 'Remembering Cities: The Role of Memory in the Culturally Sustainable Development of Dubrovnik (Croatia)', the fault line is between the protected, burnished, tourist-laden historic core and the remainder of the city, and between different communities of citizen interest and action. The successful story of the continued preservation and valorisation of the old walled city centre has been written, in some eyes, at the expense of community spirit, a more local sense of place and the spirit of creativity and cultural innovation. It is argued in this chapter that a vibrant and sustainable cultural life needs to revolve around searching for a balance between museification and innovation, as well as searching for a balance between the historical core and the city as a whole. Economic sustainability (and perhaps even environmental sustainability) can be achieved by current preservation-focused, tourism-centred policy and practice, but the Dubrovnik example strongly implies that cultural – and social – sustainability, especially at the holistic level of a whole city, not just its core, is unattainable by those methods alone.

An over-concentration on the historic centre of a town, as seen in Dubrovnik, is not uncommon, especially in difficult economic times when tourism becomes a principal generator of economic success. In large and small towns, there has been a tendency for heritage and cultural policy to create centre–periphery distinctions. A prevailing view until relatively recently was that heritage consisted of older and more ancient, as well as larger and elite, buildings and sites; this naturally drew protective action and valorisation away from the early modern and much later suburbs of towns. Several chapters discuss this problem, most particularly 'The Challenge of Cultural Sustainability in City Museums: Showing the City and Selecting the Past in Noyon (France)' and 'Social Sustainability in Historic City Centres: The Grand Place in Brussels'.

The first of these, chapter 5, uses the example of the town of Noyon in northern France to examine the processes and results of the crucial role played since the nineteenth century by city museums in the social construction of a sense of place in many if not most European towns. This role has changed through time, because as all our chapters demonstrate, heritage approaches change with prevailing social needs, and in the last few decades new museological theories have tried but not always succeeded (partly perhaps because of the changing public perceptions of experts) to bring a new more inclusive approach that promotes city museums as cultural places where identity, sense of place and equity issues can be discussed in terms of the whole town by a much wider section of the population. At a short geographical remove, but at the other end of the scale in terms of size, the tourist- and money-attracting architectural set-piece of Brussels, the Grand Place, described in chapter 6, like Dubrovnik a place on the UNESCO list, has in its social, economic and cultural shadow a large, poorly used hinterland (which is officially even called a 'buffer zone', as though its own purpose is defined solely by its relationship to the Grand Place). People-based research here has revealed a range of different social and cultural attitudes to the use and character of this area of central Brussels, highlighting some of the ways in which sustainability and heritage relate to one another, and seeking effective methods for the socially sustainable development of richly historic urban city centres without destroying their identity or causing detriment to the rest of the city.

One thread which has been seen several times so far, most strongly perhaps in the Brussels case, is the clash between global (international), or sometimes national or even merely regional perspectives, and the perspectives, ways of valuing and senses of identity, belonging and ownership that exist at a more local level. This takes very many forms, some of which are discussed, mainly at the level of the individual city, in the chapters already described, but others of which sit at the higher levels of nation or language or ethnic community. The first three chapters of Part II each focus on such issues, despite their different contexts.

First, chapter 7, 'Language Revitalisation, Sonic Activism and Cultural Sustainability: Voicing Linguistic Heritage on Jersey' gives us an account of the revitalisation of a declining Anglo-Norman language – Jèrriais – through music framed in a particularly transforming (rather than conservative) mode of cultural activity. This aims to sustain a language but at the same time to sustain inherited identities and equally to construct new identities for the present century. In the next two chapters, 8 and 9, we are shown in very different contexts the reversal of public opinion towards two quite different types of 'orphaned' heritage: the German character within the Baltic cities of Poland and Kaliningrad; and the agricultural estates of the German aristocracy in the countryside of Estonia. In both cases an initial rejection of German heritage after the departure of their original 'owners' during the various upheavals of the twentieth century has turned, for a variety of reasons, into an acceptance by today's inhabitants of 'their' heritage as 'ours'.

All three cases show the ways in which new or changing national identities can be remade through engagement with heritage, especially perhaps in relatively new, or very changed, nations. They look notably at ways in which a heritage has been reviewed, reconstituted, and recovered. In all three cases, this is not a simple story of the reclamation of a lost or stolen heritage, but a more complex tale of changing attitudes, of shifting cultural contexts, and of new attributed meanings. In all three cases, too, culture has played a big role and the emphasis has been on the intangible values attached to something else – language, history and architecture respectively. This echoes the 'new' heritage paradigm of attributed rather than intrinsic values (that, in reality, all heritage is intangible, even when it rests on tangible, physical foundations, as in the case of Estonian 'German' manor houses). It also picks up two of the major threads of this book that are seen centrally or peripherally in every chapter. First, that our assumptions, givens and verities about what we call heritage are travellers on the winds and tides of historical and cultural contingency (they depend on current opinions and needs, and are relative and potentially ever-changing, not absolute). Second, that the process of heritage-making, preserving, using, disposing – that is, the complexities of transmission from past to future – is quintessentially a participative and democratic process that requires, in order for it to be sustainable in itself and to contribute to broader sustainability goals beyond itself, a greater level of access for public involvement and engagement (assuming the public wishes to be engaged); like all democratic processes, of course, an informed and educated electorate is one prerequisite – wherein perhaps lies the new role of experts.

Many chapters in the book draw our attention to the idea of distinctive places, rather than of individual buildings, as a principal basis for heritage as well as identity. In the two 'Baltic' chapters just mentioned, the places concerned remained largely unaltered but people's attitudes and reactions to them changed.

In other cases, as shown in chapter 10, 'The Potential Space for Cultural Sustainability: Place Narratives and Place-Heritage in Rjukan (Norway)' the opposite can be the case. Here, it is the place that changed, by way of the sort of prolonged de-industrialisation that has affected many parts of Europe. As a result not only did the fabric of the place change, but so did its economy, and its social composition. Perhaps most importantly in cultural terms (because it shapes how people living there now see their region), the stories told about Rjukan, the narrative built around the place – in another word, its meaning – also changed, from a fable of success and symbolic nation-building as the cradle of modern hi-tech, electrically driven Norway, to a story of failure and decline, equally symbolic of wider trends elsewhere. In Rjukan, the heritage process, and specifically the ideological use of place-heritage, needs to be harnessed to create new, more optimistic and empowering narratives that offer a future vision, not a reference to past failure.

At several points throughout this summary of the book, the current interest in narratives, whether based on heritage or culture, has come to the fore. The next case study in the book, 'Politics, Tourism and Cultural Sustainability: The Construction of Heritage in Cyprus', is set in another relatively young and still contested state: Cyprus, a divided island. Chapter 11 looks at heritage here, insofar as it is defined by museum narratives, and the displays offered by museums on both sides of the island's Greek–Turkish divide. The narrative has been determined by national and community politics and identity – by division – and more latterly by the global–local (outsider–insider) divisions illuminated, if not caused, by high volume tourism. The particular view that different museums give of Cyprus and its history, and in particular the aspects that are not shown in the museums, creates a highly specific and selective interpretation of the place's character. Whilst not explicitly excluding, this is not a narrative that tends towards inclusion either, nor is it one that is particularly representative, nor is it likely to be particularly helpful in unfreezing the island's long-running conflicts or bridging its divisions.

Divisions; narratives; participation; ideas of place; memories lost, kept and remade; the reconstitution of heritage value; historical contingency; and pain, resentment and discomfort: these are all threads that run through the whole of the book, and most of them are brought together in the final case study in chapter 12, 'From Dissonance to Resilience: The Heritage of Belgrade's Staro Sajmište'. This is a story (still unresolved) of Belgrade's Staro Sajmište, the 'Old Fairground', built in 1937 as a national exhibition space but which was used during the Second World War as a death camp. Its history and its continuing, ever changing contemporary meaning, has not fully been taken into account in subsequent attitudes to and uses of the site, leaving it as not only dissonant but highly contested heritage. It is symbolic at many levels of many things, which simultaneously emphasises and obscures memory. Perhaps not surprisingly, and perhaps in keeping with this book's themes, little about the Old Fairground has found closure; its heritage is still contested, its interpretation still open, its future uncertain, its role in a state of flux.

References

Abraham, Y-M., Marion, L. and Philippe, H. 2011. *Décroissance versus développement durable: débats pour la suite du monde*, Montreal: Ecosociété.

Agenda 21 of Culture, IFACCA, IFCCD and Culture Action Europe 2014. Culture as a Goal in the Post-2015 Development Agenda. www.uclg.org/en/resources/policy-statements (accessed 10 February 2015).

Auclair, E. 2010. Développement culturel – développement durable, vers une plus grande démocratie locale? In Bernié-Boissard, C., Chastagner, C., Crozat, D. and Fournier, L-S. (eds), *Développement culturel et territoires*, Paris: L'Harmattan, 49–67.

Auclair, E. 2011. Revenir vers les habitants, revenir sur les territoires. L'articulation entre culture et développement durable dans les projets de développement local. *Développement Durable et Territoires*, 2:2, May 2011. On-line journal: http://developpementdurable.revues.org/8946?lang=en (accessed 10 February 2015).

Auclair, E. 2014a. Culture and Sustainable Development: A Real Dynamic or an Uncertain Relationship? In Dragićević Šešić, M., Nikolić, M. and Rogač Mijatovič, L. (eds), *Culture and sustainable development at times of crisis – proceedings*, Belgrade: Belgrade University of Arts, 15–27.

Auclair, E. 2014b. Diversité culturelle, droits culturels: atouts et ambiguités des nouveau concepts mobilisés dans les quartiers. In Bulot, T., Boyer, I. and Bertucchi, M-M. (eds), *Diasporisations sociolinguistiques et précarités, discrimination(s) et mobilité(s)*, Paris: L'Harmattan, 145–61.

Bollier, D. and Helfrich, S. 2012. *The wealth of the commons: a world beyond market and state*. Amherst, MA: Levellers Press.

Brown, L. 2001. *Eco economy: building an economy for the earth*, New York: W. W. Norton.

Brown, L. 2011. *World on the edge: how to prevent environmental and economic collapse*, New York: Earth Policy Institute and W. W. Norton.

Caillé, A. 2012. *L'idée même de richesse*, Paris: La Decouverte.

Cobb, C. and Venetoulis, J. 2004. *The genuine progress indicator 1950–2002 (2004 update): measuring the real state of economy*. www.RedefiningProgress.org.

COST 2011. COST Action IS1007. Investigating Cultural Sustainability. Action webpage at www.cost.eu/COST_Actions/isch/Actions/IS1007 (accessed 10 February 2015).

Council of Europe 2000. European Landscape Convention. European Treaty Series 176, Strasbourg.

Council of Europe 2005. Framework Convention on the Value of Cultural Heritage for Society (Faro Convention). European Treaty Series 199, Strasbourg.

Council of Europe 2009. *Heritage and beyond/Patrimoine et au delà*. Strasbourg: Council of Europe Publishing, versions in English and French. www.coe.int/t/dg4/cultureheritage/heritage/identities/PatrimoineBD_en.pdf (accessed 10 February 2015).

English Heritage 1997. *Sustaining the historic environment: new perspectives on the future*, London: English Heritage, reprinted in Fairclough, G., Harrison, R., Schofield, J. and Jameson Jr, John H. (eds) 2008, *The heritage reader*, London and New York: Routledge, 313–21 .

ESF/COST 2010. *Landscape in a changing world – bridging divides, integrating disciplines, serving society*, SPB41, Strasbourg/Brussels: ESF/COST, www.esf.org/fileadmin/Public_documents/Publications/SPB41_Landscape_ChangingWorld.pdf (accessed 10 February 2015).

Fairclough, G. 2008. New Heritage, an Introductory Essay – People, Landscape and Change. In Fairclough, G., Harrison, R., Schofield, J. and Jameson Jr, John H. (eds), *The heritage reader*, London and New York: Routledge, 297–312.

Fairclough, G. J. 2009. New Heritage Frontiers. In Council of Europe (ed.), *Heritage and beyond*, Strasbourg: Council of Europe Publishing (accessed 19/12/09 at www.coe. int/t/dg4/cultureheritage/heritage/identities/beyond_en.asp), 29–41.

Fairclough, G. 2011. The Value of Heritage for the Future. In Ünsal, D. (ed.) 2012, *Heritage in society: cultural policy and management (KPY) yearbook 3*, Centre for Cultural Policy and Management (KPY), Istanbul: Istanbul Bilgi University Press, 34–41. http:// kpy.bilgi.edu.tr/en/page/kpy-yearbook/ (accessed 10 February 2015).

Fairclough, G. 2012. Others – a Foreword. In Giaccardi, E. (ed.), *Heritage and social media: understanding and experiencing heritage in a participatory culture*, London: Routledge, xiv–xvii.

Fairclough, G. 2013. What Was Wrong with Dufton? Reflections on Counter-mapping: Self, Alterity and Community (Afterword). In Schofield, J. (ed.), *Who needs experts? Counter-mapping cultural heritage*, Heritage, culture and identity series, London: Routledge, 241–8.

Fairclough, G., Harrison, R., Schofield, J. and Jameson Jr, John H. (eds) 2008. *The heritage reader*, London and New York: Routledge.

Fairclough, G., Dragićević, S., Rogač, M., Mijatovič, L. J., Auclair, E. and Soini, K. 2014 (forthcoming). The Faro Convention, a New Paradigm for Socially- and Culturally-Sustainable Heritage Action? In proceedings of the CCCS (Centre for Culture and Cultural Studies) conference 2013, 'Cultural Memory', *Cultura (Skopje)*, IV:5.

Harrison, R. 2013. *Heritage: critical approaches*, Abingdon and New York: Routledge.

Hawkes, J. 2001. *The fourth pillar of sustainability: the essential role of culture for public planning*, Vancouver: Common Ground Publishing.

Holtorf, C. and Fairclough, G. 2013. The New Heritage and Re-shapings of the Past. In González-Ruibal, A. (ed.), *Reclaiming archaeology: beyond the tropes of modernity*, London and New York: Routledge, 197–210.

IIEDH (l'Institut Interdisciplinaire d'Éthique et des Droits de l'Homme) 2007. Cultural Rights, the Fribourg Declaration. www.unifr.ch/iiedh/fr/divers/delcaration-fribourg.

Jackson, T. 2009. *Prosperity without growth: economics for a finite planet*. London and New York: Earthscan/Routledge.

Latouche, S. 2007. *Petit traité de la décroissance sereine*, Paris: Mille et Une Nuits.

Meadows, D. H., Meadows, G., Randers, J. and Behrens, W. W. III. 1972. *The limits to growth*, New York: Universe Books.

Méda, D. 2008. *Au dela du PIB: pour une autre mesure de la richesse*, Paris: Flammarion.

Schofield, J. and Rosy Szymanski, R. (eds) 2010. *Local heritage, global context, cultural perspectives on sense of place*, Farnham: Ashgate.

Smith, L. 2006. *Uses of heritage*, London: Routledge.

Soini, K. and Birkeland, I. 2014. Exploring the Scientific Discourse on Cultural Sustainability. *Geoforum* 51:1, 213–23.

UCLG 2014. *Cultural heritage as a driver of sustainability*, UCLG Insights. http://issuu. com/uclgcglu/docs/cultural_heritage_as_a_driver_of_su/0 (accessed 10 February 2015).

UN 2002. *Report of the World Summit on Sustainable Development, Johannesburg, South Africa*. www.un.org/jsummit/html/documents/summit_docs.html (accessed 10 February 2015).

UNESCO 1996. *Our creative diversity: report of the World Commission on Culture and Development*. http://unesdoc.unesco.org/images/0010/001055/105586e.pdf (accessed 10 February 2015).

UNESCO 2005. Convention on the Protection and Promotion of the Diversity of Cultural Expressions. www.unesco.org/new/en/culture/themes/cultural-diversity/diversity-of-cultural-expressions/the-convention/convention-text/ (accessed 10 February 2015).

UNESCO 2011. Historic Urban Landscape Declaration (HUL). http://whc.unesco.org/en/activities/638 (accessed 28 February 2015).

UNESCO 2013. The Hangzhou Declaration: Placing Culture at the Heart of Sustainable Development Policies. www.unesco.org/new/en/culture/themes/culture-and-development/hangzhou-congress/ (accessed 10 February 2015).

Wolferstan, S. and Fairclough, G. 2013. Common European Heritage: Reinventing Identity Through Landscape and Heritage? In Callebaut, D. (ed.), *Heritage reinvents Europe*, European Archaeological Council papers 7, Budapest: EAC/Archaeolingua, 43–54.

Part I

Equity, inclusion, citizenship

To start at one possible beginning, and to accept 'sustainable development' on its own terms, the Brundtland definition points us towards intergenerational equity and balance (the 'needs' of future generations balanced against our own present-day needs, although at least one 'present day' need at the most personal and individual level is actually a future need – the survival of your own grandchildren). But the Brundtland definition also implicitly contains a requirement for equity in the present day, for 'horizontal' trans-society transfers as well as 'vertical' intergenerational transfer. The undefined 'needs' mentioned by the Brundtland definition are not on the whole consistent across the globe, through all levels of society, or at different stages of life, or even when filtered through ideology or faith. One person's need is another person's excess or dearth; when one set of 'needs' is fulfilled, another (often someone else's) is denied. Exclusion can be a result of perfectly well-meaning policies as well as of deliberate ill-intent. Non-representation, the absence of a voice, or its inability to be heard, is the opposite face of citizenship. Non-human 'voices' are even more silent.

All these problems and imbalances are neither fixed for ever nor are they given – they are human constructs, and they are inherited, as much 'heritage' as any great painting, national epic or cathedral church. They are also cultural, and as such, once more, solutions must be cultural. Social structures, cultural assumptions, cultural solutions are at some level chosen by people, or at the least tacitly allowed to develop. The case studies, stories and analyses that are collected in this first half of thw book illuminate some of the processes by which this happens and some of the ways in which things might become different. They are all filtered through the book's concern with heritage as an important aspect both of culture sensu lato and of sustainability; heritage, it might be argued, is the result of previous generations balancing their needs against ours. To ground the concept, most of the discussion in this book leans towards a heritage of place: the everyday presence, acknowledged or silenced, of the remains of the past, tangible or intangible. Place – and its close cognate, landscape – weaves the threads of our inheritance into something which can be used or worn, repaired and passed on; more importantly, it is a collective construct, something which is shared. Places and landscapes belong to everyone, but (unlike buildings and land) are owned by no one; multiple and plural perceptions of a single place must co-exist, thus creating yet another arena for potential imbalance and inequity. The chapters that follow argue in their diverse ways that a culturally focused sustainability offers hopeful ways forward.

1 Ordinary heritage, participation and social cohesion

The suburbs of Paris

Elizabeth Auclair

The problems of the suburbs

Suburbs are now one of the world's principal human habitats, but the term has many different meanings and can signify various types of area. Generally speaking, when people talk of 'suburbs' they mean the extensive residential urban fabric that spreads around the central cities in metropolitan areas (Vieillard Baron 2001). Although most cities are facing various economic and social changes due, for example, to de-industrialisation, urban sprawl, gentrification versus pauperisation or tourism processes, suburban towns have their own distinctive problems. They are specifically affected by rapid and uncontrolled urban expansion, large-scale 'regeneration' operations, loss of public spaces, and increased spatial fragmentation and social segregation, and as a result frequently have a negative image.

Against these problems, sustainability is currently becoming the major conceptual frame for urban development policies. Culture and heritage stand as significant issues within sustainability. Many suburban towns counter their negative and despised image by seeking to enhance local heritage, seen in a broad way as urban artefacts but also as the histories, traditions, values and aspirations of the inhabitants. It can be considered as an interesting tool for community cohesion, well-being and quality of urban life. This chapter looks at two examples, examining the policies and actions developed by two institutions in suburban towns on the south side of Paris, the Maison de Banlieue et de l'Architecture in Athis-Mons and the Val de Bièvre Écomusée in Fresnes. It analyses the conditions under which the valorisation of everyday heritage promotes inhabitants' participation, increases sense of place for the population, develops social cohesion, and reinforces links between neighbourhoods and between different communities.

Urban development and sustainability

During the twentieth century the population of the planet grew fourfold, whereas the urban population multiplied by a factor of twenty. Since 2007, more than half of the world's population has been urban, a percentage that is still increasing. In many countries, the rate has reached 80 per cent or more. The urban question has thus become one of the major issues of the twenty-first century. In industrialised countries the problems are less severe than in developing countries, but European cities are nevertheless facing economic, social and environmental difficulties. Among the core issues, the increasing amount of land taken up by urbanisation and the economic and social difficulties of some communities seem quite crucial. Many debates concern the 'economic growth' issue, and a number of researchers and scientists argue that our societies can no longer be based on a continual growth which seems to heavily impact our environment and increases social inequalities (Jackson 2009). Furthermore, some economists promote the notion of 'de-growth' in order to open new and more realistic perspectives for the future of our societies (Latouche 2007). Numerous voices also criticise the emphasis put on economic and financial issues and on the criteria of productivity, competition and efficiency. They call for the promotion of other values that aim at social equity and well-being (Gadrey 2012). The French philosopher Edgar Morin highlighted the tension between the prosaic and the poetic dimensions of our societies. He considers that greater attention must be given to poetic, symbolic and spiritual values (Morin 2000). According to him, there is an urgent need to organise decent living conditions for the population, with greater attention given to cultural issues.

Since the publication of the Brundtland Report in 1987, urban matters have become fully integrated in the discussions on sustainable development. The articulation between the different issues appears complex, however: is it possible in urban territories to ensure the simultaneous achievement of economic development, social cohesion and environmental quality? It seems that the concept of sustainable development, supposed to cover the 'needs' of the present and future generations, does not include all human needs. Notably, the cultural dimension is not sufficiently taken into account in urban policies. Environmentally friendly housing developments, often presented as the best illustrations of sustainable development applied to urban territories, generally focus on ecological issues. The high cost of housing in these so-called 'sustainable sites' frequently leads to gentrification and social segregation (Emelianoff 2008). Culture is rarely considered as a significant topic in those urban projects. Nevertheless, in times of economic crisis, culture can also be considered as an instrument for economic development. Thus, the concept of 'creative cities' developed by Richard Florida has been widely mediatised (Florida 2002), even though many researchers have pointed out the limits and ambiguities of this approach, and the risks inherent in the instrumentalisation of art and culture (Vivant 2009).

However, the situation seems to be progressively changing. For some time already cities have been aware that supporting culture – arts and creativity as well as heritage – is an essential component for local development, and presently many are interested in increasing the articulation between culture and sustainable development (Auclair 2010). A number of cities use Agenda 21 of Culture, a policy frame developed in 2004 by UCLG (United Cities and Local Governments), as a means to reinforce the place of culture within local policies, to promote cultural diversity, and to strengthen local democracy and inhabitants' participation. Ten years after its first launch, UCLG intends to present a new version of the Agenda 21 for Culture in 2015, in order to help more local communities adopt this tool. Participation has clearly become a major issue for cultural and heritage policies, even though this notion is vague and can signify different approaches ranging from plain information to genuine co-construction of urban projects with the population (Arnstein 1969). A greater attention to the expectations of the local population seems currently to be appearing in public policies dealing notably with urbanism, sustainable development and culture.

The turn to people-centred and place-based approaches

For the past ten years research work has emphasised the general trend in favour of people-centred and place-based approaches. These approaches are being encouraged by a number of international documents and are being developed by different actors, cultural institutions and local governments (Auclair 2011). The aim is to take account of the needs and opinions of the population and to promote new values. Several documents from the Council of Europe and UNESCO have underlined the importance of culture and heritage for sustainability, and have contributed to a widening of these concepts, in particular by proposing people-centred processes with a focus on collective governance and inhabitants' participation. The European Landscape Convention (ELC), for example, considers landscapes as both the result of and the interaction between natural and human elements, and defines new categories of heritage which shift from a kind of nostalgia favouring mostly ancient and natural landscapes, towards a prospective vision of contemporary territories (Council of Europe 2000). This directly concerns suburban areas. The ELC encourages all actors to take into consideration 'ordinary' landscapes and not only exceptional ones, that is landscapes as they are perceived and experienced daily by their inhabitants. Additionally, the Faro Convention on the Value of Cultural Heritage for Society explicitly gives a greater place to citizens in heritage policies (Council of Europe 2005). It requires us to think about indicators other than just aesthetic and historical ones, and to recognise as heritage all elements that make sense and create identity for local populations. Thus, the Faro Convention also introduces the notion of 'ordinary' heritage. Both texts suppose a modification of accepted approaches: the ambition is to have citizens and communities participating together with experts in defining the values of heritage, with inhabitants outlining what heritage means for them.

Besides, for UNESCO's 2005 Convention on the Protection and Promotion of the Diversity of Cultural Expressions, enhancing urban heritage means taking into account the plurality of individual and collective opinions, values and identities. It leads to the valorisation of those social, economic and cultural elements which contribute to shaping urban territories. This can facilitate the dialogue between different neighbourhoods, between communities, between generations, between newcomers and former inhabitants, and promote social cohesion. More recently, in its 'Recommendation on Historic Urban Landscape' (HUL) UNESCO has adopted this emerging discourse and aims to promote the integration and valorisation of culture and heritage in urban development policies (UNESCO 2011). HUL also enlarges the range of elements to preserve, and encourages the turn from merely architectural and historical monuments towards social and cultural practices. Thus local policies should be based on 'respect of the inherited values and traditions of different cultural contexts'. This means mapping 'the city's natural, cultural and human resources' and assessing their vulnerability by means of sustainable development criteria such as socio-economic stress or climate change. The objective is to consider urban areas as 'common cultural heritage'.

Against a general deterioration in the quality of urban environments, heritage, including its tangible and intangible components, is thus coming more and more to be viewed as 'a key resource in enhancing the liveability of urban areas', to continue using the words of the HUL recommendation. HUL furthermore encourages the inclusion of more partners in the decision making and the involvement of inhabitants in the process. The intention is 'to reach consensus using participatory planning and stakeholders' consultation on what values to protect for transmission to future generations', and 'to establish the appropriate partnerships and local management frameworks for each of the identified projects'. The matter is important because there remains a perception in society that there is real conflict between urban development and heritage preservation – either protecting heritage appears to be an obstacle to new urban projects and is therefore no longer guaranteed, or on the contrary, heritage is considered as a valuable component and finds itself instrumentalised. In both cases, the choices seem determined by economic issues. Indeed, heritage valorisation and cultural tourism has often been considered as just another tool used by cities as a means for economic development. Until recently heritage policies have rarely taken into account local populations.

Even though all these texts and conventions have not yet been signed up to by the French government, they are contributing to the spread of new ideas and values, and are therefore inducing transformations in cultural and urban policies. These changes are taking place relatively slowly in France, however, mainly because of the persistence of the strong ideological structure developed by André Malraux for the Ministry of Culture over fifty years ago. This conceptual frame is characterised by a relatively narrow definition of culture and heritage, by the importance of state policies, and by top-down approaches. 'Traditional' cultural policies seem currently to be facing a significant crisis that is linked to serious financial problems as well as ideological issues. Indeed, the common evolution towards a more anthropological meaning of culture presupposes some changes, and the decentralisation process is giving increasing responsibilities and power to local governments. Against this fragile background, sustainability appears as a kind of lever leading to new representations and projects (Auclair 2014a). A report established in 2002 by the French Commission for Sustainable Development indicated that culture should be fully integrated into the sustainable development policies. Though few actions have yet been implemented at the state level, many cities and cultural institutions are developing various projects related to what can be called cultural sustainability. Indeed, it means analysing the everyday life of the local population, considering their environment in broad terms, and keeping in mind what effectively matters to people. This approach is also based on a wider meaning of culture, since it leads to recognising 'ordinary' heritage and landscape.

Beyond negative stereotypes: the emergence of suburban heritage

In France and especially in the Paris agglomeration, suburbs often have a particularly despised image. Though in reality suburban towns present a wide diversity of situations – there are some very wealthy cities mostly situated west of Paris which can be termed suburbs – the word *banlieue* is very often currently interpreted in common usage to indicate deprivation and economic and social difficulties (Stébé 2010). In the context of competition that exists between cities wanting to lose their negative image, one method for increasing their attractiveness is to enhance their heritage. What, though, can be considered as heritage in towns where few 'famous' historical and architectural monuments exist? What are the different elements that might be used to portray the towns located on the outskirts of Paris? Beyond the clichés spread by the media, there are undeniably some deep-seated problematic characteristics. The consequences of de-industrialisation include the transformation of economic activities, an increase in the unemployment rate, and a multiplicity of neglected sites. Uncontrolled urban sprawl is responsible for a progressive loss of open spaces, forests and agricultural land. Massive regeneration operations carried out in the last ten years under the housing policy of ANRU (Agence Nationale pour la Rénovation Urbaine) have often radically transformed social housing areas and suburban landscapes. In addition, these territories are often traversed by important urban infrastructural elements which increase spatial fragmentation and social segregation.

On the other side of the picture, suburban towns are also composed of quiet housing estates, where solidarity and social life are significant, with residual areas of woodland and agriculture, and fragments of nature surprisingly preserved, 'shared gardens' and small, single-family houses appreciated by newcomers leaving the high urban densities of Paris (Figure 1.1).

More generally, suburbs offer another way of life that lies between that of the town and that of the countryside. Suburban towns therefore cannot only be viewed through one lens as a succession of indeterminate urban areas that daily commuters just pass through; they are also territories where inhabitants live every day and develop social relations. These suburbs constitute complex urban landscapes which are delicate interweavings of various stories, memories and identities. Consequently, all these elements constitute what the towns themselves acknowledge and valorise as 'ordinary heritage'. This term is sometimes considered a negative term in opposition to 'extraordinary heritage', referring to well-known historical buildings and famous cultural events. Nevertheless the expression refers to place-based approaches and to the existing relation between the inhabitants and their heritage. The spread of this concept – at least in the scientific and policy-making world – has now given it a positive connotation.

Figure 1.1 A typical residential area in Athis-Mons

Source: Collection of the Maison de banlieue et de l'architecture of Athis-Mons.

Thus, paying attention to ordinary heritage and embracing the histories, traditions, values and aspirations of the population as well as the urban fabric is seen nowadays as a means to promote quality of life, social cohesion and well-being. Many initiatives have been taken by municipalities and cultural institutions in order to promote local heritage and to stimulate the participation of the population. In the Ile-de-France region, approximately fifteen cultural institutions and museums (including, for example, the Museum of the *Département* of Seine-et-Marne, the Écomusée of Saint-Quentin-en-Yvelines, the Museum of Social and Urban History of Suresnes and the Écomusée of Savigny-le-Temple) situated in the outskirts of Paris have joined together since 2003 to create an informal network called 'Les Neufs de Transilie'. The aim is to propose a new vision and image of the suburbs. The challenge is striking because of the antagonism between Paris with its overwhelming heritage (Paris remains one of the major worldwide tourist destinations with more than 32 million visitors in 2013) and the frequently despised suburbs. Therefore the ambition is not to engage with Paris in a vain competition for tourists (although some outlying cities like Versailles of course attract almost equivalent numbers – six million people visited the royal palace in 2013), but to valorise local heritage primarily for the inhabitants themselves.

The members of Les Neufs de Transilie are cultural institutions that share an interest in how people live – or have lived in the past – in these towns, with subjects related to housing, work, transport, health, education, food, and many similar topics. The purpose is to conduct research and reflection on 'suburban heritage' and to organise common activities, such as exhibitions, conferences and seminars. Besides recalling local elements such as nice parks, ancient churches or edifices built by well-known architects, in order to improve the image of the towns, the aim is to consider these territories such as they actually are 'practised' every day by the population. Attention is also given to promoting links between the past and the present. These structures differ from the main cultural institutions and museums of Paris through their particularly strong relations with the geographical and social reality of their territory. Among the different institutions of this network, two of them will be analysed here: the Maison de Banlieue et de l'Architecture in Athis-Mons, and the Val de Bièvre Écomusée.

The Maison de Banlieue et de l'Architecture: enhancing ordinary landscapes

The Maison de Banlieue et de l'Architecture is a locally run cultural institution in the suburban town of Athis-Mons in the *Département* of Essonne, south of Paris. It is not a museum as there is no collection; rather it is an interpretation and education centre on urban environment, suburban heritage and architecture (www. maisondebanlieue.fr/) (Figure 1.2).

Its focus is on the territory and its resources: 'our collection is the territory and its inhabitants', explains the director. The approach can be compared to the interpretation centres first developed in the United States and Quebec in the 1950s, and then generalised in other countries, that aim to valorise and explain specific

Figure 1.2 The Maison de Banlieue et de l'Architecture in Athis-Mons, housed in the former town hall (the *mairie*)

Source: Collection of the Maison de Banlieue et de l'Architecture of Athis-Mons.

sites. The main key words of the *Maison* are art, culture, history and urbanism. Since 2001, it has been financially supported by local, regional and state bodies. Initially it only concerned the town of Athis-Mons, but now covers a wider territory, the 'Communauté d'agglomération Les Portes de l'Essonne', a grouping of five *communes* that numbers roughly 100,000 inhabitants.

Defining a strategy in order to valorise suburban heritage

At the start, the strategy of the municipality of Athis-Mons was based on several observations. The suburban towns have heritage and history which are generally unknown, and the inhabitants of these suburban towns have little knowledge of the territory where they live. Moreover, many inhabitants were not born in the town, and come from other regions or even other countries. Besides, suburban towns often have a negative image. So the first actions initiated in the 1990s were linked to a regeneration project planned by the municipality in a disadvantaged social housing neighbourhood. The aim was to set up a project with school children in order to work on the memory of the area, by collecting pictures, photographs, and interviews with inhabitants. The methodology was based on a specific approach that can be called 'learning to look' (*l'education au regard*). Similar activities using this approach are often used by artistic institutions in order to help children, as well as adults, understand and appreciate dance or theatre plays. The purpose is to give preliminary information and to help the children learn how to look at their environment, and thanks to being given explanations and to open discussions, to become more aware of their neighbourhood and their town. After that first experience many other projects have been developed with school children and subsequently with the whole population. The method was gradually extended to other areas of the town and to a wider territory. The intention is to develop a global approach which articulates two issues: the history, memory and heritage dimension on the one hand, and the recent and future urban and architectural projects on the other. These suburban towns are concerned by rapid changes which can be considered either as a handicap or as an opportunity. As the director says: 'Our territory is an unfinished work of art under permanent transformation: our job is to help the inhabitants discover this richness'.

The Maison de Banlieue et de l'Architecture aims to develop research and increase knowledge concerning suburbs, and to share this with the population as well as with outside visitors. The library hosted by the institution is open three days a week, with books, films, photos and various documents concerning suburban districts; it is aimed at researchers, students and school children, but also simply any local inhabitant. The ambition is to make citizens more familiar with the history, heritage, architecture and landscapes existing in their town. The goal is to develop an understanding of the various changes which have marked these areas and to counter the stereotypes concerning suburbs. In an allusion to the label 'Villes et Pays d'Art et d'Histoire' given by the French Ministry of Culture to cities and territories with a grand and famous architectural and historical heritage, the *Maison* seeks on the contrary to valorise '*villes d'art modeste et d'histoires simples*' ('cities of modest art and simple stories') – to enhance ordinary heritage.

Activities based on the values of citizenship, participation and social cohesion

The approach of the Maison de Banlieue et de l'Architecture is based on several key values. The goal is to help the inhabitants act as citizens: the idea is that inhabitants aware of the history and changes of their locality can be more involved in the city, can participate in debates and give their opinion concerning urban issues. The hypothesis is that the more you know about your town the more you like it and respect it. Therefore the aim is to help people to be proud of the place where they live. The objective is also to promote social cohesion by increasing exchanges and relations between different neighbourhoods and between the various communities (the city centre, the social housing neighbourhoods, the individual housing estates, etc.). Thus, the institution organises various activities for children and adults such as exhibitions, artistic workshops, conferences and visits.

Every year several thematic exhibitions take place, some organised by the *Maison* itself (there is at least one major exhibition each year, accompanied by the publication of a book), and others by other institutions and simply hosted at the *Maison*. The exhibitions generally concern specific architectural elements which are typical of the suburbs, such as the houses of local stone (*meulière*) built mainly between 1880 and 1930 in the Ile-de-France region (Figure 1.3), the large high-rise social housing estates built in the 1960s and 1970s on the outskirts of the cities, or the factories that form part of the industrial belt constructed all round Paris around the turn of the twentieth century and that are now deserted due to de-industrialisation.

Exhibitions also feature the numerous stone, wood or metal bridges erected over rivers, roads or highways, as well as the parks, gardens and remaining agricultural land. These exhibitions aim to provide a better understanding of the design and evolution of Les Portes de l'Essonne. Although the topics of these exhibitions are mostly related to intangible components, they also feature the social and economic dimensions of the territory. Recent exhibitions have focused on – for example – the social impacts of the de-industrialisation process, activities related to the river Seine, high-rise buildings considered as familiar landmarks and skylines, and the place of nature in the suburbs. In addition, different activities related to the exhibitions are organised, such as outside visits, conferences, film shows followed by discussions, scientific seminars, and pedagogical projects led by artists and aimed at children.

As well as drawing people into it by means of exhibitions, the *Maison* goes out into the townscape. 'Urban walks' are regularly organised for groups, with the participation of 'experts' invited to talk about specific topics. This type of activity has become very popular these last few years in the Paris suburbs: people seem eager to learn more about their city, to meet other people and to exchange views on local issues. Some of the walks are organised in collaboration with locals who act as guides and supply information about their own neighbourhood, and with students of the local art school. A social project already similarly developed in other towns of the Paris region has recently been tested in Athis-Mons: the idea is to work with

Figure 1.3 A *maison en meulière*, a highly typical Ile-de-France cottage built in the local stone (*meulière* + 'millstone grit')

Source: Collection of the Maison de Banlieue et de l'Architecture of Athis-Mons.

social structures and to ask young people aged 16–25 who are facing unemployment or other social difficulties to act as guides in their home town. More generally, the Maison de Banlieue et de l'Architecture develops projects with many local partners, and especially with cultural and social structures such as the 'social grocery' and various other associations dealing with disadvantaged people.

The Écomusée du Val de Bièvre: promoting everyday heritage

The Écomusée du Val de Bièvre is also situated south of Paris, in the suburban town of Fresnes in the *Département* of Val de Marne. The museum was created in 1979 by an association of several public bodies. It is officially recognised as an eco-museum and consequently it respects the rules and principles defined by the International Council of Museums in 1971. The aim of an eco-museum is primarily to valorise the intangible and tangible heritage of a territory and of its population. It is therefore a tool for conserving and transmitting the memory of an area, but it is also expected to participate in contemporary social life, by promoting activities and debates. The participation of the inhabitants is one of the major principles. While most of the eighty-four French eco-museums are devoted to rural or industrial areas, and highlight ancient traditions and handicrafts now belonging to the past, the Val de Bièvre Eco-museum is dedicated to suburban areas, along with the Eco-museum of Saint-Quentin-en-Yvelines. The institution serves the Communauté d'agglomération du Val de Bièvre, a grouping of seven towns with approximately 190,000 inhabitants.

Everyday life as heritage

The Val de Bièvre *Écomusée* has a slightly different scope than the *Maison* at Athis-Mons because it is a genuine museum with its own collection of pictures, photos and objects (http://ecomusee.agglo-valdebievre.fr/). The collection numbers more than a thousand objects, but unlike most museum collections each object is accompanied by a specially recorded interview with its former owner. As the director explains, '[w]e can collect all sorts of objects. The object is not interesting in itself, but talking with its owner enables us to understand its use and its meaning, and this is the interesting part'. The emphasis here is less on architecture and urban landscapes, and more on traditions and everyday life. However, in a similar way, the focus is on emphasising the value of suburban heritage and in the process promoting the participation of the inhabitants. In the towns covered by this museum, few elements can be considered as heritage in the traditional sense of the term (no famous buildings and no touristic places to visit). So the objective is to map and take into account what is significant for the inhabitants themselves, such as is clearly shown through the 'presentation text' of the museum: 'Val de Bièvre Eco-museum, Words of Suburban Inhabitants'. The aim is to collect histories, memories and objects which form part of the population's heritage and which relate to the past. However, heritage in this case is not only considered to be the past, it also relates to the contemporary issues of these suburban areas. 'We want to avoid nostalgic approaches in the representations of the area; we want to focus on the social issues, the disadvantaged populations, the minorities, the young people', explains the museum's director.

So, as in the previous example, the topics are mostly connected to the ordinary lives of the inhabitants, and concern tangible and intangible elements. The Eco-museum highlights various urban patterns specific to different periods of history (ancient city centres, estates composed of small single-family houses with gardens, high-rise social housing from different periods), industrial constructions, remnant agricultural zones, family gardens, suburban landscapes, etc. The subjects are linked to local stories and social practices, such as work, television, women's condition, and so on. The objective is to talk about the suburbs without negative stereotypes but with a truthfulness that allows difficulties (such as drugs, noise, pollution, unemployment, commuting, or the proximity of Fresnes prison) to be highlighted. The aim of the museum is not so much to defend a specific identity for suburban towns, but to show how people actually live – and have lived – in the region, with no nostalgia and with a focus on social topics. The Eco-museum is careful to take into account the social minorities and disadvantaged categories of the population.

A museum made for and by the population

Various activities are organised by the Eco-museum, such as exhibitions, conferences, debates, film screenings, concerts and shows. There are three types of exhibition which are all linked to the territory, and all have a clear social dimension. One type concerns history, ethnology and social sciences, and many of these are co-constructed with the local people. Another type is devoted to contemporary art and creativity (including commissioning work from artists), and concern paintings, sculptures, posters, etc. The third type of exhibition is dedicated to photographers (such as Robert Doisneau or Willy Ronis) whose work has featured the Ile-de-France region. Participation is a major issue for the museum: locals are invited to cooperate during the different stages of the process and particularly in collecting objects and stories. The principle is to collaborate with the inhabitants in defining the heritage of their town and to let the population decide what should be transmitted to the following generations. The Eco-museum organises outdoor visits, pedagogical activities and artistic workshops for the children, and offers a resource centre with books, journals and films. Moreover, the institution participates with other partners in national or international events such as the 'European Heritage Days' in September and the 'European Night of Museums' in May.

Towards new concepts and tools for sustainable cities?

These two examples illustrate various ways of dealing with 'ordinary heritage'. Both the Maison de Banlieue et de l'Architecture and the Écomusée du Val de Bièvre aim at creating and promoting stronger links between the inhabitants and their territory. But the challenge is great in the Paris region where the suburbs often have a stigmatised image: the term *banlieue* itself – which literally means 'rejected by the city', 'put beyond the boundaries' ('mis au ban') – has for many people (for example, politicians and the media) come to contain a negative meaning. The objective of both the institutions just described is not to create an artificially positive identity for these towns, but to overcome the clichés and to work alongside their populations to uncover the reality of these districts. Participation in the *banlieue* remains a delicate task, however, especially regarding the disadvantaged social categories of the population. As with most museums and cultural institutions, there is a small number of middle- or upper-class people who are interested and who participate in the proposed activities, but an important part of the population does not seem concerned, in spite of the relations developed with social associations. Moreover, while many children from the local schools come with their teachers, relatively few young people visit these institutions on their own. These questions relate to more general issues of citizenship as well as participation.

The activities organised by these cultural institutions go far beyond the objectives of traditional museums. They reflect a recent dynamic promoting new methodologies for sharing open spaces, landscape, culture and heritage, and thereby increasing the role that local populations play in defining heritage and the extent to which citizens understand and engage with decision making for urban transformations, which are particularly rapid and drastic in the suburbs. Making links between the past, the present and the future can contribute to developing a stronger sense of place. Thus, working with the population on heritage issues appears as a relevant approach because it gives the inhabitants some means to become actors in their own territory. This can be a major challenge because in France there is still a gap between a general wish to encourage participation and the reality of local actions. Although a shift from top-down projects to bottom-up procedures is recommended in many texts and laws, and in particular those concerning social policies and sustainable development, inhabitants' participation is often limited to transmitting information to those people concerned with urban projects (Desponds et al. 2014). Research has also pointed out the limits and risks of some participative cultural projects which seem to 'use' the inhabitants for a specific political purpose, notably in the case of urban regeneration operations (Auclair 2014b).

'New' concepts – in reality not so new but now becoming popular – have been developed by sociologists, philosophers and economists, and are currently being discussed in France in order to improve tools and approaches for public policy. Two of these seem particularly interesting for promoting citizens' participation and engagement in the city's affairs. The concept of 'empowerment' has recently been mediatised in France by the sociologist Marie Hélène Baqué (Baqué and Biewener 2013), notably during debates concerning urban and social policies in deprived areas. Originally, this concept was developed in the United States forty years ago to help communities and social minorities express their needs and expectations and defend their rights. In France, the message currently being promoted is that no thorough improvement can be accomplished in the suburbs without an active engagement of the population, and that radical changes must be brought to participation methods. Furthermore, the concept of empowerment can be related to the concept of 'capabilities' developed by Amartya Sen (Sen 1985) and by Martha Nussbaum (Nussbaum 2011). The 'capabilities approach' aims at helping people become aware of their potential to gain more power and to change their living conditions. The ambition is to reinforce human dignity and social justice. Hence, these approaches can be relevant to helping people understand and appreciate their local environment, acknowledge their existing ordinary heritage, and become proud of where they live.

Another significant concept which can be used in order to protect and enhance local heritage and to support social cohesion is that of 'commons'. It is becoming extremely popular, especially among NGOs and civil society, particularly since Elinor Ostrom received the Nobel Prize for Economics in 2009 for her work on the commons in developing countries (Ostrom 1990). Commons is a useful concept for supporting a community by identifying resources considered as essential for the whole group – such as tangible and intangible heritage – and setting up collective governance methods in order to protect and valorise these resources for the well-being of all. It was originally applied for managing natural resources (such as forests, water, biodiversity, and so forth) then for sharing knowledge and software, and more recently for urban development (Bollier and Helfrich 2012). At present, all over the world, various groups and networks related to the anti-globalisation movement, the 'Global Justice Movement', the South American movements promoting the notion of *buenvivir*, or more recently the international 'Occupy' movement, are contesting the privatisation and exploitation of resources due to neoliberal processes and are protesting against the resulting social and economic inequalities. These movements have contributed to the emergence of new ideas and values, and particularly to the popularisation of the concept of commons. For some researchers this concept appears as a possible 'political alternative' for the twenty-first century (Dardot and Laval 2014).

An international network of associations, the 'Réseau Francophone autour des Biens Communs' was created in 2012 in order to gather information on activities and best practices related to the concept of commons and to valorise and spread this concept. In November 2013, more than 150 events were held in 40 towns, during what was called the Festival des Villes en Biens Communs ('Festival of Cities as Commons'). At present the concept of commons is starting to be used for preserving culture, heritage and landscapes (Sgard 2010). Indeed, with this theoretical frame, heritage can be considered as a common resource, and acknowledged as such in order to be shared by the population. It belongs to everyone but is 'privately' owned by no one. So these concepts seem useful for promoting sustainable urban development.

Conclusion

In many suburban towns which are often without too much thought despised and characterised by a negative image, 'ordinary heritage' is becoming a genuine type of heritage which needs to be protected and enhanced. This new approach reveals a shift from the more traditional top-down heritage policies focusing on famous historical and architectural buildings. The major challenge is to encourage inhabitants' participation in defining this ordinary, everyday heritage. The aim is to identify what really counts for people, and by taking into account the real aspirations and expectations of the population, to promote well-being and social cohesion. But these goals are difficult to achieve and alternative participation methodologies are needed in order to reach certain categories of the population. However, the concepts of empowerment, capabilities and commons appear at present as interesting tools to be used for promoting sustainable cities.

References

Arnstein, S. 1969. A ladder of citizen participation. *Journal of the American Institute of Planners* 35(4), 115–34.
Auclair, E. 2010. Développement culturel – développement durable: vers une plus grande démocratie locale? In *Développement culturel et territoires*, eds Bernié-Boissard, C., Chastagner, C., Crozat, D. and Fournier, L-S. Paris: l'Harmattan, 49–67.

Auclair, E. 2011. Revenir vers les habitants, revenir sur les territoires. L'articulation entre culture et développement durable dans les projets de développement local. *Développement durable et territoires* 2(2), May. At http://developpementdurable. revues.org/8946?lang=en (accessed 10 February 2015).

Auclair, E. 2014a. Culture and sustainable development: a real dynamic or an uncertain relationship? In *Culture and sustainable development at times of crisis – proceedings*, eds Dragićević Šešić, M., Nikolić, M. and Rogač Mijatovič, L. Belgrade: Belgrade University of Arts, 15–27.

Auclair, E. 2014b. Les projets mémoriels en banlieue: participation ou instrumentalisation des habitats? *Francosphère* 3(2) (in press).

Baqué, M. H. and Biewener, C. 2013. *L'empowerment, une pratique émancipatrice*. Paris: La Découverte.

Bollier, D. and Helfrich, S. 2012. *The wealth of the commons: a world beyond market and state*. Amherst, MA: Levellers Press.

Council of Europe 2000. European Landscape Convention. European Treaty Series 176, Strasbourg.

Council of Europe 2005. Framework Convention on the Value of Cultural Heritage for Society (Faro Convention). European Treaty Series 199, Strasbourg.

Dardot, P. and Laval, C. 2014. *Commun, essai sur la révolution au XXIe siècle*. Paris: La Découverte.

Desponds, D., Auclair, E., Bergel, P. and Bertucchi, M. M. 2014. *Les habitants, acteurs de la rénovation urbaine?* Rennes: PUR.

Emelianoff, C. 2008. Pour un partage de la fabrique urbaine. *Urbanisme* no. 363 (Dossier: La ville durable en question[s]).

Florida, R. 2002. *Cities and the rising class*. London: Routledge.

Gadrey, J. 2012. *Adieu à la croissance. Bien vivre dans un monde solidaire*. Paris: Alternatives Économiques.

Jackson, T. 2009. *Prosperity without growth: economics for a finite planet*. New York/ London: Earthscan/Routledge.

Latouche, S. 2007. *Petit traité de la décroissance sereine*. Paris: Mille et Une Nuits.

Morin, E. 2000. *Les sept savoirs nécessaires à l'éducation du futur*. Paris: Seuil.

Nussbaum, M. 2011. *Creating capabilities: the human development approach*. Cambridge, MA: Harvard University Press.

Ostrôm, E. 1990. *Governing the commons: the evolution of institutes for collective action*. Cambridge: Cambridge University Press.

Sen, A. 1985. *Commodities and capabilities*. Amsterdam: North Holland.

Sgard, A. 2010. Le paysage dans l'action publique: du patrimoine au bien commun. *Développement durable et territoires* 1(2) (online).

Stébé, J. M. 2010. *La crise des banlieues, sociologie des banlieues sensibles*. Paris: Presses Universitaires de France.

UNESCO 2011. *Recommendation on the historic urban landscape*. At www.icomos.org/ en/what-we-do/focus/more-themes/historic-urban-landscape (accessed 10 February 2015).

Vieillard Baron, H. 2001. *Les banlieues, des singularités françaises aux réalités mondiales*. Paris: Hachette Supérieur.

Vivant, E. 2009. *Qu'est ce que la ville créative?* Paris: Presses Universitaires de France.

2 'Keeping it real'

Social sustainability in the Homeless Heritage project in Bristol and York

Rachael Kiddey and John Schofield

Introduction

Heritage, as a social process, has been likened to a 'conversation' (Fairclough 2012, xv). Seen in this way, heritage work is no longer limited to a concern for the conservation of objects or landscapes associated with grand (often simplified) nationalist histories. Instead, heritage is people-centred creative action in which everyone can be involved, a principle engrained in English Heritage's (2008) Conservation Principles (that heritage is a 'shared resource' in which 'everyone' should have the opportunity to get involved), and in the Council of Europe's (2005) Faro Convention on the Value of Heritage for Society (Council of Europe 2009). The Faro Convention connects everyone's 'right' to a heritage with which they can identify with the right to actively participate in the broader heritage process, and claims both as part of basic human rights. This was the theoretical foundation of the Homeless Heritage project 2008–2013. In this chapter, we critically appraise the Homeless Heritage project in terms of its social sustainability. We review collaborative methodologies and argue that heritage work can play an important role in developing social sustainability through increasing equity and enhancing social cohesion within communities. We identify ways in which heritage as a social process can involve working with communities on perspectives that at once challenge dominant narratives about the built environment and function therapeutically for the people involved, promoting redemption and enabling people to move on from traumatic experiences.

The Homeless Heritage project (2008–2013)

The Homeless Heritage project started organically in 2008 in Bristol in southwest England, one of the UK's largest cities with a population of over 400,000 (about the tenth largest by population). The project later became the subject of the first author's doctoral research (Kiddey 2014a) and expanded to York in northeast England, a city of about 200,000 people with a massive seasonal tourist influx. The objective of the project was to see whether homeless people would be interested in undertaking a collaborative archaeological study of the material culture of contemporary homelessness; that is, the landscapes, routes, places and things significant to those homeless people with whom we worked. A further objective was to see whether such a study might have anything useful to add to existing literature on contemporary homelessness. A central concern was for this to be a recording of homeless heritage by homeless people, in words and ways meaningful to them. In Bristol, homeless people were approached directly, on the street, and the project worked with whoever expressed a desire to take part in the project. In York, homeless people were contacted through an established homelessness centre in the city (Arc Light) where all residents were homeless at the time or had recently experienced homelessness. In Bristol, the project worked with around twenty-five homeless people overall and seven regularly. In York, where the population of people who consider themselves to be homeless is far smaller than in Bristol, the project worked with ten homeless people, but three remained fully engaged for the duration.

Collaborative methodologies

A distinctive aspect of archaeological approaches to the contemporary past is that the people who created or used the material culture, or who occupied sites of interest, are generally still around to speak to and work with. Other disciplines have been working with communities for many years, and ethnographic approaches that have been developed across other fields (especially in the social sciences) were usefully applied throughout the Homeless Heritage project. However, it was important to move beyond 'participant observation' to operate truly collaboratively. Thus, all aspects of the project, from initial field walking to the publication of findings, were open to all members of the 'research team', a team comprised of homeless people, academics and student archaeologists.

Having first established contact with homeless people, the purpose of the project was made clear. Kiddey explained that in documenting contemporary homeless heritage collaboratively, we would actively put homelessness 'on the map' and stake 'claims' to parts of the city through continued or historic use and through representing attachment to particular areas or places within the city. To some homeless people, this was a 'crazy idea' that sounded like it would be fun to take part in for an hour or two; to others, the project became something they owned and drove forward. Either way, these homeless people quickly became known and referred to as 'colleagues' rather than 'respondents' or 'subjects' – the word 'colleague' more accurately representing the nature of relationships within the project team. This seemingly minor descriptive detail was later proven to have significant impact on the success of the Homeless Heritage project in relation to its contribution to social sustainability, as we will show later in the chapter.

The next stage of the project involved undertaking a 'survey' of each city (Bristol and York). This took the form of walking and talking around the city with colleagues, individually and sometimes working in small groups. At first, it was hoped that homeless colleagues would take notes, and draw and annotate maps. However, it was soon evident that although colleagues were keen to talk about their perspectives and show us the landscape according to their points of view, few were keen to write or draw or operate a camera or Dictaphone. Instead, colleagues often suggested (to start with, at least) that Kiddey should write, draw or record what was said (Figure 2.1).

This corresponds with the experience of sociologist Nels Anderson, almost a century previously. Anderson, a pioneer of the method that became known as 'participant observation', studied 'hobos' in Chicago in the 1920s and recalls:

> At first the writer tried to gather his data by revealing his identity and purpose and asking the [homeless] individual to fill out the case card, upon which were about twenty five questions of a general nature. He was not long learning that such a method was not practical, as the reactions of the men were generally negative.
>
> (Anderson, cited in Rauty 1998, 81)

To the authors, working out how we would work together – agreeing processes for recording what we found – was an important part of developing a truly collaborative methodology, and being willing to adapt conventional working practices was integral to achieving the research objectives. Once the method for recording had been agreed upon, we took note of routes and shortcuts taken, recorded how our colleagues described places, and the names they gave particular sites or areas; we documented what was significant to whom and why, and to what things or places in the area they felt attachment or laid claim. These 'field walks' through homeless landscapes led to the creation of maps (annotated and hand drawn), thousands of photographic images and hours of audio recordings.

Figure 2.1 Andrew Dafnis and Rachael Kiddey 'counter-mapping' in Bristol
Photo: R. Kiddey, 2009.

The next stage of the Homeless Heritage project evolved from a conversation that took place one afternoon on a small tract of land, at the time synonymous with homelessness, known colloquially as 'Turbo Island' (Bristol). Several homeless people had an animated discussion about the history of the site. Had it been a place where pirates were hanged? Was it a kind of Speaker's Corner? Did it house a secret entrance to the largest crack den in Bristol? An archaeological excavation of the site was arranged and took place in December 2009. Work was undertaken by a collaborative team comprising between five and ten homeless people (the number changed daily), three professional archaeologists and ten archaeology students from the University of Bristol. Two local policewomen also joined the team for one day of the excavation, which greatly contributed to the sense that the excavation was a community focused project, open to all local people. A similar excavation of a contemporary homeless site was undertaken in York. 'The Pavilion', as the York site became known, featured on all the maps made during field walking, which arguably made it a landmark of homeless culture, ripe for collaborative excavation. These excavations have been written about in detail elsewhere (see Crea et al. 2014; Kiddey 2014a). Post-excavation work was then conducted with the same focus on prioritising collaborative working methods (Figure 2.2).

Everyone who wanted to remain actively involved in the project was encouraged to attend a series of finds washing and interpretation days held at the University of Bristol and the University of York respectively.

Figure 2.2 Martyn (a student at the University of York) undertaking finds analysis with Dan Clarke, York

Photo: R. Kiddey, 2011.

Therapeutic potential of collaborative heritage work

From the outset, it was never intended that homeless people would be the subject under study; rather the project's subject was their homeless material culture. Correspondingly, it was decided never to ask colleagues how they came to be homeless although if people wanted to talk while we undertook fieldwork, others were happy to listen. However, seated around the table cleaning finds in York, some colleagues felt motivated to speak about their experience of homelessness in a detail they had never previously entered (at least in the present company). As he cleaned a decayed polystyrene cup found at 'The Pavilion' (York) excavation, one homeless colleague noticed it read 'Women's Royal Voluntary Service' (RVS). 'They [the Women's RVS] used to run the cafe in the hospital when I was an inpatient there [Bootham Park Hospital]', our colleague proffered. He then spoke candidly about his experience of having spent time at Bootham Park Hospital (York) several times during the 1980s. He remembered the medication he had been given (Largactyl) 'known as the liquid cosh'. He talked about other patients who were given electroconvulsive therapy: 'You'd see someone led away from the ward and then wheeled back. It was scary', he told us. All the time, he continued to carefully clean artefacts and place them in the tray to dry, his eyes and hands occupied while he spoke. It was as though handling material connected to the time he spent living homeless and in and out of the Bootham Park mental health hospital gave his experience authenticity, made his memories more real. Part of our colleague's self-identity was, in a small way, confirmed by the tangible remains of a polystyrene cup.

Throughout fieldwork it was made clear to homeless colleagues and students that the intention was to present findings collaboratively. This has indeed been achieved through a variety of co-authored articles in diverse publications including *The Big Issue* (a magazine sold by self-employed homeless vendors) (Kiddey and Schofield 2009) and *British Archaeology* magazine (Kiddey and Schofield 2010). Two further co-written papers were published in the academic journals *Public Archaeology* (Kiddey and Schofield 2011) and the *Journal of the Society for Post-Medieval Archaeology* (Crea et al. 2014) alongside a chapter in the book *Who Needs Experts? Counter Mapping Cultural Heritage* (Kiddey 2014b). All publications contained verbatim comments (of varying lengths) from homeless colleagues and some (e.g. Crea et al. 2014) are co-authored with homeless colleagues. These colleagues were also encouraged to co-present findings at a variety of conferences (Figure 2.3).

For example, homeless colleagues Jane (Hallam), Danny, Deano and Whistler co-presented a paper titled 'Punks and Drunks: Counter Mapping Homeless Heritage' at the conference of the Theoretical Archaeology Group (TAG) at the University of Bristol in 2010, and Andrew (Dafnis), Jane (Hallam), Dan (Clarke) and Mark co-presented a paper called 'Stories from the Street: Contemporary Homelessness as Heritage' at the postgraduate conference in historical archaeology at the University of Leicester Centre for Historical Archaeology in 2011. Papers were put together by homeless colleagues and Kiddey collaboratively, with each

Figure 2.3 Jane Hallam presenting findings at the University of Cambridge
Photo: R. Kiddey, 2011.

colleague taking responsibility for a particular theme or aspect of homelessness about which they felt comfortable speaking. For example, Jane gave a presentation on her 'hot skipper' at the Theoretical Archaeology Group conference 2010, in Bristol. The word 'skipper' is widely used by homeless people in Bristol to denote a sleeping place. Jane's 'hot skipper' was so called because it was a sleeping place beside a hot air vent. In Leicester, Andrew explored the theme of 'anti-homelessness tactics' using photographs of locations where sheltered areas had been fenced or grilled off and rendered inaccessible.

Responses to these co-presented papers were illustrative of the powerful way archaeology can function as socio-political action and bear witness to a plurality of ways to experience places. They revealed archaeology to be an effective tool through which counter narratives may be materialised and used to challenge dominant heritage interpretations. Similarly, responses to co-presented papers revealed a wider appetite for non-traditional heritage, that is, appreciation of human experiences that have commonly been disregarded by the heritage industry. For example, at TAG 2010 Deano spoke for a short while about busking (street performing) as a homeless work practice upon which he relied for his living and then performed on guitar an extract from the song 'The Boxer' by Simon and Garfunkel. The conference session audience were moved to spontaneously join in the chorus, revealing an uncommon emotional and physical response to an academic paper. Negative stereotypes were challenged in both directions. For example, at the conference in Leicester in 2011 our co-presented paper was received well. During the plenary, historical archaeologist Dr Sarah Tarlow said that our paper had 'made her think'. Jane was pleasantly surprised by this comment because, as Jane perceived it, she had spoken in front of a room full of 'top people who've written books', people she perceived to be 'posh' and had imagined would look down on her (and other homeless colleagues). Jane said the experience had challenged her preconceptions about 'posh' people in much the same way that conference audience members spoke of the way in which each presentation 'made them think' differently about homelessness and addiction. In both cases, collaborative archaeological methodologies and co-presentation of findings led to the creation of a productive platform which centralised the humanity of the individual homeless people involved and facilitated a more critical, nuanced appreciation of the concept of homelessness and its phenomenological physical reality. Homeless knowledge, like academic knowledge, is not a coherent body but rarely do such diverse dialogues converge. A coming together in the way described can be shown to have had positive therapeutic outcomes for individuals and the broader public understanding of homelessness.

It is suggested that there are several significant factors to consider which might perhaps have more profound consequences. The group situation inspired by working as a collaborative heritage team was a safe and supportive one. It was not based on a 'cold' group of people brought together by mutual alcohol or drug problems as many 'group therapy' sessions available to people with addictions, well represented among the British homeless population, seem to be. Instead, it was a group of people brought together by a mutual and emerging interest in archaeology, and the focus of and reason for being together was not a negative one, such as addiction or the trauma of homelessness, but rather a positive social and cultural initiative. The social process was itself important – shared cultural activities, such as working together on site, sitting around a table to clean and interpret finds, and constructing papers and talks, made members of the group comfortable in one another's presence and greatly aided the nurturing atmosphere. Some people spoke and others listened in turn.

With regards to finds cleaning specifically, it is a fiddly process that requires a person's hands to remain occupied. Hand to eye co-ordination is important, and thus visual communication within the group is fleeting. The 'front brain' is occupied – in everyone around the table – and attention is focused on the 'mundane' job in hand, for example, cleaning the mud from artefacts. This allows the 'back brain' to wander in a similar way to that induced through meditation. There was no expectation that people should 'open up' or recall traumatic experiences but when they did, the group was supportive, which, it is suggested, took a lot of the pressure from the situation. Equally, there was no expectation that anyone should respond verbally to a colleague's story, or make a suggestion, diagnosis or comment. Rather like a Quaker meeting, the words, the scenarios, some of which were quite frightening images of loneliness and desperation, were able to 'just be' – and the group returned to the task in hand, that of finds cleaning. Finds cleaning, this mundane but necessary stage of the archaeological process, thus functioned to keep people 'on track' and to reach the wider objective of discovering the archaeological process as a social process (for example, preparing artefacts for analyses, identifying themes and emerging narratives) and provided a comforting path to which we returned regularly.

The supportive and nurturing social environment in which post-excavation processes – finds cleaning and interpretation, data analyses, putting together presentations and papers – took place was paramount. Following finds cleaning and a process of collaborative interpretation, two interactive public exhibitions were produced at which we showed the collection of material resources that the project had generated, for example, films about the project, photographs, maps and artefacts from the excavations. Each exhibition was organised thematically, open to the general public and hosted and curated by homeless colleagues.

As a social process in which homeless people were encouraged to contribute their perspectives and to recognise their experience of place to be as valid as that of anyone else, the project can claim to be very effective. Five dimensions of *measurable urban social sustainability* have been defined (Dempsey et al. 2011, 294) and the project (in retrospect) has been measured against these. One of them – community stability – was not relevant to the project; the homeless population within Bristol and York fluctuates to such an extent that to speak of a homeless 'community' is to misinterpret the degree to which homelessness is a social status experienced by individuals. But the Homeless Heritage project fulfilled all four of the others; it:

1   enhanced *social interaction* and increased 'social capital' for the individuals involved through widening and strengthening social networks;
2   constructed 'homeless heritage' as a team and involved the creation of a new collective who *participated* in activities and organised events *within the local community*;
3   exposed how contemporary homelessness manifested itself in Bristol and York, which allowed homeless colleagues to share their *sense of place* and identify their '*right to belong*' (Talen 1999, 370, quoted in Dempsey et al. 2011) in each city; and
4   *enhanced the perception of safety and security* within the local neighbourhood through increasing social interaction between homeless people and other members of the local community (including two policewomen) and fostering an attitude of respect for the shared built environment. For example, Andrew planted thirty daffodil bulbs in the top soil of Trench 1 after the excavation and backfilling of Turbo Island, saying that when they bloomed 'everyone could enjoy them'.

Undertaken collaboratively, heritage as a social process bears witness to a plurality of ways to experience places. To those involved in the Homeless Heritage project, heritage became a therapeutic conversation, a way to communicate experiences and perspectives and a process through which aspects of the past, fundamental to their constructed identities as British homeless people, could be re-examined and in some cases, moved on from.

The importance of legacy

The Homeless Heritage project may be considered to have been highly successful methodologically in terms of engaging a much-marginalised group in collaborative heritage work and to be commendable for positive therapeutic results for those individuals involved. The issue of how community archaeology and heritage projects archive the materials they generate must be more fully investigated if the counter stories that are produced are to remain accessible, and not simply drift back into the unknown at the culmination of a project or close of an exhibition. Without a deliberate strategy for ensuring the ongoing accessibility of materials generated through community heritage projects, the whole exercise becomes pointless except for the fun those involved might have had and the skills that they learnt. This is particularly true of politically driven heritage work that seeks to challenge 'authorised' or expert heritage perspectives and present alternative viewpoints (for example, strike histories, black and minority ethnic histories and working-class histories). Ensuring heritage projects have genuine legacy and retain momentum may broadly be considered to involve concerns over custodial relationships (for example, decisions on where archaeological or heritage material is deposited and on its ongoing accessibility).

'Community', like 'sustainability', is a slippery word, open to multiple interpretations and able to resist definition. Common criticisms of 'community' heritage or archaeological work include that it is too often a 'box-ticking' exercise that arose from politically correct notions of 'social inclusiveness', something that results in numerous case studies which do little more than uncritically demonstrate the 'importance' of community engagement (Watson and Waterton 2010). There are numerous important reasons for undertaking community heritage work, as we have seen above. There is, for example, value inherent in accessing previously marginalised bodies of knowledge, diversifying heritage audiences and perspectives on places, events and artefacts. Engaging people from non-specialist backgrounds in archaeological work, as was the case with the Homeless Heritage project, can aid interpretation of material remains and help to reveal multiple perspectives on place. The process enriches our wider understanding of how archaeological sites come into being and allows complex and, at times, contrasting viewpoints to be given equal representation, if not regard. However, without ongoing involvement of members of the source community (in this case, homeless people from Bristol and York) and the ongoing accessibility of archival materials generated throughout the project (for example, the photographs, maps, films and collections), one might argue that the work was, from a counter narrative point of view at least, futile.

Until relatively recently, many community heritage projects have had few options but to take materials (for example, boxes of artefacts and files of photographs, flyers, videos and recordings of oral testimonies) to a local archive or records office. Handing over material to 'official' repositories is sometimes considered problematic due to the colonial habit of appropriating and accumulating material culture, and subordinating people whose material it is, by manipulating and controlling it or simply hiding it from view, and preventing its stories from being told (Stevens et al. 2010, 67). Similarly, stuffing archival material into a box and storing it in a cupboard, or in a loft or garage, is equally likely to result in the stories remaining 'hidden' and inaccessible.

At the close of the Homeless Heritage project there was optimism for its legacy. Enthusiasm was high among the team, several homeless colleagues continued to regularly attend public archaeology lectures, and two homeless colleagues went on to undertake further community archaeology as volunteers. A comprehensive website constructed by the team (www.arcifact.webs.com) played host to photographs, films, audio recordings, maps and relevant other information. Accessing materials was made easy through having them all in one place, freely available online to anyone who wished to view them. Exhibition materials, including boxes of labelled bags of finds and other artefacts, hand-drawn maps, interpretation panels and exhibition memorabilia, were stored together, ready to be used in further exhibitions and later archived more permanently. Findings and results were co-published in a variety of formats, ranging from articles in popular magazines (Kiddey and Schofield 2009; 2010) and peer reviewed journals (Kiddey and Schofield 2010; Crea et al. 2014), a book chapter (Kiddey 2014b) and an unpublished but online Ph.D. thesis (Kiddey 2014a). The most telling outcomes, however, are those experienced by the individual people involved in the project and the groups with which they were directly associated (for example, probation services and other established public health and well-being services such as drug and alcohol rehabilitation and housing programmes).

Of those homeless colleagues with whom the authors worked in Bristol, Andrew, Jane, Punk Paul, Disco Dave and Ratty are now housed. Of York colleagues, Mark, Dan and Richard have now moved into independent housing. Several colleagues now have employment. Punk Paul is employed delivering vegetables and newspapers in Bristol and Mark is a full-time delivery driver for United Parcel Service in York. After spending time as a volunteer on a community archaeological excavation of a Roman site, Richard secured a full-time job as a cleaner at a hotel in York. Dan has part-time work as a gardener, works as a volunteer in a charity shop, and continues to give self-devised lectures on homelessness as heritage at several schools in York. Of those colleagues who suffered addiction to alcohol and/or drugs, several people have reported that their consumption has decreased markedly since taking part in the heritage project. Reasons include that they feel happier and continue to benefit from widened social circles, which now include people who do not have addictions, an uncommon luxury for the majority of homeless people in Britain. Furthermore, several colleagues reported that involvement in the heritage project inspired them to engage with existing addiction services in Bristol and York. This outcome is particularly valuable because it suggests that colleagues have chosen to make this move freely and actively rather than as the result of punitive external pressures such as threats from a law court. It is suggested that collaborative heritage work of the type described here can aid the rehabilitative process where 'realising for oneself' is a far more powerful way to learn or accept something than is absorption of information through lecture or punishment (Lacan 1977).

Further to those positive outcomes described above, important identity work was undertaken by colleagues as a function of the archaeological process. Andrew, for example, cited the project as having directly enabled and inspired him to reject his 'street name', Smiler (by which he had been known for twenty-five years) in favour of his birth name, Andrew. He explained that the experience of counter-mapping Bristol made him realise that he was tracing his *former* self, Smiler, the homeless heroin user. At that time, Andrew was moving into independent accommodation and no longer used heroin. The collaborative heritage process, by which places were mapped according to *memory and meaning*, led Andrew to the realisation that the places – the social activities, people and 'things' which constituted them – were aspects of his *past*, even if it was a recent past. This is a good example of the powerful way in which archaeology can aid construction (or reconstruction) of identity through locating aspects of it in space and time. The difference between Smiler and Andrew is fewer than five years, but Andrew remained haunted by his street name and its associations. The active experience of being directly involved in the heritage process insisted that change had occurred. Following this powerful realisation, Andrew spent Christmas Day 2012 with his parents for the first time in over thirty years.

Reconnecting with family is a strong and happily recurrent theme among the positive outcomes from the Homeless Heritage project. Jane made contact with her children through Facebook in April 2012, and has since seen photographs of her grandchildren and made plans to visit her family in Brighton. Deano decided to look for regular work in Bournemouth and, still busking for a living, has moved to the city full time so that he can see his children more regularly. Richard resumed contact with his family in York and now shares a house with his father. Dan, now housed independently, had his parents to stay for a weekend for the first time in twenty years and had them back again for Christmas 2013. If only one colleague had been motivated to resume contact with family following engagement with the Homeless Heritage project, we might see no correlation. However, several colleagues were motivated to reconnect with their families and cite the project directly as having influenced their actions. For this reason, it is argued that involvement in collaborative heritage work can have therapeutic outcomes perhaps more familiar to fields of psychology and counselling, where reminiscence and restoration are central features of the approach. Although by no means an anticipated legacy at the start of the project, increased 'social sustainability' is a significant positive outcome and suggests there is potential for archaeology to function more explicitly as a therapeutic material memory practice in the future.

Conclusion

Translating those Conservation Principles (English Heritage 2008) relating to social value and the laudable but challenging aims of the Faro Convention (Council of Europe 2009) into practice was never going to be easy. Heritage practice has an accumulation of expertise when it comes to managing things – curated objects, places and buildings – but it has less experience of working with people, managing and facilitating their wishes and expectations. Some 'heritage communities' (after Council of Europe 2009) are willing and eager volunteers, never shy of expressing an opinion, or getting involved in workshop events and outreach. These are 'the converted', with whom the heritage sector has a continued dialogue long after their conversion. But what of the many others who also have a heritage (or heritages) but for whom the heritage sector seems alien, or who are less willing to engage with established heritage practice, or who are suspicious of those community-minded, authorised 'experts'? How can those working in the 'official' heritage sector – and in other sectors, for example that of sustainable development – involve them, and should they even try? The argument presented through this fieldwork is that we should and can, because whilst never easy it is possible to achieve real and meaningful results.

This project also demonstrates some of the clear benefits in persevering, both for a sector that should be creative in establishing inclusive methodologies, and for the participants. In this chapter the emphasis has been on the participants, whose real-life stories are genuine beacons of hope, and an illustration that heritage can help. The challenge is to move beyond a position where one project can help a dozen participants, to a situation where one sector can help another. This is where cultural and/or social sustainability kicks in – the points beyond which a project begins and ends, and people benefit, to the preferred end game, where one project leads to another, and where the beneficiaries pass on their knowledge and their stories to new groups. That happened here, on a small but significant scale. As the Bristol project was drawing down, and the York project was coming alive, several members of the Bristol team, all homeless, travelled up to York to persuade members of York's homeless community to engage with the project. This transfer of expertise and enthusiasm allowed the project to move from one city to another. Mark, a York-based homeless colleague, explained:

> We're always being told to 'get involved' in activities by Support Workers and probation officers ... but to hear about the [Homeless Heritage] project from people who'd actually been homeless, knew that game, that's what made me get involved and not just sack it off at the start.

It is a small example of what is possible. The challenge for the heritage sector is now to invest in this possibility. Heritage is one of those things that everybody has, irrespective of their cultural, social and economic backgrounds. In a society within which divisions are often given prominence, heritage has the capacity to unite and create a common sense of purpose. We have shown that this can be done, with some of the hardest-to-reach members of our society. For this approach to prove sustainable, we need to up our game – to do more, and work harder around the margins.

Acknowledgements

We are very conscious of writing this on behalf of the colleagues in our project, to all of whom we owe thanks. It will be noticed that we sometimes use colleagues' full names and sometimes we refer to them by first names only or by their 'street' names. Equality within the team was and remains paramount and the difference in how we name people in publications reflects their personal choices. In some cases, involvement in the Homeless Heritage project directly influenced colleagues' decisions to revert to using and preferring to be known by their full, given name (see Kiddey and Schofield 2011, 20).

References

Council of Europe 2009. *Heritage and Beyond*. Strasbourg: Council of Europe.

Crea, G., Schofield, J., Dafnis, A., Hallam, J. and Kiddey, R. 2014. Turbo Island: Excavating a contemporary homeless place. *Post Medieval Archaeology*, 48(1), 133–50.

Dempsey, N., Bramley, G., Power, S. and Brown, C. 2011. The Social Dimension of Sustainable Development: Defining urban social sustainability. *Sustainable Development*, 19, 289–300.

English Heritage 2008. Conservation Principles, Policies and Guidance for the Sustainable Management of the Historic Environment. *English Heritage* (www.english-heritage.org.uk/publications/conservation-principles-sustainable-management-historic-environment/conservationprinciplespoliciesguidanceapr08web.pdf; accessed 25 January 2015).

Fairclough, G. 2012. Others: A prologue. In Giaccardi, E., ed., *Heritage and Social Media: Understanding heritage in a participatory culture*. London: Routledge, xiv–xvii.

Giaccardi, E., ed. 2012. *Heritage and Social Media: Understanding heritage in a participatory culture*. London: Routledge.

Kiddey, R. 2014a. Homeless Heritage: Collaborative social archaeology as therapeutic practice. Ph.D. thesis, University of York (http://etheses.whiterose.ac.uk/6262/; accessed 18 July 2014).

Kiddey, R. 2014b. Punks and Drunks: Counter mapping homelessness in Bristol and York. In Schofield, J., ed., *Who Needs Experts? Counter mapping cultural heritage*. Farnham, Surrey: Ashgate, 165–79.

Kiddey, R. and Schofield, J. 2009. Rough Guide. *The Big Issue*, 23–29 November, 14–15.

Kiddey, R. and Schofield, J. 2010. Digging for (Invisible) People. *British Archaeology*, July/August, 18–23.

Kiddey, R. and Schofield, J. 2011. Embrace the Margins: Adventures in archaeology and homelessness. *Public Archaeology*, 10(1), 4–22.

Lacan, J. 1977. *The Four Fundamental Concepts of Psychoanalysis*. London: Hogarth Press.

Rauty, R. 1998. *Nels Anderson: On hobos and homelessness*. Chicago: University of Chicago Press.

Stevens, M., Flinn, A. and Shepherd, E. 2010. New Frameworks for Community Engagement in the Archive Sector: From handing over to handing on. *International Journal of Heritage Studies*, 16(1–2), 59–76.

Watson, S. and Waterton, E. 2010. Editorial: Heritage and community engagement. *International Journal of Heritage Studies*, 16(1–2), 1–3.

3   The burden of history

Living heritage and everyday life in Rome

Anna Laura Palazzo and Antonio Pugliano

Similarities and specificity of the Roman case

The treatment of archaeology in Rome is a major issue for several reasons. The sheer extent and richness of the city's heritage and the likelihood (or, for planners and builders, the 'risk') of any development in Rome encountering unexpected structures and sites requires spatial planning and 'development control' practices to be designed in the light of a protection, conservation and 'rescue' mentality. In a broader sense, however, the inherent significance or 'social relevance' of archaeological or historic remains should also be framed within decision-making concerning possible re-use, incorporating both formal and functional values. In this respect, a major concern is the cleavage between the set of value judgments endorsed by specialists in historically focused disciplines which associate 'relevance' with research, knowledge and original meanings, and the significance arising from people's perceptions and informal understandings, that is to say the 'visibility', 'legibility' and 'imageability' of surviving archaeological remains.

If we go deeper into the division between expert and common knowledge, from the specialists' point of view ruins often constitute exclusive and irreplaceable evidence for past societies and for history. This very attribute tends to focus on the past and can obscure ongoing relationships between past and present, especially when dealing with remains brought to light by excavation. The 'documentary' or evidential value afforded by archaeological remains, however, only rarely attracts a general or public rather than a specialist audience. This is the case for the thousands of visible, still 'silent', remains that occupy the metropolitan area of Rome. Paradoxically such plenitude allows for indifference. Despite or perhaps because of being surrounded by such plentiful heritage, Italian people, and notably Romans, seem unaware of the values and potentialities of their legacy. At the same time, a crucial aspect of our regulatory framework is the fact that protection is conceived and perceived as a system of regulations set up in order to avoid almost all new development according to a conformative approach, rather than to achieve a better living environment in consonance with a performative one.

The treatment of physical remains from the past should in fact go far beyond their material survival into the realms of intangible heritage related to cultural and symbolic values. Monuments can provide communities with a new sense of memory while keeping alive the awareness of present times, but an interruption in the use and functionality of archaeological remains can be a major obstacle to this. Individual and collective perceptions of what has vanished and what still remains, are at stake along with new learning experiences, and of course other dimensions such as critical interpretation and communication.

The conservation theories of Brandi (1963) and Manieri Elia (1998) have been influential in Italy; in these, the interpretation, restoration and planning of archaeological heritage is seen as a possible solution to the problem. This starts by recognising the irreducible ambiguity of the 'ruin', that is always a fragment but has inherent *imageability*, that is, 'the quality of a physical object, which gives an observer a strong, vivid image' (Lynch 1960). When perceived as part of landscape, the artefact somehow becomes involved in the natural aging processes of its environment. Such an association between ruins and nature only works if the ruin has an appropriately defined surrounding area that can act as its *contesto di accoglienza*, its 'welcoming frame' or 'setting'.

On a different conceptual level, the complexity of dealing with archaeological remains in a city such as Rome arises primarily from the uncertain location and unpredictable physicality of the remains. Even though indirect, remote and non-invasive techniques such as photo-interpretation and geophysical prospecting now exist, and preventive knowledge can keep risk within limits (Palazzo 2008), unexpected remains can still suddenly force new choices and costs; 'archaeological risk' is therefore a crucial issue in any urban planning or development process.

Another factor is that the intrinsic complexity of urban places through time requires 'urban archaeology' to be a 'global archaeological research that deals with a living city, or an entire settlement sequence, from its foundation to the present day, without privileging one period over another' (Francovich and Manacorda 2000, 350, authors' translation). Such an approach requires contributions from many disciplines and the engagement of civil society within a participatory approach. In practice, however, the distinctive and sometimes conflicting perspectives and philosophies of different specialists such as archaeologists, restorers and urban planners can create a major arena for ambiguity. Each professional group can have a different role in the same project, with differing opinions on the inherent relevance of archaeological remains or of their formal and functional value, on conservation measures and on their future treatment in the urban fabric. This segmentation of knowledge is deeply rooted in positivism; but although the different action fields and competences may appear to be exclusive, they are in practice overlapping or contradictory, with resultant potentially negative effects on decision-making.

The successful combination of expert and common knowledge to help find a balance between continuity and innovation remains a challenge, and especially so in urban contexts. In this chapter, our overview of Roman experience is framed in the light of the European Landscape Convention – the 'Florence Convention', of which Italy is one of the instigators and a great champion – that notably defines 'the aspirations of the public with regard to the landscape features of their surroundings' as being critical to the management and planning of well-functioning, socially responsive landscapes.

Rome: past ways of handling the problem

Archaeological pre-surveys to identify archaeological needs and avoid unplanned variations during urban construction projects have only been mandatory in Rome since 1997. Moreover, decision-making is dispersed and fragmented, at institutional (municipality, region, state), administrative and even disciplinary levels, which can produce outcomes detrimental to the archaeological remains and ultimately to the city itself and to its citizens' lives. This section will describe the evolution in Rome – first in the ancient walled centre and then in its suburbs and surrounding countryside – of ways of managing the rich repositories of vestiges of the past that are still relevant to the millions of people who use, visit or live in Rome. These remains include not only major remnants (such as public buildings, aqueducts and ancient roads), but many scattered 'memories' (such as towers, walls, dwellings, smaller temples and churches) across a broad region within the city's wider hinterland that are indicative of how heritage affects everyday life.

Within the walls: the historic centre

For Rome's core area, there is a long history of trying to come to terms with the archaeological heritage. In 1813, during the Napoleonic occupation, the architect Louis-Martin Berthault drew up ambitious plans for a large area of Rome next to the Italian garden of Horti Farnesiani on the northern side of the Palatine Hill. He was loosely inspired by the principles of English landscape gardens by following the instructions of the Minister of the Interior, Jean-Pierre de Montalivet, to take into consideration all the monuments and those which provided their setting, to manage access to the most celebrated from their most picturesque viewpoints without neglecting the lesser monuments – already, therefore an impossibly large task (Boyer 1943). His grand proposal was to carry out a large-scale and extensive clearance to create a new promenade – 'un Jardin du Capitole' – that would connect all the monuments in the Forum area between the Capitoline Hill and the Colosseum. Berthault began his work with extensive clearance and excavations, but the project was never completed.

In 1887, however, after the proclamation in 1870 of Rome as the capital of the new Italian nation, a series of programmes were launched to clear away the later layers of the city, including streets and houses, and to incorporate the resultant isolated classical-period ruins within a so-called 'Monumental Area'. By then, there had been major steps towards a sensible treatment of memories linked to the value of complexity and recognition of heritage as a 'palimpsest'. Although the passage of time had carried out some selection of what should survive, it was seen as the task of specialists to decide what should be given priority to create understanding and readability for the non-experts. Such assumptions, although exposed to radical reversals during the Fascist period, were reflected in the archaeologist Rodolfo Lanciani's *Forma Urbis Romae* (1901) created in the late nineteenth century, an outstanding and very detailed representation of ancient

Rome within the Aurelian walls, laid out on the modern city map at a scale of 1:1,000. Lanciani's main source for this map – the surviving fragments of the massive Severan (early third century) 'Marble Plan' – was matched with a meticulous documentation of the archaeological discoveries that had come to light during hectic construction activities. In connecting the reconstructed ancient city plan to the present-day plan, Lanciani created a practical tool for planners and restorers. Soon after, in the early twentieth century, stratigraphic excavation methods and extensive restoration techniques (*anastylosis*) were introduced into the Monumental Area by archaeologist Giacomo Boni. This included the didactic use of plants and greenery (such as bunches of evergreens cut in the shape of columns or exedras, for example) to support a virtual reconstruction of the layout and structure of buildings that had been entirely or partly lost.

The 'liberation' of the major ruins of the ancient city from everyday life by creating the Monumental Area, however, was in fact also an 'exile', separating past from present. It caused major destruction of the urban fabric and the deportation of thousands of inhabitants from the centre of the city to distant suburbs, the so-called *borgate*. After the Second World War, increasing social awareness led to a cultural debate more focused on the 'use of history', within the broad range of options and positions between the treatment of the Monumental Area's archaeological remains as 'monuments' to be preserved as a civic or national symbol, and their interpretation as 'documents' to be handed over to public enjoyment under specific rules and conditions. The cleavage between the two options has gradually softened, according to the shared statement that 'the modern city must connect with, but not damage the ancient city, enabling the two cities, the old and modern, to touch and communicate with each other' (Panella 2014, authors' translation).

During the 1980s and 1990s, municipal initiatives led to a much more radical conflict. A competition for the re-arrangement of the Monumental Area was the occasion for a strong debate between the needs of the living city and arguments for protecting archaeological remains. A proposal to expand the Forum area by 'restoring' – or, more accurately, reconstructing – the Velia Hill, that had been 'cleared' in the Mussolini period during the construction of the Via dei Fori Imperiali, would have meant sacrificing this great monumental artery of the city, and further damaging mobility throughout the municipality (Insolera and Perego 1983; Benevolo 1985). Almost thirty years later, construction sites of the new C-line of the metro, excavated below the archaeological levels, invade the spaces of a busy, if not chaotic city. Interruptions and changes to the building of the metro caused by unexpected archaeological discoveries take the discussion back years.

Beyond the walls: the suburbs and the Agro Romano

In the 1960s, the entire municipal area was for the first time placed under zoning regulations focused on protective restrictions affecting not only single sites and ruins but also their wider settings and contexts. Despite this, the planning process was manifestly careless with regards even to documented remains such as the numerous structures of the Roman era along main roads from the city. Compulsory alignments and 'non-buildability' constraints were defined but have seldom been enforced. This is despite a series of inventories and cartographic and topographic studies focusing on the Roman countryside, culminating in the 1980s with the *Historical Archaeological Monumental Map of the Suburbs and Roman Countryside* (known as the *Carta dell'Agro*, or the *Agro Map*).

The *Agro Map* inventoried at a scale of 1:10,000 several thousand artefacts of historical-monumental, natural and/or landscape interest, both above ground and buried, and formally controlled or not. It offered some protection even to elements at high risk of being transformed or destroyed, such as sites with pottery fragments. Just as Lanciani's *Forma* nearly a hundred years earlier, the *Agro Map* makes immediately visible the coincidence between the pre-existing archaeological elements and new proposals and provisions. Coloured symbols defined site type, period, condition and conservation status. For ancient linear elements such as paths and aqueducts (often only visible intermittently, even on aerial photos), a 'hypothetical' – or predictive – factor was introduced reflecting reliability of knowledge. The map project also included a census of the farmhouses which were a characteristic element of Rome's countryside. Although some results were achieved, the *Agro Map* should have been treated as an in-progress tool requiring continuing research in order to assess whether isolated findings belonged to more extended and complex structures, such as villas, funerary complexes, archaic settlements still waiting for re-constructive hypotheses (Fazzio 2005).

In 2008, a new city plan, supported by a *Map for Quality* (2008), combined information from the *Agro Map* with a *New Forma Urbis Romae* (2001) that had been produced for the area within the Aurelian walls. The *Map for Quality*, which was intended to address the main weaknesses of previous legislation, was not limited to a census of cultural heritage. It also provided criteria and guidelines for a range of possible interventions according to preservation needs and transformation criteria. It laid out, by means of a handbook, the case-by-case transformation processes needed, subject to differing site conditions – public land or private areas – and the legibility of ruins; further, pre-approval processes were specially conceived to reduce the impact of new development on structures that are not visible on the surface.

In real practice, the biggest discrepancies between conservation and transformation occurred in a number of social housing neighbourhoods. Archaeological risk played a part in ongoing development processes by determining 'compromise solutions' in alignments and layouts of urban fabric. In the case of urban gaps in the suburbs recently incorporated into the city, there has been some disruption in the continuity of the remains and a loss of coherence, and some more or less accidental demolitions of minor finds. Trivial solutions are common, almost routine, however: so far, mostly within the urban fringe, when remains are secured, often in a fragmentary state, they are fenced off and isolated from 'real life'; this broadly ensures physical preservation and avoids degradation, but diminishes other, social and cultural, values.

When ruins are preserved in squares, plazas and public gardens, they do not always have a true dialogue with their surroundings. Their locations may even represent a deterrent to good preservation as they are often associated with urban decay rather than with urban regeneration. Where monuments are not integrated with their surroundings, there is a risk that in the absence of pro-active conservation the degradation process may paradoxically intensify, as shown by a series of cases. The many gaps that were left in the urban fabric in order to protect some major remains, as well as the trivial shelters covering scattered remnants of larger structures, are seldom accessible and are likely to become rubbish dumps, not to mention the deterioration caused by atmospheric agents and vandalism. Conversely, when protection is too effective, it isolates remains from the real city and its developments, encouraging citizens to disregard cultural heritage in their leisure time; the way that archaeological fragments are 'preserved' within the main hall of Italy's largest shopping mall, the 'Porta di Roma', puts them out of sensible context and mainly generates indifference (Figure 3.1).

In the late 1990s, in order to overcome these difficulties, the Municipality of Rome enacted the so-called 'Programma Centopiazze' with the intention of creating or recovering several public spaces. This initiative ought to have taken an overview of the entire urban context in both historic and current functional and access terms, but in practice it was little more than a series of unconnected ideas, which mostly proved that a bench, some trees and a memorial stone do not create a sustainable plaza. Even when a good design concept was found, implementation fell short of planning, as in the Piazza Castano in the deprived neighbourhoods of

Figure 3.1 Archaeological fragments in the main hall of the Porta di Roma shopping mall, said to be the largest mall in Italy: the cultural asset is out of context and is not a point of interest, thus generating indifference

Photo: A. Pugliano, 2012.

Tor Bella Monaca far away from the city centre, which included a stretch of the ancient Via Gabina, still paved with ancient slabs but completely ignored except for vandalism and drug trafficking. The Piazza Castano concept was in fact co-produced through a series of thirty public meetings during which community hostility and distrust gradually turned into curiosity and interest, and produced a dialogue that socially validated the project and met local needs. The archaeological authorities were gradually convinced of the added value of allowing the Via Gabina to be brought back into use as a pathway, to connect the Piazza with other places in the neighbourhood, while the architects borrowed form and materials (travertine and coloured concrete aggregates) from the classical period as well as utilising traditional elements of the Roman landscape such as pines, cypresses, and Tibetan cherry (*prunus serrula*). The design worked well for a while, until undermined by poor maintenance, thus increasing the indifference of the inhabitants (Figure 3.2).

Figure 3.2 Piazza Castano and the Via Gabina – co-production and continued maintenance. Despite good co-produced design, this attempt to bring archaeological remains into a living relationship with the modern city, as part of the 'Programma Centopiazze' of the Municipality of Rome, has been compromised by poor maintenance leading to indifference on the part of local inhabitants; after several years the Via Gabina is neglected, and the sensitive landscaping is fading into invisibility

Photo: A. L. Palazzo, 2010.

Looking forward: how should heritage work in Rome?

Several proposals have been made in the past ten years for the regeneration of the central Monumental Area, but without extensive realisation. One, the project 'Ancient Rome, a Value for Modern Rome: Regeneration and Enhancement of the Monumental Area', aimed to improve the use and accessibility of underused sites within an area of 107 hectares including the Circus Maximus, the Theatre of Marcellus, the Capitol, the Imperial and Roman forums, the Palatine Hill, the Valley of the Colosseum, and the Oppian and Celio hills. The basic intention was to offer the citizens' community a wide and rich archaeological context of the centre of Rome, in compliance with the local road network that, especially in the early twentieth century, had determined the fragmentation of that archaeological site. The goal was a balanced urban structure both respectful of the archaeological background and consistent with the contemporary city and well linked to outer city areas.

The latest initiative was advertised by the municipality as 'Roma Capitale' and presented to the press as a cultural plan based on educational issues. It aims at recomposing the archaeological landscape of Rome in a unitary path of utility and knowledge, addressing social issues whilst enhancing sense of place. One sub-programme, the 'Rome Grand Tour European Programme' (March 2014), concerns ten sites, mostly in the city centre (the Celio Park, the Oppian Hill, the Tor de Conti, Trajan's Market, the Capitol, the Theatre of Marcellus, the Via dei Cerchi and the Circus Maximus) with two (Pliny's Villa in Castelfusano and the Centocelle Park, Ad Duas Lauros and Piscina Villas) in the outskirts. The programme characterises contemporary use by defining for each location a predominant function. Thus, the Capitol represents the place for *Public Life*, Trajan's Market *Progress*, the Circus Maximus *Free Time*, the Theatre of Marcellus *Art*, the Via dei Cerchi *Identity*, the Tor de Conti *Welcoming*, the Oppian Hill *Welfare*, the Celio Park *Life Styles*, Pliny's Villa *Leisure and Meditation*, the Centocelle Park *Domestic Life and Agricultural Production*. The project, however, shows no strategy consistent with the initial hypothesis of educational purposes and recovery or strengthening of place-identity. In other words, it fails to meet the challenge of conveying within each location their multiple narratives of place, but rather threatens to impose a simulated reality rather than authentic experience.

The main objective, in contrast, ought to be to demonstrate the cultural meaning of the environment (historic, anthropological and social) to help motivate and support particular options for enhancement. The foundations of thematic itineraries should be laid by offering to the community the historical data about formation and growth processes, the social organisation of human settlements in the different periods, and by highlighting past ways of living and artistic expressiveness. That is to say, archaeologists and planners should today put the narrative potential of sites and ruins into practice. The cultural value of urban artefacts is fully understandable only when they are placed in some sort of wider context or network of related places. Understanding and appreciation, and thus use and valuing, of the Monumental Area, for example, would benefit from further exploiting its connection with the Appian Way and from a more efficient relationship with the

Tiber, thus enabling fuller enjoyment and use of the cultural landscape of the ancient suburbs and countryside southwest of the city as far as the extraordinary complex of Portus and Ostia on the coast.

This is not an easy task. It is a matter of conceiving the city and its significant contexts as if together they were a dispersed landscape museum system – perhaps on the analogy of some eco-museums – comprising three principal foci: a Museum of the Ancient City in Ostia and Portus (Pugliano 2011), a Museum of the Tiber in the countryside (Palazzo and Rizzo 2013) and the long-desired Museum of the Historical City in the centre. Such a museum network would be usable in everyday life through different levels of participation and even real experiences. A tourist plan could be drawn up to use specific forms of slow, eco-sustainable and efficient urban and suburban mobility able to connect service centres and cultural hubs through a series of selected paths, also devoted to thematic tours.

A complementary transport system might use the banks and floodplains of the Tiber to develop the river's accessibility and navigability and to rediscover urban and suburban railway lines for reaching Ostia and Portus and Fiumicino (Leonardo da Vinci) Airport. Generally speaking, it would be a matter of connecting isolated monumental contexts by physical and cultural links which would physically intersect with 'ordinary' urban mobility and allow better access to archaeological areas from underground stations and urban railways. The point would be to reclaim unused areas of the city, and its interstitial tissues, by facilitating the development of sites related to the character of urban and suburban places, but above all to make the ancient remains begin to live as part of the modern city, to bring them into daily life. Activities should be evocative of relevant ancient practices (agriculture, traditional local crafts) and functional and useful in modern-day terms (accommodation, facilities for tourism).

The creation of such a broad museum system, diffused and centred upon the City of Rome, could generate many opportunities for development in the spheres of restoration, economic regeneration, social inclusion, cultural and professional training as well as employment. In order to implement the urban economic and social development, relationships between training and employment have to be re-balanced within the cultural heritage sector. The topic is crucial. Italy stands out in Europe (indeed in the world) as the country with the largest number of UNESCO World Heritage Natural and Cultural Sites (fifty) and has Europe's highest national percentage of students (24 per cent) – but it records the lowest percentage of employees in the sector (1.1 per cent) (Modena 2013). This consideration led to a university teaching experience in the Ostiense site (Pugliano 2011) that tested an important educational model by combining conservation practices with the training of operators involved in decision-making and production processes. The initiative aimed to set up sustainable conservation and planning projects in Ostia and Portus, through a series of integrated research and training actions which also built stronger bridges between the university and social and economic life in the territory (Pellegrino and Pugliano 2012). Action was focused on 'organised forms of learning' (a digital platform equipped with a special cartography and with the thesaurus of reference for the database compilation), useful to manage the site and suitable for quick conversion into activities of enhancement (Figure 3.3).

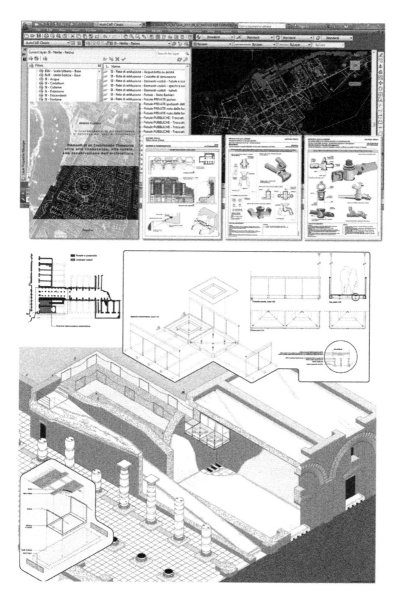

Figure 3.3 Ostia Antica and Portus. Preparatory surveys for the enhancement of the archaeological sites. Above: The digital platform (GIS) equipped with the thesaurus of reference for the database compilation. Below: Operational proposals for the enhancement of Portus; the restoration of the warehouses near the Portico of Claudius

Source: Research and graphic elaboration by Elisabetta Moriconi (above) and Simone Diaz (below) for: Pugliano, A., *Programme of integrated research and training actions for the documentation, conservation and enhancement of the archaeological site of Ostia. Convention between MiBAC-SSBAR Seat of Ostia and 'Roma Tre' University of Rome – DiPSA [2010–2012].*

The experiment led to the organisation of an International Postgraduate School, an on-site training opportunity for architects, restorers, landscape architects and archaeologists to work on the sustainable conservation of archaeological contexts. Its future success, however, demands conspicuous, enduring, costly and fundamental efforts from both the government and the scientific community: these efforts should be directed to allow training and academic institutions to root themselves more strongly in the territory and in local communities.

Networks based on archaeological remains within and outside the city, linked by tourist paths, will need to follow effective scientific and communicative behavioural models using up-to-date tools. The model will conceptually differ from past protection and conservation practices that generate a cultural distance between the ruins and the modern city that surrounds them, which ensures that ruins are isolated and inaccessible, 'silent' and unintelligible, and discouraging of community interaction. Yet, properly explained and communicated, the monumental highlights and the archaeological substrata could be re-integrated with the living city and its citizenry in perception, even though not always physically.

If the material expressions of different historical phases of the territory were thus to be enhanced, residents and visitors could more readily experience a stimulating and living environment that is emotionally and aesthetically rich and symbolically informative. In such a well-organised living environment, the vestiges of the past would no longer appear as foreign objects that limit and complicate the citizens' daily life; rather, they would become the essential components of the everyday theatre of their existence. The memory of the past could play an active role in contemporary culture and citizenship. An example can be found in the Theatre of Marcellus, recently re-embedded in its setting, or 'welcoming frame', displaying a sequence of open spaces within the urban scene, notably by adapting the excavated remains to the urban context through an efficient pedestrian path. The Theatre area has become part of the local urban road network and is now easily usable by tourists and citizens alike. It has been given back to the city in the form of a cultural/urban site, suitable for hosting cultural events too.

The richness and depth of Rome's historical and archaeological palimpsest is indeed particularly suited to such a project of reconnection. Rome, like other major cities, is the expression of a highly complex evolutionary process based on the continued influence of its ancient and medieval predecessors. It has for 2,000 years been the norm in Rome for an inherited genetic code of townscape, or of urban planning, or of architectural masses, to dictate the next layer. The continual redevelopment within the constraints of the ancient street blocks – the *insulae* – has been one method; another has been the 'consumption' of monuments, metabolised or reinvented through reoccupation and overwritings, throughout the Middle Ages. In Rome, therefore, antiquity coexists with many phases and layers, creating peculiar mutations; the separation of past from present with which we have become familiar is a new, not a traditional, situation.

In the history of Rome, there are numerous cases of reuse of ancient urban spaces and buildings, such as the Circus Agonalis (Piazza Navona) which was re-appropriated from the ninth century onwards by secular estates and the churches of St Nicholas of the Lorrains and St Agnes in Agone, both repeatedly transformed. Another example is the transformation process affecting the church of St Barbara of the Librarians, which owes its geometry to the fact that it is hosted by one of the Theatre of Pompey's spans, whilst the curvilinear development of the Via di Grottapinta has been generated by the layout of Pompey's theatre, the very nature of the Theatre thus becoming a permanence, conveyed also by the name of the street referring to its ancient vaulted and frescoed arches.

The ancient city, or at least its real memory, thus lives extensively within the current one. It defines layouts of buildings and the shape of open spaces in the historical districts, where it is common to observe specific evolutions of the urban fabric that result from the presence of previous objects such as ancient structures or boundary lines. The city's archaeological facts are just the emerging part of a relational system deserving investigation in order to reach an interested and educated public, through selective occasions of information and direct knowledge.

The strong coexistence, perhaps too briefly cited here, between antiquity and subsequent phases of the history of Rome has left countless traces that are an important feature of the city's heritage and give the city a crucial and unavoidable role in the diffusion of scientific knowledge. In his contribution to 'Medioevo Negato', a forum organised by the Italian Historical Institute for the Middle Ages, Michel Gras, Director of the Ecole Française de Rome, spoke for the centrality of the cultural role of the city in the context of demonstrations against the funding cuts to cultural institutions after the 2010 Stability Law (Gras 2011). He argued that the presence in Rome of so many research and cultural institutions from almost every European country is due to the city being a key point of reference in the field of archaeological, monumental and artistic heritage; its primacy is also supported by the presence of invaluable public and non-public archives. Since 1946, soon after the Second World War and before the Treaty of Rome in 1957, therefore, all the non-Italian cultural institutions, together with the most representative Italian ones, met in Rome to discuss the repairing of some of the damage caused by two world wars, and to give life to an international coordination network, to which Italian universities, the monuments' curators and the large archival centres are still closely linked. Rome therefore hosts a very active microcosm from all over Europe whose aim is to foster valuable contributions to European culture and identity. Research programming, knowledge diffusion, training of students of all nationalities willing to share working knowledge day after day, form a setting in which the Italian language plays an essential role as, according to Gras, it is the proper tool needed for the development of such a cultural project.

From Michel Gras' words, one can understand which energies should be involved in the planning and implementation of the enhancement of Rome's heritage, and what kind of expectations from civil society, even the non-Italian one, should be addressed. The methodological basis of the initiative is the Code of Cultural Heritage and Landscape (Legislative Decree of 22 January 2004, no. 42), which identifies enhancement as a complex, mainly economic and regulatory system, designed to achieve greater use and social benefits from heritage, or to realise the appropriate information flow and implement experiences. Good communication is also required, to connect enhancement to potential users, and not surprisingly heritage education has recently been fully integrated within EU initiatives aimed at promoting a shared European culture.

The Framework Convention on the Value of Cultural Heritage for Society (Faro Convention, Council of Europe, STCE no. 199/2006) is a cornerstone of future policy, emphasising the two-way relationship between heritage education and citizenship. The Convention synthesises all the previous elaborations in terms of culture, society and environment, from the Universal Declaration of Human Rights (1948) to the European Landscape Convention (2000, Florence Convention, Council of Europe, STCE no. 176/2000). In particular, the Faro Convention sets out principles to which states may refer in order to establish a virtuous relationship between communities and their tangible and intangible culture, in space and over time. Heritage is made of history, traditions and territory, together with its components of value and significance: the territory becomes a landscape when it is recognised as a significant product coming from the interaction between populations and their natural and non-natural environment. Cultural heritage is understood as a legacy to pass on to future generations through appropriate policies guaranteeing a sustainable use. Technical choices concerning restoration should take into account their ability to express information on the cultural significance or value of the object to which they are referred. For this reason, the Convention establishes deep relationships between heritage issues and the multiple sectors of education, training and scientific research in the fields of architecture, archaeology, art, environment, tourism, political and social sciences, economic planning and, last but not least, the comparative study of European languages and laws.

Amongst necessary communication tools, the Convention identifies the digital as the one able to generate data dissemination in a very democratic and attractive way. The pragmatic commitment to mono-linguistic standardisation, however, might endanger other languages, but could perhaps be countered by producing multi-language dictionaries and thesauri as evidence of different cultures. On this subject, the Ministry for Cultural Heritage and Activities (MiBACT) also has been active, producing and spreading a thesaurus of traditional Italian architecture with the objective of structuring real tools of linguistic sharing, considered as a useful basis for planning urban restoration (Pugliano 2009).

Conclusion

Heritage enhancement and transmission in Rome would benefit from substantial reform to make historical and cultural knowledge of the past more pervasive. It is crucial to reach the general public. Participation planning processes at the neighbourhood level became mandatory in 2006, but they have not been appropriately enforced. Nor is achieving participation the only problem. We have emphasised that the enjoyment and use of historic remains is being curtailed by lack of information and the poor organisation of their exhibition space or settings (Figure 3.4).

Figure 3.4 Ostia Antica. A fallen column reveals its composite construction, and our predecessors' craft skills and tastes; the abrasive skin of the porbeagle shark (*Lamna nasus*) was used to obtain fresh texture effects in order to emphasise the marbling on the exterior

Photo: A. Pugliano, 2012.

These drawbacks could be partly overcome by presenting ruins and monuments through multiple stories related to the material culture, technologies and lifestyles of our predecessors, and through place-based approaches developed from the concept of 'imageability'. By doing so, a deeper knowledge of the past could be embedded within common perceptions, and foster inherent cultural experiences. Such knowledge can be shared by transferring methods of experimental archaeology to experiential learning activities based on excavation and restoration stages and on research and documentation activities, in addition to the learning of Latin and Italian by foreigners. The institutions in charge of protection can find a synergy with national and international organisations responsible for training: educational paths are traced so that schools and universities, by adopting a part of the heritage, develop scientific knowledge about it, while providing the disclosure of cultural data, thereby facilitating protection and development practices. Communication and comprehension also depend on reuse practices, and restoration can serve this very aim, shaping and forming the most reliable interpretations of heritage. The goal is to establish a sense of familiarity with history and ancient culture, gained by familiarity with the material objects that are such a major part of heritage. This would be matched by the reconnection – as described above, following the age-old practice of reusing buildings and streets in new townscapes – of the ancient and the new, the past and the present, within Rome's cultural and social life.

Acknowledgements

The authors conceived and developed this chapter cooperatively. The first and last sections are attributable to both authors; the second section to Anna Laura Palazzo and the third to Antonio Pugliano.

References

Benevolo, L. ed. 1985. *Studio per la Sistemazione della Zona Archeologia Centrale*, Rome: De Luca.

Boyer, F. 1943. La conservation des monuments antiques à Rome sous Napoléon. *Comptes Rendus des Séances de l'Académie des Inscriptions et Belles-Lettres*, 87e année, 1, 101–8.

Brandi, C. 1963. *Teoria del Restauro*, Turin: Einaudi.

Fazzio, F. 2005. *Gli Spazi dell'Archeologia. Temi per il Progetto Urbanistico*, Rome: Officina.

Francovich, R. and Manacorda, D. eds. 2000. *Dizionario di Archeologia, Voce 'Archeologia Urbana'*, Rome and Bari: Laterza.

Gras, M. 2011. Relazione. In *Medioevo Negato*, ed. Istituto Storico Italiano per il Medioevo. www.isime.it/medioevo_negato/Gras_2011.02.03.pdf.

Insolera, I. and Perego, F. 1983. *Storia Moderna dei Fori di Roma: Archeologia e Città*, Rome and Bari: Laterza.

Lanciani, R. 1901. *Forma Urbis Romae*, Rome: Tipografia Salomoni.

Lynch, K. 1960. *The Image of the City*, Cambridge, MA: MIT Press.

Manieri Elia, M. 1998. *Topos e Progetto*, Rome: Gangemi.

Modena, G. 2013. Da Ostia Antica all'Ager Ostiensis. Un Laboratorio Progettuale nel Territorio. In: Camera del Lavoro Territoriale di Roma Centro-Ovest Litoranea, Convegno: 'La centralità del patrimonio artistico, culturale, ambientale nel piano del Lavoro della CGIL per la conservazione, la tutela e la valorizzazione dei beni comuni, per lo sviluppo integrato del territorio, per il lavoro'. Ostia Antica, Sala Riario, 1 July 2013.

Palazzo, A. L. 2008. L'intervento nelle aree con presenze archeologiche. In *La Progettazione Urbana. Declinazioni e Strumenti*, eds Colarossi, P. and Latini, A. P., Milan: Edizioni del Sole 24 ore, 209–22.

Palazzo, A. L. and Rizzo, B. 2013. Assetti e prospettive di valorizzazione del territorio. Presented at the conference, 'Il delta del Tevere: 3000 anni di storia, le sfide del presente', May 2013. Avaiable at http://romatevere.hypotheses.org/713 (accessed 25 January 2015).

Panella, R. 2014. *Roma la Città dei Fori*, Rome: Prospettive.

Pellegrino, A. and Pugliano, A. 2012. Proposte di Azioni Integrate di Ricerca e Formazione per la Conservazione e la Valorizzazione del sito archeologico di Ostia, in *I luoghi della memoria. Interventi di conservazione e restauro*, MiBACT.

Pugliano, A. 2009. *Elementi di un Costituendo Thesaurus Utile alla Conoscenza, alla Tutela, alla Conservazione dell'Architettura. Vol. 1: Il Riconoscimento, la Documentazione, il Catalogo dei Beni Architettonici*. 2 vols. MiBACT-Iccd, Rome: Prospettive.

Pugliano, A. 2011. Ostia. Un museo della Città Antica. *Ricerche di Storia dell'Arte*, nos. 103–4, pp. 94–169. DOI: 10.7374/71516.

4 Remembering cities

The role of memory in the culturally sustainable development of Dubrovnik (Croatia)

Anka Mišetić and Sara Ursić

Introduction

There are several reasons why it is worth remembering that the principle of sustainability includes the living community and must take into consideration the vitality as well as the materiality of a place. It seems that historic cities represent the greatest challenge in this regard (Ardakani and Oloonabadi 2011; Murzyn-Kupisz and Gwosdz 2011). Dubrovnik, on the eastern Adriatic coast, is a city whose historic core has been carefully protected for many decades and since 1979 has been inscribed on the UNESCO World Heritage List. The preservation of its value for future generations and the use of its past as a role model for the harmonious life of a city and a community is a key issue for its residents. For these reasons, society has decided to remember to make the city original and authentic but at the same time vital and alive, and changeable according to the actions and needs of the contemporary community. Ways to do this can be found within the concept of cultural sustainability.

To understand cultural sustainability to its full extent, comparison is needed with the concept of social sustainability, a concept widely accepted by academics and planners as a framework for planned development in modern societies (Redclift 2005; Jordan 2008; Boström 2012). Whilst most authors will agree that there is no unified definition of social sustainability, we can say that it aspires to the establishment of a socially balanced community, affirms the importance of dialogue and increased social inclusion, and exists within a balance between the local and the global, and between public and private spheres. In other words, social sustainability can be connected with other ideas and concepts in social theories such as social justice and equality, social cohesion and social diversity, cultural values and identity, human rights and human potential, cultural capital, civil participation and many others (Elliot 1999; Jabareen 2008).

With such a broad definition, it is possible to apply the concept of social sustainability in the analysis of different sectors, including the cultural sector. In that regard, *cultural* sustainability can be interpreted as the balance between different cultural models, identities, global and local influences, cultural heritage and modern culture-production. In an urban environment, it is manifested through different dimensions of social life: in the relationship between 'urban memory', for example, and in a post-modern re-semanticisation of heritage, or through the role of public spaces in cultural transfers, or in the processes and consequences of 'gentrification'.

When considering protected city cores such as that of Dubrovnik as a particular type of cultural asset we are faced with the use of revitalisation (or what might be termed regeneration) as a method of combining heritage and modernity in a joint life. Each revitalisation is to a certain extent a re-semantisation of what we are reviving in a new social and temporal context. The question is not so dramatic when we are faced with specific objects, structures or artistic artefacts (paintings, books, sculptures, special buildings or music, for example) which are autonomous and resilient in their own separateness, but what happens when the cultural artefact is a whole city? In this regard, especially when we are dealing with issues which can help us understand cultural sustainability in the urban context, the dynamic of city–culture–community–remembrance has to be developed.

Based on these starting points, we have taken on the task of analysing the contemporary treatment and use in society and in culture of Dubrovnik's historic core. Our methodology has been based on semi-structured participative interviews with selected cultural actors. Many participants have been involved in cultural heritage revitalisation processes and their contributions as well as opinions are important for the success of such a project. In this chapter we shall focus on a particular community of participants, 'cultural actors', the professionals and artists who are most active in the city's cultural life, and who maintain, create, and produce culture. In the first part of what follows, the issues outlined above will be analysed by way of three different discourses or debates, and through theoretical concepts such as memory and heritage, and the concept of 'historic core' with all the implications it has for the rest of a city. In the second section, an empirical contribution to the debate on cultural sustainability will attempt to answer the questions from the perspective of different social participants and their experience.

Framing discourses

A discourse of artists

In writing about the history of the Danube, and following historical trails in Budapest, a central European city which made its mark on European culture in a special way, Claudio Magris mused on the dynamic relationship of the city and its history:

> The Danube flows broad, and the evening wind passes through the open-air cafés like the breath of an old Europe which may already be at the brink of the world and no longer produces history but only consumes it ...
>
> (Magris 1989, 387)

To oppose the idea that a city can stop 'producing' history and live only by 'consuming' its own history and culture requires a turn towards the concept of cultural sustainability. There is a sense of nostalgia surrounding historic cities, from which Dubrovnik is not exempt. This nostalgia is particularly inspiring for the literary genre, which gladly interprets the relationship between the city and its history, through which numerous cultural phenomena, in the broad sense of the term, can be examined. If we take as examples Pamuk's *Istanbul* with its subtitle *Memories and the City*, or the novel-guidebook *Venice is a Fish* by Tiziano Scarpa, it seems that these authors recognise the city–memory connection as the basis upon which heritage can be built and as a model through which culture can be preserved and passed on to new generations. Jure Kaštelan, a Croatian poet, wrote about Dubrovnik as a place of 'stone and light', which in his perception is a 'unique stage on which the past and the future have the same meaning, and their own creative power. ... not only a work of art, but ... also a creator itself, and it has been so throughout the centuries ...' (Krtalić 1984, 33). In other words, a city which creates culture is a city which 'produces' history.

To such ideas we can add the thoughts of Neven Šegvić, an architect whose significant architectural oeuvre was created in Dubrovnik. His commitment to modern Croatian architecture in the historical surroundings of Dubrovnik faced issues of urban memory and the commitments they represent to the modern architect. It has been said that Šegvić's starting point was that 'the memory of a city can primarily be read in literature ... it is the writers, not the architects who petrify the illusion about it' (Uchytil 2007, 19, authors' translation). But architects, if orientated towards the city as a whole, are constantly faced with relationships of 'the old' as well as 'the new', and are continually assessing what they find while seeking to resist traps of petrification. They attempt to organise city life in an optimal, i.e. sustainable, way in a given space. In his article 'The Specificities of Architecture in Dubrovnik', Šegvić gave an overview of how the city came into existence: its architecture and urbanism as a witness of the 'immanent human desire for harmony and creation' (in Uchytil 2007, 47–55). For him, however, Dubrovnik is not only a museum-like image of the past harmony of function, structure and form; rather, the city for him is a constant source of inspiration and a stimulus to continue the production of history.

> Its harmony and unity of urbanism, architecture, life and art, dream and reality, its rhythm of proportion and completeness within the city walls, all these aesthetic and life categories, all these different forms of life and artistic reality have found their balance because they have been creatively inserted into the living organism which fascinates us, and which seems to be even more contemporary as time passes.
>
> (Šegvić 2007, 47, authors' translation)

A discourse of legislation

Dubrovnik is a city in which the continued influence of its ancient past has been ensured through multiple cultural–ethnic continuities more than through direct links with the original location of its ancient predecessor. This shows the ability of cities to internalise creatively different cultural influences from their very beginnings. This is the strongest attribute of the historical development of Dubrovnik, as of other long-lived cities, which has resulted in a special urban and social identity. The community of residents in Dubrovnik, whose interests were crucial in forming the city in the period from the thirteenth to the seventeenth century, have been important to the city's evolution (Delalle 1997); their early urban planning can be read in the first statute of the city dating back to 1272. This outlined the unity of the spatial component of the urban centre, and the community's way of life, which reveals the principles of a socially sustainable city and a city which has the capacity for creating a particular culture. Which principles mentioned in the first statute are in use today and are useful to mention in discussions on cultural sustainability? Besides the generally mentioned principle 'give people what belongs to them', the need to establish a relationship between individual and common interests is definitely useful ('the distribution of street usage according to which one-third of the width belongs to the houses, and the middle of the street belongs exclusively to the community'); the statutes also discuss issues relating to quality of life ('regulations of the community drainage system') and heritage ('the owner is responsible for repairs and maintenance of ruins and damaged parts').

If we take a leap across a long period in history, after a number of centuries we find a modern equivalent, 'The Strategy of Protection, Preservation and Economic Usage of Cultural Heritage in the Republic of Croatia 2011–2015' (MKRH 2011). This document from another time period has a different purpose and style, but just like the first city statute, it reveals the author's vision and the values to which it corresponds. It sets out three main goals from which our relationship and treatment of heritage should emerge: (1) protecting, preserving and finding sustainable uses; (2) obtaining material income from sustainable use; and (3) raising individual and community awareness of the importance of cultural heritage and its sustainable use. Even a superficial analysis shows that 'sustainable use' is a very important part or an important social value in all three proclaimed goals. With this it becomes an important part of the framework for all individual and separate legal regulations and for everyday treatment. The continuity of a 'happy coexistence' of the community and the urban seems to be ensured as a permanent and unquestioned value. However, the implementation of these values into practical actions and the sustainable usage which they always imply, and the bringing-in of the new, is a part of a complex process of revitalisation without which there is no continuity of the previously mentioned 'production' of history – and without which in turn 'sustainable usage' is merely the consumption of an old part of history which we have petrified and, by that act, separated from the vital, living part of the city.

The Strategy grew from an economic assessment of the fact that the Dubrovnik city core, because it has been listed as a World Heritage Site, offers opportunities to improve the city in other ways and areas, especially in the further development of small companies, cultural tourism and cultural management:

> Recent changes indicate the importance of that strategic goal which shows that an important part of the wealth of developed countries in the next few

decades will be generated in exactly these areas which are encompassed by an economy based on cultural heritage which includes cultural industry, cultural tourism, and cultural management. The predictions of the World Tourism Organisation also indicate a constant increase in cultural tourism worldwide. According to some estimates, the average growth rate for cultural tourism in 2020 will be 15 per cent.

(MKRH 2011, 52, authors' translation)

The idea of heritage as a facilitating process prevails in the discourse of the Strategy; it is seen as a value to be preserved and economically exploited. If we focus the analysis of the discourse towards what is not said, however, to what is not present in the Strategy, then we have to mention Mumford's classic interpretation of the role of the historic core in the development of the city, which should not be just an opportunity for servile imitation, but a basis for original ideas for application in planning other architectonic units (Mumford 1968, 480). In this sense, the Strategy for cultural development fails to see heritage as an inspiration and incentive for new creative actions and the continuation of cultural production.

A dialogue between the past and the present

Most authors who deal with the phenomenon agree that the relationship of cities towards their history is now becoming very specific, and that a preoccupation with history is characteristic of our era. For example:

> Never before have there been so many amenity groups, preservation societies, genealogists, museums, historians amateur and professional, conservation areas, and listed buildings. The past is everywhere and it is nowhere.
>
> (Crinson 2005, xi)

Furthermore, as Crinson also recognises, a general characteristic of post-modern urbanism is the selective quotation of history, most commonly through the revitalisation of some segments, such as individual buildings – for example, neglected industrial buildings – which are being given a new function and meaning, but also through remembering some past forms of public social life.

One of the first contacts with history, in which the entire city community is included in the most democratic way, is displayed through the relationship to the city core – the historic centre. Even though interest in historic centres is often attributed to post-modern urbanism, its roots can be identified even in the era of modern urban planning. The urban sociologist Ivan Rogić suggests that during the twentieth century this interest evolved into a

> true concern about the deterioration of the old city cores which was present in the forties and fifties, it is easy to conclude that the restoration of the old historic core is essential in (post) modern as well as in modern urban planning conception.
>
> (2002, 12)

By identifying processes of long-term deterioration in historic city cores along the eastern Adriatic coast, Milan Prelog identifies the revitalisation problem in the second half of the twentieth century with regard to historic cores that have not successfully been brought back to life: 'with all due respect towards old buildings, we still do not see them as formative parts of our cities' development, as parts of their future' (Prelog 2003, 80). Similarly, Rogić diagnoses the phenomenon of the 'peripheral pulse in the city core' through analysis of numerous signs of deterioration in the Dubrovnik city core in the second half of the twentieth century. Population decline, ecological neglect and residential deterioration turn the historic core into a developmental periphery. Processes of gentrification at the end of the twentieth century gave historic city cores a new meaning but with negative as well as positive consequences. In other words, the importance of involving participants and social actors who are connected with the issue of vitality and see opportunities for affirming the concept of social sustainability, has been confirmed by the changes to the social structure of residents, their way of life, and the symbolic meaning of identity which have resulted from gentrification processes in many European cities (Enyedi and Kovács 2008).

As previously mentioned, experience has shown that the process of revitalisation cannot be separated from live actors, the city community and its memory. Crinson (2005, 13) uses Halbwachs' definitions of memory concepts: '[m]emory, for Halbwachs, bound groups of people together, recharging their commonality by reference to the physical spaces and previous instances, often a founding moment, of that collective identity'. To neglect the idea that memory is a formative element of a community means to increase the chances for revitalisation to become synonymous with museification, or as Rogić says (2002) to 'de-dramatise' daily life.

From a sociological point of view, the importance of the historic core today is confirmed through at least two aspects of urban daily life: as a symbol of identity, and as a contribution to sense of a place, a specific group of attributes which ensures a distinctive sensation, which cannot be repeated in another place. This group of attributes is based on the interaction between people and places, and it is always about identity. 'Identity is the extent to which a person can recognise or recall a place as being distinct from other places – as having a vivid, or unique, or at least a particular, character of its own' (Lynch 1981, 131). The perception of an area is a creative act, and never just a passive reception. In this creative act, the identity of a city and the identity of an urban community are formed: '[u]rban landscapes are an expression of identity and also shape the identity of those who live in them' (Hall 2006, 189). If we understand the city core as a special place in which sense of place and identity are formed through the interaction of the community, then it is determined by the role of cultural, historical, and special social values. There is a connection with the growth of tourism, and the so-called industry of experiences (Figure 4.1).

The pressure of the desire to experience the special sense of a place, the beauty of a city or the uniqueness of its environment, to participate experientially in something that has become the world's heritage, at the same time leaves the

Figure 4.1 Through the eye of a tourist: Stradun, Dubrovnik's main street
Photo: Roko Mišetić.

possibility of affirmation and creates a new threat to the city of becoming a 'destination' instead of a 'place'. 'Tourism and memory obviously intersect in the niche area of heritage tourism, where historical sites and preserved artefacts as embodiments of collective memory are commoditised to attract tourists' (Marschall 2012, 2216). Even though the range and potential of economic benefits from participating in the tourist industry are alluring, the threat of museification, banality, commercialisation and prevalence of spectacle are also there. This is surely the most intense way of 'consuming' history, and it is worth recalling here that the economic use of cultural heritage and the related increase in income is set out as a special goal in the Republic's Strategy mentioned above for the 'Protection, Preservation and Economic Usage' of cultural heritage.

An inside look

Cultural actors

To gain an in-depth, insider perspective, we interviewed selected cultural actors, namely professionals and artists who are engaged in different aspects of cultural life in the city. Interviewees were chosen because of their important role in the culturally sustainable development of Dubrovnik. A number of cultural actors in Dubrovnik's cultural scene are part of official cultural policies, and depend for support on the Ministry of Culture and culture departments at the local level. Their cultural activities and projects are numerous and aspire to officially present culture: museums and galleries in Dubrovnik, the 'Dubrovnik Summer Festival' and similar things. The Summer Festival is paradigmatically prominent as a theatrical and musical manifestation. Founded in 1950, it is now a sort of official symbol of the city. The vision of the Festival has been described in these terms:

> The Dubrovnik Summer Festival will be recognised as the main producer of high-end cultural events in the city of Dubrovnik, as a leading cultural institution in Croatia and as one of the five most prominent cultural festivals. Based on a rich and vital heritage of the Institution and the City, the Festival will persist on ambientality, the correlation of tradition and modernity and the correlation of local, national and international.
> (www.dubovnik-festival.hr, accessed 8 March 2014)

At the same time, however, there are other actors in the cultural life of Dubrovnik who appear as a sort of alternative to the dominant cultural policies, being independent of individual or civil initiatives and not subject to standard institutional procedures. In connection with the concept of independent artists there are museums, non-profit organisations, which are according to some opinions essential for modern art because they provide space for new kinds of expression, new practices, and the development of new methods which step out of the framework of generally accepted standards: 'such organisations often allow artists to explore, and work with several different local art scenes, through their more or less formal affiliation with international networks of artists' mobility and residence programmes' (Blessi et al. 2011).

Whereas the Dubrovnik Summer Festival is a project through which the Dubrovnik and Croatian culture scene tries to position itself in an international context, over the past twenty-five years the independent art scene within Dubrovnik has been formed through a smaller, more local network, the Art Workshop Lazareti (AWL). The AWL is more oriented towards production which will enrich the local community. Although it started as a completely informal artists' initiative, today it is a relatively well organised independent cultural centre. It defines its mission in terms of the 'improvement of life-quality in Dubrovnik in the artistic, cultural and social sense through artistic, cultural and other public activities, as well as the encouragement of a quality development of a civil society in Dubrovnik and Croatia' (www.arl.hr/o_nama/about.shtml, 8 March 2014). This statement emphasises the connections of culture and civil society which articulate some elements of cultural sustainability very well (Figure 4.2).

Figure 4.2 A lively market, right in the heart of the old city of Dubrovnik
Photo: Roko Mišetić.

To understand the relationship to culture in Dubrovnik more fully, we analysed the opinions of cultural actors taken from interviews with members of Dubrovnik's cultural scene who have cooperated with the AWL. This was an opportunity for dialogue with people who have experience of working in an independent art scene. Five in-depth, semi-structured interviews were conducted – with two artists, two members of NGOs in the field of culture, and a museum worker. This proved to be a good way of gaining insight into the opinions and experiences of experts who create culture (Kovacs 2011; Bade 2011).

Cooperation not exclusion

The attitudes of cultural actors suggest that each of their projects has a specific task and responsibility. In the words of one of the cultural activists interviewed, 'classical music, theatre and drama are represented throughout the Summer Festival. Art hasn't been used very well; on the other hand, there are some activities in the independent scene, in the field of conceptual art'. Even though both the official (represented by the Dubrovnik Summer Festival) and the independent scene (represented by the Art Workshop Lazareti) have a clearly defined goal of promoting cultural activities and the cultural presentation of the city, there are differences between them which can easily be noted. The Art Workshop has shown some complementary advantages in comparison to the so-called official culture. One cultural activist said that the *independent scene in the historical suburbs of Lazareti (which was once upon a time a quarantine) has been successfully realised in the organisational and contextual sense, while all other aspects of culture which depend on the state budget produce occasional and not fully developed cultural projects.*

A freelance artist explained how AWL had '*nurtured its own audience and created an unusually active scene for such a small community. It has also served as a platform for events relevant in the international scene*'. The role of the independent scene for affirmation of different cultural identities was also emphasised in the interviews, and comparisons show the main objection to official culture, in the words of a freelance artist, as being that

Aspects of independent culture have been well realised through the work of the Art Workshop Lazareti and definitely through the high quality programme of the Art Gallery Dubrovnik ... The Summer Festival is still the Festival of the privileged and those obedient to the government, and not a responsible high-budget art festival.

Research investigating how cultural workers in Dubrovnik assess the consequences of the city core being a part of the UNESCO's World Heritage concept has shown that there is still enough space for a stronger involvement of the local community in the culture (Mišetić and Miletić 2014). It has indicated a low level of local community participation in projects connected with cultural heritage, as well as a general lack of interest among the population in historic and cultural heritage. Even though the Art Workshop Lazareti is not exclusively focused locally, it definitely contributes to the strengthening of ties between citizens and culture. These opinions are good indicators that it would be more appropriate for different models of cultural action in a city's life to be intertwined and not to exclude one another.

Living with/from heritage

From the perspective of cultural actors, the concepts of museification and innovation are constantly reviewed as two complementary practices. Trends in conservative practices, which are oriented towards 'reviving' heritage, are no longer a novelty either. Here we are discussing something that Škarić describes as 'the living heritage, one that surrounds us, and is a part of our daily life, makes us happy and makes our lives richer' (2008, 74) (Figure 4.3).

In order to make it continual, cultural identity is realised through the dialogue of the past with the present, which is sometimes hard to achieve. However, if that dialogue is seen as a part of cultural sustainability of a community, then its role has a new meaning. On the same note, 'there is often an implicit discourse of continuity between past and present, between older uses and meanings of space and newer ones' (Belanger 2002, 74).

Figure 4.3 Everyday life in a World Heritage Site, Dubrovnik
Photo: Roko Mišetić.

Even in the early analysis it was possible to detect that the connection between the protected city core and the remainder of the city is a dynamic relationship which could be the key to the cultural sustainability of the city. However, when we are talking about Dubrovnik, the above-mentioned research on cultural actors' attitudes (Mišetić and Miletić 2014) has shown some disparities. Most of the interviewees did not agree with the claim that 'the city core has been revived', even though they did identify an increase in different activities in that core, from cultural events to commercialisation, investment, demand for real estate and emigration of the local population. In other words, even though some elements of gentrification, as defined by Zukin (1987) and Miles (2007), have undoubtedly been recognised, it seems that even that process has not been finished because the outward movement of inhabitants from the centre has not been compensated for by new social groups moving in. From the perspective of the local community, it has left the city core socially empty. 'Unlike the city of Dubrovnik, whose structural development after World War II was positive, the historical core has been experiencing a constant transformation and a negative population growth for some time' (Djukić and Jerković 2008, 210). One interviewee, a cultural activist, explained the imbalance between activities in the core and its perception in the context of the city as a sustainable unit:

The lack of vision at the management level of the city as a unit, short-term functioning and orientation towards short-term income coming from tourism (seasonality) and the non-existence of a cultural audience, in the true sense of the word, are the main obstacles which today's actors who work in the field of culture and art in Dubrovnik are faced with.

This statement can be interpreted in the light of the phenomenon of 'transitional gentrification' which is characteristic of post-communist societies. Its characteristics have been well described by Čaldarović: '[c]hanges in the urban environment are recently almost everywhere, with almost no discussions on the concepts, ideas, programs and plans, in many transitional societies' (Čaldarović and Šarinić 2009).

The people we have interviewed have not positively graded the interaction of citizens and the heritage in Dubrovnik, as in this response from a cultural activist:

The brand of Dubrovnik as a museum-historical entity impedes innovations, which the residents could take part in through education, entertainment or simply by participating in the realisation of cultural programmes. There are too many similar existing contents.

The opportunity to create an original production on the basis of inherited culture is a goal which is not always easy to achieve; indeed, according to one cultural activist: 'Dubrovnik as a city, despite its glorious past, does not have enough potential to create high-quality culture'. Some of the interviewee's answers radiate pessimism of that sort, a feeling of entrapment in their own glorious past. They emphasise the fact that they cannot enter a discourse in which they would be equal, and also lack the opportunity to form sustainable cultural identities on such a basis. Others have made similar comments: 'it is the present assault on memory, with the constant bombardment of commercial images eroding a sense of continuity between past, present and future, that can lead to pessimism concerning the possibility of the construction of meaningful identities' (Neill 2004, 10).

The perception of the city as predominantly the city core, with its cultural heritage which we expect to ensure for the future, distances itself from the concept of the social sustainability of modern cities, which aims to cover the city as a whole. This is proclaimed, for example, through the Urban Renaissance movement in the UK (e.g. Mace et al. 2007). Therefore it is appropriate to end by quoting one of the interviewees (a freelance artist) who summarised all the elements through which the connections of the city, culture, and community are created:

I would like it to remain what a city basically is – a living city, inhabited by different kinds of people. This is the starting point for everything. Therefore, life should be the most important symbol of cultural identity. Since there is no life, the only thing that remains is the souvenirs.

Figure 4.4 The night lights of Dubrovnik
Photo: Roko Mišetić.

Conclusion

In this chapter we have shown a few of the different points of view that can exist
in relation to the city, heritage and remembering. Each one of them deals with the
city whose memory binds, inspires, and gives the potential for the creation of not
only personal but also social and cultural identities. The participants in our
research were writers, architects, art historians, cultural activists and members of
the so-called official culture, but also independent, non-official artists; we also
interrogated laws, strategies, statutes and programme objectives. All of them
undoubtedly have one common goal, which was formulated by the first town
planners: to enable the continuity of coexistence between the community and the
urban environment (Figure 4.4).

Our investigations show that the concept of cultural sustainability could be
related to locally based sustainable development. It would include recognition of
local cultural values, use of participatory approaches and creation of a stronger
sense of place. But participatory models of planning and decision-making need to
be improved, so that they include a range of different participants such as experts,
cultural actors and politicians, as well as ordinary citizens. Moreover, many of
those respondents we listened to see culture as fundamental for development. For
them, it can be concluded that heritage has been used for representing the cultural

identity of Dubrovnik at the national and global level, but so far the opportunity has not been utilised for heritage to appear as an integrating factor in the community of Dubrovnik. The interviewees identified a series of disparities, which still have not been well balanced; life is not just 'the most important symbol of cultural identity', as one of the interviewees said, but the most important element of every principle of sustainability. These opinions lead us to interpret cultural sustainability as the balance between different cultural models and identities, global and local cultural influences, cultural heritage and modern cultural production. It similarly includes the community of citizens (which simultaneously 'consumes' and 'produces' history), the vital community which is oriented towards a future, and the community which remembers.

Heritage is obviously an obligation and responsibility, but heritage also brings a lot of opportunities for local community development. According to this view, culturally sustainable development is considered to be a complex process of revitalisation, especially in historic cities, which promotes culture as the foundation of all policies. Besides the recognition of traditional cultural values, cultural development implies and produces new cultural values and artefacts. It could be recommended that this is the appropriate way to maintain continuity of cultural heritage and to reinterpret a unique part of history as the vital, living component of the city.

References

Ardakani, M. K. and Oloonabadi, S. S. A. 2011. Collective Memory as an Efficient Agent in Sustainable Urban Conservation. *Procedia Engineering* 21, 985–88.

Bade, D. 2011. An Approach to Researching Cultural Heritage Management on Conservation Islands in New Zealand. *Graduate Journal of Asia-Pacific Studies* 7(2), 62–77.

Belanger, A. 2002. Urban Space and Collective Memory: Analysing the Various Dimensions of the Production of Memory. *Canadian Journal of Urban Research* 11(1), 69–92.

Blessi, G. T., Sacco, P. L. and Pilati, T. 2011. Independent Artist-run Centres: An Empirical Analysis of the Montreal Non-profit Visual Arts Field. *Cultural Trends* 20(2), 141–66.

Boström, M. 2012. A Missing Pillar? Challenges in Theorizing and Practicing Social Sustainability: Introduction to the Special Issue. *Sustainability: Science, Practice and Policy* 8(1), 3–14, available at http://sspp.proquest.com/archives/vol8iss1/TOC.html (accessed 9 March 2014).

Čaldarović, O. and Šarinić, J. 2009. First Signs of Gentrification? Urban Regeneration in the Transitional Society: The Case of Croatia. *Sociology and Space* 46(3/4), 369–81.

Crinson, M. 2005. Urban Memory: An Introduction. In *Urban Memory: History and Amnesia in the Modern City*, ed. M. Crinson, London and New York: Routledge, ix–xi.

Delalle, R. 1997. *Traganje za Identitetom Grada*, Rijeka: Izdavački centar Rijeka.

Djukić, A. and Jerković, S. 2008. Some Contemporary Socio-Geographic Processes in the Historical Old City of Dubrovnik. *Geoadria* 13(2), 207–25.

Elliott, J. 1999. *Introduction to Sustainable Development*. New York: Taylor & Francis.

Enyedi, G. and Kovács, Z. 2008. Social Sustainability of Historical City Centres in Central Europe: An Introduction. In *Social Changes and Social Sustainability in Historical*

Urban Centres: The Case of Central Europe, eds G. Enyedi and Z. Kovács, Pècs: Centre for Regional Studies of Hungarian Academy of Sciences, 11–20.

Hall, M. 2006. Identity, Memory and Countermemory: The Archaeology of an Urban Landscape. *Journal of Material Culture* 11, 189–209.

Jabareen, Y. 2008. A New Conceptual Framework for Sustainable Development. *Environment, Development and Sustainability* 10(2), 179–92.

Jordan, A. 2008. The Governance of Sustainable Development: Taking Stock and Looking Forwards. *Environment and Planning C: Government and Policy* 26(1), 17–33.

Kovacs, J. F. 2011. Cultural Planning in Ontario, Canada: Arts Policy or More? *International Journal of Cultural Policy* 17(3), 321–40.

Krtalić, I. 1984. *Trideset i Pet Godina Dubrovačkih Ljetnih i Gara*, Zagreb/Varaždin: Zavodza Kulturu Hrvatske/Časopis Gesta.

Lynch, K. 1981. *Good City Form*, Cambridge, MA: MIT Press.

Mace, A., Hall, P. and Gallent, N. 2007. New East Manchester: Urban Renaissance or Urban Opportunism? *European Planning Studies* 15(1), 51–65.

Magris, C. 1989. *Danube*, London: Harvill Press.

Marschall, S. 2012. Tourism and Memory. *Annals of Tourism Research* 39(4), 2216–19.

Miles, M. 2007. *Art, Space and the City: Public Art and Urban Futures*, London and New York: Routledge.

Mišetić, A. and Miletić, G. M. 2014. *Participacijski Proces na Pilot Području Dubrovnika*, Dubrovnik: Institut Ivo Pilar.

MKRH 2011. Strategija Zaštite, Očuvanja i Održivog Gospodarskog Korištenja Kulturne Baštine Republike Hrvatske za Razdoblje 2011–2015 ('The Strategy of Protection, Preservation and Economic Usage of Cultural Heritage in the Republic of Croatia 2011–2015'). Ministarstvo Kulture Republike Hrvatske, Zagreb, available at: www.min-kulture.hr/default.aspx?id=6 (accessed 9 March 2014).

Mumford, L. 1968 (1961) *Grad u Historiji: Njegov Postanak, Njegovo Mijenjanje, Njegovi Izgledi*, Zagreb: Naprijed.

Murzyn-Kupisz, M. and Gwosdz, K. 2011. The Changing Identity of the Central European City: The Case of Katowice. *Journal of Historical Geography* 37(1), 113–26.

Neill, W. 2004. *Urban Planning and Cultural Identity*, London and New York: Routledge.

Prelog, M. 2003. *Tekstovi o Dubrovniku*, Institut Zapovijestum Jetnost, Društvo Prijatelja Dubrovačke Starine.

Redclift, R. 2005. Sustainable Development (1987–2005): An Oxymoron Comes of Age. *Sustainable Development* 13(4), 212–27.

Rogić, I. 2002. Historic Core and Post-modern Urban Planning. In *Split Historic Core: Neglected Heart of the City*, eds Anči Leburić and Maja Maroević, Grad Split, Gradsko Poglavarstvo, Služba za Staru Gradsku Jezgru, 13–19.

Šegvić, N. 2007. The Specificities of Architecture in Dubrovnik. In Uchytil, A., *Dubrovačke poruke arhitekta Nevena Šegvića*, UHA, Arhitektonski Fakultet Sveučilišteu Zagrebu, 47–52.

Škarić, K. 2008. Zaboravljena Baština ('A Forgotten Model'). *Kvartal* 5(4), 73–5.

Uchytil, A. 2007. *Dubrovačke Poruke Arhitekta Nevena Šegvića*, UHA, Arhitektonski Fakultet Sveučilišteu Zagrebu.

Zukin, Sh. 1987. Gentrification: Culture and Capital in the Urban Core. *Annual Review of Sociology* 13, 129–47.

www.arl.hr/o_nama/about.shtml (accessed 8 March 2014).

www.dubrovnik-festival.hr/hr/o-nama (accessed 8 March 2014).

5 The challenge of cultural sustainability in city museums
Showing the city and selecting the past in Noyon (France)

Anne Hertzog

The museum in society

City museums convey a process of the 'heritagisation' of urbanity by identifying urban artefacts and imagery to be protected, and by creating a certain public image of the city by exhibiting it through the materiality of artefacts (Poulot 1997). Narratives and methods of exhibition vary considerably according to the context, the personalities involved, and the current but changing urban social representations of the city. In city museums, the local urban heritage is constantly reinterpreted according to the way that urban communities select the past that is deemed to be worth remembering, in order to deal with their present and anticipate the future of the city. Since the nineteenth century, museums dedicated to particular cities have been playing a crucial role in the social construction of a sense of place in the French and European cultural context. Exhibitions reflect the professional museological standards, but they can also be considered as an expression of the social representation of space and selective readings in urban history. In this perspective, museums are political instruments in the construction of a collective identity symbolically dominated by personalities imposing a *legitimate* image of the city in the public space.

New theories of museology have emerged in recent decades in both Europe and North America, before being diffused across much of the rest of the world. During this evolution, city museums have progressively been seen as places of intercultural dialogue and spaces of negotiation (e.g. Bodo et al. 2009), where identities and social and political issues could be discussed and debated through new kinds of exhibitions, content and cultural practices based on the empowerment of local communities. The appearance of the eco-museum movement in the 1960s showed how French theoreticians (such as G.-H. Rivière) were particularly involved in this re-conceptualisation of museums at large, promoting the participation of local communities. In spite of the success of these new 'participative theories' (Arnstein 1969), however, the shift from expert visions to a local community's expertise has often remained difficult in museum practices. In the case studied in this chapter, this difficulty appears to be rooted in three types of reasons: the museum professionals' posture, the role of local social hierarchies and power struggles, and the central role played by the museum in the construction of local tourism narratives in a context of urban crisis. As a result, what kind of selective image of the city is presented in the museum through the exhibition of artefacts, eclipsing many aspects of the 'collective memory' and ignoring many dimensions of the place?

This chapter is based on qualitative field study (interviews, archives, observations) in and around the city museum of Noyon, a small town of less than 15,000 inhabitants, located in the Oise department of Picardy in northern France (Figure 5.1). It first describes the changing role of city museums over the past century or so, and then focuses on the renewal of the museum in the early 1990s: it will show how this time of transition turned out to be a failed attempt to build a more 'inclusive' vision of urban heritage. It is argued that this failure is explained less by conflicting visions of heritage between amateurs and professionals (inhabitants vs. curators) than by the selective, local tradition of heritage-making in which it is rooted, and that it also reflects the social and political organisation of the community.

Figure 5.1 The Noyon museum in the former Episcopal Palace, partly rebuilt after World War I, and the cathedral of Noyon

Photo: Anne Hertzog, 2012.

The city museum: between a 'dominant' vision of heritage and urban nostalgia

Showing one's 'own' city: class-dominated visions in the museums of the nineteenth century

In the nineteenth century, museums in France were mainly of three types: encyclopaedic private collections, small 'provincial Louvres' conceived on the model of the Louvre in Paris, and local history museums preserving and interpreting the history of their local territory. These museums were mostly founded by local residents interested in art, archaeology and local history, usually 'erudite', upper class or aristocratic male town-dwellers. Until the middle of the twentieth century, municipalities were not very involved in local museums. In Picardy such collections, as legacies of the past, were often considered unwieldy.

City museums were places for upper-middle-class notables to display 'their' city and their collections of archaeological fragments, monuments and memorabilia of 'local heroes', local folklore and local landscape paintings. Objects and images, often labelled as the gifts of local collectors, illustrated the most glorious episodes of the city's history, in the process revealing the tastes and values of its dominant social classes. These museums exhibited 'typical' and picturesque representations of the city in order to promote a singular identity. At the same time, however, local history museums in the nineteenth century were also a collective response to the social, urban and economic transformations of cities, and their collections and activities and displays were coloured by nostalgia and local patriotism. Local history, the exaltation of great local figures and the definition of a territorially specific heritage were also used to affirm the status of each city as a 'small provincial capital', revealing the competition between cities and sometimes triggering tourism policies. City museums were in themselves, for example architecturally but also in terms of function and symbolism, an essential component of being urban, a part of the urban core, as attested by their monumental architecture and location in the town centre in and adjacent to buildings associated with social, political or economic power.

This first generation of city museums participated in the definition of a 'collective' heritage that affirmed urban dominant categories and imposed their representation of the past through collections influenced by the eclectic, private collections of eighteenth-century aristocrats. Many of today's urban museums, especially in smaller towns, are the direct heirs of these first local history museums, inheriting with that mantle a powerful conservatism in their way of dealing with the past.

Urban nostalgia on display: the aftermath of wartime destruction

The period after a war in destroyed cities has always been a crucial moment of heritage valorisation and museum growth, and World War I presented just such an occasion on a large scale. In the devastated areas of the former Western Front after 1919, the reconstruction of ruined buildings and monuments and the reconstitution of destroyed museums or dispersed collections went hand in hand as an important part of the rebuilding of the country. The reconstruction of old or the creation of new city museums was an attempt to rebuild the collective memory of local communities which the war had totally disorganised, if not broken, in both material and symbolic ways. In cities that had been completely transformed by demographic loss, the exodus of former elites and the physical destruction of economic activities and urban landscapes, the (re)creation of a museum could provide a collective re-invention of the city 'before' the disaster as well as an illustration of the city's suffering. Noyon, our case study, was almost entirely ruined by the 1914–18 war, and was even designated a 'Pompeii of the North' (Panni and Jagielsky 2000); its new city museum was seen as an illustration of the *ville-martyre*, the martyred town, an official status given to devastated cities, along with the award of the Légion d'Honneur, which Noyon received in 1920. Although the 'German atrocities museum' wished for by the mayor in 1919 was never created, the collection gathered by representatives of the local cultural society nevertheless illustrated the city in post-war ruin (paintings, photographs, pieces of destroyed monuments) as well as during its golden ages (Gallo-Roman, medieval, Renaissance).

Both victim and hero, the city became the central 'figure' in its museum's collection, its history related chronologically from the origins of the city to the recent war. This was quite a new way of thinking of the city museum, in contrast with the first generation still influenced by the encyclopaedic model. Henceforth, the 'museum of the city' was seen as a stage on which to exalt the 'biography' or the 'portrait' of the city. The sense of loss and renewed attachment to vulnerable places can explain this 'personification' of cities, but another hypothesis could be the influence of comparative representations of the city conveyed by French geography in the early 1920s, which has had a big impact on scholarship.

The eclipse of the city in the 1970s: museums as stages for urbano-phobia?

During the 1970s, French museums were deeply transformed in line with contemporary concepts of cultural heritage, a better acknowledgement of popular culture, and the emergence of new categories of cultural professionals competing with the traditional elites. Traditional city museums (especially art museums) that seemed to be at a remove from the general public (Bourdieu and Darbel 1966) were often considered as elitist, unlike the *écomusée* which offered a renewed model (Poulard 2007). This new model had been theorised by the French men George Henri Rivière and Hugues de Varine, as a 'mirror of the territory and its local people', and was only possible with the democratic participation of the inhabitants. In France only a few of them were urban: for example, the *écomusée* of St Quentin in Yvelines was integrated into urban planning in order to evoke the social, economic and architectural transformation of the suburbs. It was also used to preserve the collective memory of the former town, as well as to participate in defining the identity of the present city with the active collaboration of residents.

In Picardy, these renewed models of museums were mainly located in rural areas, which had been deeply transformed in the 1960s by agricultural modernisation, urban growth and sometimes industrial decline. Most of the ethnographic museums or *écomusées* created during the 1970s and 1980s expressed a deep attachment to an idealised countryside, and reinvented popular rural traditions often in a rather nostalgic way. These numerous museums created by residents defending their idea of local identities (including ideas of regional autonomy, and a defence of linguistic particularism) strongly claimed that the 'authentic' Picardy was to be found in rurality and in nature. Museum and other narratives often therefore presented a negative interpretation of urbanity and urbanisation, presenting them as factors of destabilisation and a cause of a loss of authenticity and 'true values'. These popular museums illustrate a reactivation of 'urbano-phobia' or 'city detestation', a cultural anti-urban imaginary, grounded for a long time in occidental philosophy (Rousseau) or literature (Dickens) (Salomon Cavin and Marchand 2010).

This is perhaps why one must wait until the 1990s to witness a slow and controversial recognition of a specific urban heritage in Picardy, the industrial heritage, very visible in one of the most industrialised regions in France. The region had been dramatically impacted by de-industrialisation since the 1970s, an economic decline which affected many cities, leading to demolitions, social crisis and urban regeneration. Tourism and heritage were put forward as new resources for urban development, but former factory workers or managers have not generally been active in museum projects related to industry. According to local associations and former factory workers, industrial heritage is linked with the urban working classes or immigration memories. However, in many industrial sites or museums realised in the 1990s in Picardy, these social aspects have to some extent been recovered by nostalgia for the lost prosperity. Even if narratives do not wholly avoid the difficulties and hardships of past working conditions or the class inequalities of the time, both being unavoidable dimensions of the industrial past, these museums are often still focused on celebrating technology, and illustrating modernity and innovation.

Changing the city museum to transform city life

The city in the expert's eyes: new theories in the 1990s

In 1993, the first international conference devoted to city museums was organised by UNESCO at the Museum of London. The subsequent issue of UNESCO's journal *Museums International* that was dedicated to this conference reveals how professionals and experts were developing new kinds of reflections in a context of increasing global urbanisation. The experts' visions of urbanisation were rather negative, even catastrophist, reflecting a dominant approach in the social sciences at that time, especially towards cities in the Global South:

> UNESCO's concern with cities is thus a response to this overwhelming, critical and inescapable fact of urban life. Today it is no longer the factory and the enterprise that reflect social conflict, but the urban fabric itself – the

city – that is the locus of new rifts in society. Cities, which have been the wellspring of such vital concepts and practices as urbanity, civilization, politics and democracy, community solidarity and social bonds, are seen by many today as unwieldy agglomerations of disorder, chaos, violence and pollution.

(Editorial [Marcia Lord] to 'City Museums' special issue,
UNESCO 1995, 3)

Moreover, the dominant preoccupations and visions of Anglo-American experts at the conference produced a view of the 'city' that was mainly reduced to the multicultural and cosmopolitan metropolis. The emerging international debates about city museums in the 1990s seemed to crystallise around the concepts of 'integration of citizens' and 'cultural diversity'. The social and political role assigned to a city museum (showing the diversity of the city in order to integrate every citizen) was thus reaffirmed and re-theorised (as 'new museology') on an international level. One of the principal architects of the conference, Nicola Johnson, who was in charge of the Museum of London's Department of Later History and Collections in 1993, wrote that:

[a]ccepting that the city museum cannot be all things to all people all of the time, however, does not absolve it of its responsibility towards all citizens. That responsibility demands that the museum attempt to take account of the histories, aspirations and urban experiences of citizens from many different cultural, economic and ethnic backgrounds and to retrieve lost or suppressed aspects of those histories.

(Nicola Johnson, in UNESCO 1995, 5)

These new or re-conceptions were largely taken up in France, where eco-museology had been a tradition among museum curators, administrators and experts since the 1960s. The need to modernise an old institution – the city museum – was also due to the departure of the previous generation of traditional museum actors and their replacement by a new generation of young museum experts nurtured in a context of professionalisation amongst the cultural spheres in France (Poulard 2010). Moreover, the gap between the image of the city set out by the traditional local history museum and the reality of the contemporary city was still growing wider than ever. Consequently the social role of the city museum was coming to be reconsidered in the context of urban changes that were widely seen mainly as a series of urban crises (the suburbs crisis, urban unemployment, exclusion, de-industrialisation, and many others).

The seminar on 'City Museums' initiated in 1996 within the Direction des Musées de France (DMS), the French state museums service, testified to this willingness to reinvent the city museum and to expand its capacity to account for urban change. The museum, it was believed, should begin to present total urban history, and to make understandable the spatial and social organisation of the whole city. It should also include social aspects such as migrations, evolution of

90   *Anne Hertzog*

social structures and economic activities, and should act as a 'guide for reading the city' and a means of encouraging citizens to analyze their feeling of belonging to the city (Joly 1998). This conception of the museum is political: it should be a tool for 'cultural democratisation' and 'social cohesion', as well as a 'school of citizenship'. The project is social and it is also scientific: city museums should take account of recent scientific or social sciences approaches in urban studies (urban geography, history or socio-anthropology), even if most of the time the new professional curators have no complete training in such fields (especially geography), as their studies and diplomas were in the great majority of cases centred on art history.

Presenting identities, common heritage and collective memory in the contemporary city

More recently other types of reflections have emerged among museum professionals and experts in a context of important urban transformations. Metropolitisation processes (such as the concentration of population and activities in the most important cities, peri-urban sprawland urban expansion) have added new scales of urban planning based on grouping of districts, and led to new questions about territorial identity, new scales of urbanity and a definition of a 'common' heritage. In this changing context, it was asked whether city museum narratives might look to the old historical city centre to integrate the new 'multi-communal' territories, the expanding suburbs and the peri-urban zones beyond. How could city museums adapt to this new complex urban context, involving actors referring to these new scales in urban planning? Such questions were the main points of a congress held in Nantes in 2010 by FEMS (the Fédération des Ecomusées et Musées de Société). How can the museum develop its scientific and cultural project in coherence with new territories, whether they are political, administrative, planning, inhabited, or virtual territories? What is an effective scale in the European and globalised context?

These recent debates about museums underlie more general questions and doubts about collective identities and their construction, about the construction of a sense of belonging and the collection, preservation or transmission of collective memory in the contemporary changing city. It is all the more challenging to present the contemporary multi-scalar city since social, cultural and spatial identities seem far more complex and uncertain than in the past.

Re-interpreting museum collections, inventing urban fictions

During and since the 1990s many public museums of the first generation have been reorganised and redeveloped. These transformations have been in keeping with the process of professionalisation already mentioned, but also with a willingness to set new norms in order to modernise French museums. One of the new requirements has been the Scientific and Cultural Project (1992) imposed on museum curators to find coherence within the collection based on a link with the local territory. The principles of eco-museology ('museums as a mirror of the territory') were to some extent applied in other types of museums and especially to those city museums that were often generalist or encyclopaedic. Collections have thus been strictly sorted, selected and reordered in order to give support to coherent narratives, reinventing the history of cities. This has changed the status of the object and challenged the definitiveness of the collection.

Such transformations of city museums into museums *of* a city, remembering the case of Noyon after World War I, also demonstrate the essential role of museums from a tourism and economic point of view in urban planning. Public stakeholders and urban planners have developed a renewed interest in city museums as a tool of urban planning in a symbolic and concrete way. The French geographer Michel Lussault suggested that urban planning participates in building 'urban fictions' and that city museums in particular are used to promote this 'symbolic register of public action' (Lussault 1997). They are often considered as efficient – and magical – tools in urban planning: 'mirrors' of the city, that enable the construction of a coherent image of the city and thus of an ideal of social cohesion. Inventing urban fictions gives a sense to places and facilitates the feeling of belonging to the city; they are a means of territorial development, in the same way that culture and heritage are now considered to be new urban resources in post-industrial cities.

The city museum of Noyon: challenging cultural sustainability?

'The scooter must have its place as much as the beautiful piece of earthenware': theories of exhibition

The city museum of Noyon was entirely redeveloped around 1996. The curator, a new professional recruit and active member of the Seminar on City Museums, aimed to bring both new standards of 'professional' museological exhibitions (standardised furniture, clarity, balance between objects, pictures and texts) and new city museum theory to his new cultural project (Panni 1997). The museum collections that had been on display since 1949 were reordered to illustrate in a pedagogic way a new interpretation of the city story. The traditional model of the museum had been questioned by the curator.

> How can a local history museum become a place of interpretation of the urban environment? Is the staging of decorative arts and collections of 'old souvenirs', in which the museums are often rooted, relevant enough to cast light on the urban phenomenon? ... What about contemporary history and the recent expansion of the city, and its new residents with their own memories? Should they be dismissed? If the purpose of the museum is really to testify to urban history, shouldn't the scooter have its place as much as the beautiful piece of earthenware?
>
> (Author's translation from Panni 1997, 20)

The city museum should give '*as much importance to the scooter as to the beautiful piece of earthenware*'. In other words, give equal value to popular culture and to high culture, to recent (and present) and to ancient heritage, to street objects and more traditional art pieces. Furthermore, it should do this in a more metaphorical way, giving an equal place to the history of 'other' urban categories (young, popular, migrant categories) as well as to that of upper-class residents. This rather provocative project thereby aimed to break many barriers and divides between urban social categories, but also between outsider and insider, popular and high culture, object and art. By reconciling opposite categories the curator aimed to frame a city museum that could expose a non-fragmented and multidimensional city and thus could be a concrete tool for 'social integration' and 'urban cohesion', a local transposition of the theories that were arising in museums at that period.

Does the scooter have its place? Exhibition in practice

The renewed organisation and display of the collection still refers, however, to narratives that privilege the long history of the city, from its Gallo-Roman origins to World War I. The emphasis is on antiquity (with an important archaeological exhibition), the Middle Ages (through displays of catholic religious objects and art) and the Renaissance (as can be seen on the museum's web page, at www.ville-noyon.fr/Le-musee-du-Noyonnais.html). Traditional narratives (for example of the French Revolution or the Industrial Revolution) dominate many more recent periods too. The narratives of World War I continue to reinforce the vision of an urban continuity brutally brought to an end by this event. This urban story is disconnected from the present-day life of the city.

Moreover, the choice of the objects exhibited shows a monumental and material conception of the city's heritage, and evades most economic, sociological or political dimensions of the city's story. The territorial approach is far more selective. Despite the presentation of a model of the whole town (especially devoted to revealing the traces of Roman roads) and several aerial photographs, the narrative remains centred on the old historical town centre and more precisely on the cathedral area. Historically and visually, the renewed museum offers a fragmented representation of the city, excluding all the outlying areas such as the post-1960 residential estates, the working-class areas and tower blocks, and the industrial districts, and overlooking everyday life approaches or aspects of popular culture. The scooter, finally, in fact, does *not* have its place next to the beautiful piece of earthenware! Presented as a museum of the 'whole city and its environment', indeed bearing the broader title 'le Musée du Noyonnais', the museum nevertheless privileges the city centre. Thus, the museum has finally chosen a rather traditional form of museology that is generally justified by the various material constraints linked to the specific organisation of the building, which is an ancient episcopal palace, and the various financial constraints that restrict the ability to obtain new acquisitions. This 'new' museology is the result of a drastic selection process carried out on the collection, resulting in a focus on pieces of 'historical and artistic' value. This shows the power of the disciplinary traditions (history of art, importance of archaeology, attachment to the chronological approach, etc.) that influence the work of curators. Analysing the renewal process, Panni finally concludes that

> ... [v]iewing the museum of Noyon as a tool to interpret the city's identity, our aim was to reorganise the museum as a 'city museum' ... [a] museum following the traditional model of collections on display in a building can be a good answer to many questions about the city ... But we have to find *other places* in the city to show other aspects – more contemporary aspects – of the city's history.
>
> (author's translation of Panni 1997, 20)

Making a museum, imposing a legitimate image: the city museum as symbolic arena

What is particularly interesting, indeed, is that this renewed museology is in line with the local museographic tradition constituted in the 1920s and 1930s, as if collective memory was entangled with these fixed interpretations of the past, in a permanent reactivation process without any possibility of integrating new memories. The process of renewal undertaken by the new curator was supported by the municipality, and involved many professionals and experts (architects, exhibition designers, museologists) who were mostly not locals. This underlay a rupture in the management of the museum, hitherto largely dominated by the traditional local cultural 'amateurs' (belonging to local societies of archaeology and history). The 'professional' transition led to tensions and conflicts between the new curator and the amateurs, a classic phenomenon. As the conflict over redesigning the exhibitions showed, the amateurs felt dispossessed and marginalised by the new professional values and practices. But, as 'authentic' residents of the city they also felt to some extent dispossessed of 'their' collective memory by new categories of actors who could easily be considered 'outsiders'.

Choices made in the renewal project testify, however, to the desire not to erase completely the local historiographical tradition, and thus not to break off with those who built it (the 'insiders'). Local research and local history were centred on a few main topics like religious history (the cathedral), the Gallo-Roman period and, much later in date, World War I. Local urban historiography has been rooted in topics that have shaped a culture of local knowledge which had also been valorised in the museum since the 1930s. The museological renewal can thus be seen as a crucial moment of confrontation between different representations of the city. The reactivation of a traditional vision of the urban 'mythology' (its golden ages), even though 'rewritten' by professional practices and narratives, revealed a strong control exercised by representatives of the rooted local authorities over the production of knowledge about the past, and thus over the definition of legitimate common heritage. But museum practice is not only a consequence of this social and cultural domination. It is also influenced, with the support of the municipality, by an 'institutionalised' image of the city that emerged from the development of urban planning and tourism in the 1980s and 1990s.

During those two decades, Noyon suffered from economic crisis and industrial decline. The city became a bastion of the extreme-right political party, the Front National. The city suffered from major social and urban divisions, mainly between the historical centre and the populous but often underprivileged suburbs. In this context, questions of social cohesion and cultural development became major issues in municipal politics. Culture and heritage were mobilised in urban regeneration in order to integrate every citizen and struggle against socio-spatial exclusion. The museum's transformation took place in that political context.

The economic stakes were important, as the renewal of the museum had to contribute to a strategy of tourism development clearly affirmed at the same period. An inventory of architectural heritage was made in order to develop cultural mediation and tourism programmes in the town. The aim of this inventory was also to win the official label of 'Ville d'Art et d'Histoire 1998' ('City of Art and History 1998') (www.ville-noyon.fr/-Ville-d-art-et-d-histoire-.html). Whereas outlying suburbs were only concerned with social politics without any specific cultural action, culture and heritage were essential dimensions of urban planning in the city centre. In 2001 the patrimonialisation process led to the creation of a *Zone de Protection du Patrimoine Architectural, Urbain et Paysager (ZPPAUP)*, a zone of rather strict legal and planning controls that covered the whole historical centre (heritage district), especially around the town's iconic monument, the cathedral.

This urban planning included heritage as a tool to reinforce socio-spatial contrasts between this ultra-protected and thus ultra-valorised old centre and other parts of the town which by implication lacked comparable qualities and values. The manner in which the renewal of the city museum was implemented to some extent mirrored this inequality in urban politics and its policies of qualification and valorisation, with the risk of losing the integrating vision that had been clearly stated in the early 1990s.

Conclusion

Whereas the 1960s and 1970s were decades of obliteration, the 1980s and 1990s were decades of 'over-exposure' of the city in museums, dependent on the need to make the more complex and multidimensional urban territories more intelligible. A modernisation process for outdated institutions was also undertaken by new professionals and experts, and supported by public actors according to the renewed social, economic and political purposes of the city museum.

The renewed city museums that frame a positive image of the city rooted in heritage and urban mythology expose, however, a selective and fragmented vision of urbanity. This is especially so when the dominant social and professional elite reactivate only the more traditional conceptions of the city story and transfer them into the new narrative. Exhibitions of the city are always socially and spatially rooted. The example of Noyon shows that it is less the inertia of museums that must be questioned than the inertia of urban representations, carried by those with the authority to impose and transmit their vision as the most legitimate.

In the case of Noyon, three types of reasons converge to explain why its own city museum failed in the attempt to present a more inclusive vision of urban heritage and of the city: the professional curatorial posture, the role of local social hierarchies and power struggles, and the central role played by the museum in its search for strong local tourism narratives during a time of economic and urban crisis. As a result, a culturally, socially and spatially selective image of the city is presented in the museum through the exhibition of artefacts, hiding many aspects of 'collective memory' and ignoring many dimensions of the place, especially in the geographic (but not necessarily civic) peripheries of the city. To find a different pathway in future is the challenge of cultural sustainability.

References

Arnstein, S-R. 1969. A ladder of citizen participation. *Journal of the American Institute of Planners* 4(35), 216–24.

Bodo, S., Gibbs, K. and Sani, M. 2009. *Museums as places of intercultural dialogue: selected practices from Europe*, London: Museums as Places for Intercultural Dialogue (MAP for ID Group). ISBN 978-0-9564752-0-6.

Bourdieu, P. and Darbel, A. 1966. *De l'amour de l'art: les musées et leur public*, Paris: Editions Minuit.

Joly, M.-H. 1998. *Des musées d'histoire pour l'avenir*, Paris: Editions Noesis.

Lussault, M. 1997. Des récits et des lieux: le registre identitaire dans l'action urbaine. *Annales de Géographie* 597, 522–30.

Panni, F. 1997. Un musée de ville: le musée du Noyonnais. *Bulletin de la Société Historique Archéologique et Scientifique de Noyon* nos. 257–58, December–January, 20.

Panni, F. and Jagielsky, K. 2000. Les ruines en images: Noyon et Soissons. *Coll. Reconstructions en Picardie après 1918*, Paris: RMN (La Réunion des Musées Nationaux), 204–19.

Poulard, F. 2007. Les écomusées: participation habitante et prise en compte des publics. *Ethnologie Française* 3–3, 551–57.

Poulard, F. 2010. *Conservateurs de musées et politiques culturelles: l'impulsion territorial*, Paris: La Documentation Française, coll. 'Musées-Mondes'.

Poulot, D. 1997. Le musée dans la ville. *Le musée dans la ville*, Actes du colloque des Musées Protestants (1996), La Rochelle: Société d'Histoire du Protestantisme Français.

Salomon Cavin, J. and Marchand, B., eds, 2010. *Anti-urbains: origines et conséquences de l'urbanophobie*. Lausanne, Switzerland: Presses Polytechniques et Universitaires Romandes.

UNESCO 1995. City museums. *Museum International* XLVII(3), 187. Paris/Oxford: UNESCO/Blackwell.

6 Social sustainability in historic city centres

The Grand Place in Brussels

Maria Leus and Leen Kosatka

Introduction

The topic of celebration chosen for the 40th anniversary of World Heritage in 2012 was 'Sustainable development: the role of local communities'. From the outset of the World Heritage programme it was claimed that World Heritage Sites can contribute to ecological and cultural sustainability and thereby to the quality of life and to social sustainability. The Conclusions of the 2012 meeting made an appeal:

> We call for the practice of conservation to incorporate a new multi-disciplinary and inter-sectoral approach, which would be based on a fully participatory approach and integrate a consideration of social and economic dimensions through appropriate methodologies and indicators. Unless such a sustainable development perspective is integrated in the management of a World Heritage property, in the long run it would be difficult to ensure the conservation of its Outstanding Universal Value.
>
> (UNESCO 2012, p. 1, conclusion no. 16)

Within this concept, historical urban sites are considered in a broad context with a layering that goes beyond the pure architectural aspects and also integrates immaterial aspects, and social and cultural values; in other words, '[c]ultural heritage must be understood as part of the larger sphere of socio-cultural processes' (Avrami et al. 2000, 11). It is important to emphasise that sustainable development is an anthropocentric concept and is linked with the perception of people: '[t]he best we can achieve is to acknowledge the centrality of people' (Bell and Morse 2010, 43). Sustainable development offers new opportunities for cultural heritage to our society, but robust demonstrations are needed of how it improves the quality of life for communities.

The Grand Place in Brussels, a major set-piece of historic urban design, has been inscribed on the UNESCO World Heritage List since 1998. But Brussels, like many other cities in Europe, is subject to the phenomenon of urban shrinkage and an increase of vacancy in heritage buildings (Banzhaf et al. 2007), and this is a particular problem in the area surrounding the Grand Place. UNESCO has remarked that many World Heritage properties 'face problems that directly or indirectly derive from the situation of their buffer zone' (UNESCO 2008) and the striking vacancy of the Grand Place buffer zone is a threat to the outstanding values of the World Heritage Site (WHS). According to Setha Low (2010) social sustainability refers to the preservation of relations and significances which reinforce the cultural system. Different communities only remain connected with the cultural heritage if their values and meanings are also preserved; after all, cultural heritage is an aspect that contributes to our identity and is influenced by the communities we are part of (Ashworth and Howard 1999, 8–10). It is precisely because cultural heritage contributes to our identity that it is important to involve local people in the management of cultural heritage sites. We might wonder if the large vacancy rate in the historical town centre of Brussels is a possible indicator of the fact that the local population is not so concerned about this heritage. Vacancy can reduce the feeling of connection with heritage and thus influences one's identity.

Historic cities like Brussels were originally supported by the economic and social benefits of urban concentration, which is a sustainable strategy in itself. The protection and conservation of the site under UNESCO guidelines carries therefore a clear risk of establishing a frozen city, which is at odds with sustainable development. To freeze a WHS or to neglect its sustainable development can have a harmful impact in the form of decreasing the legibility of the space due to too many tourist facilities, dissolution of the social fabric, loss of employment, and reduced aesthetic quality because of vacancy and degradation. This is likely to have legal or juridical consequences and finally to result in less intergenerational responsibility and no participation or voluntarism (Verhelst 2014). In this case, unsustainable heritage management can have a destructive effect on the broader life of a city, causing perceptions of a harsh setting, environmental pollution, safety problems and inefficient use of space and buildings. This example not only illustrates the importance of the sustainable development of cultural heritage but also shows that a holistic approach is necessary.

The new WHS management plan of Brussels (UZMPB 2012) has a strong focus on the preservation of the historical urban landscape and safeguarding of the spatial quality, but hardly any attention is paid to the social aspects of sustainable development. This is a missed opportunity. The research discussed in this chapter therefore used the Grand Place to explore the role of the social context in the valuation and preservation of remarkable cultural heritage sites such as World Heritage Sites. It utilised detailed questionnaire-based interviews with thirty residents of the Grand Place neighbourhood and thirty tourists, of different ages and backgrounds, carried out in June 2013 during the day on weekdays and at weekends. The characteristics of the respondents were compared with the sample population and visitors to this site.

Two research questions were asked concerning the tension between sustainable development and historic preservation and conservation: What are the relationships between sustainability and cultural heritage? Are there methods by which socially sustainable development could be reconciled with heritage conservation? A conceptual framework of social and cultural heritage aspects was created so that the complex character of sustainability could be translated into concrete standards. This framework of social and cultural heritage indicators was used to describe integrated sustainable development in a holistic way. There was particular focus on the presence of vacancy, an important subject in research into sustainability because it also determines the values that society ascribes to World Heritage Sites. Vacancy (and degradation, neglect, disrepair) also depends on many other aspects of society, and the study also therefore considered demographic factors. The framework used acts as a barometer for identifying the core problems of sustainability and those aspects of WHS management that integrate cultural heritage in the sustainable development debate.

Life in the Grand Place and its buffer zone

The Place and its environs

The Grand Place is characterised by a high level of architectural homogeneity, mainly in the baroque style of the late seventeenth and early eighteenth century (De Pange 2011) (Figure 6.1).

Figure 6.1 The Grand Place, Brussels
Photo: L. Kostatka.

The UNESCO statement of significance claims that it meets two criteria (ii and iv) for inscription on the WH List (UWC 1998). Criterion ii: 'The Grand-Place is an outstanding example of the eclectic and highly successful blending of architectural and artistic styles that characterise the culture and society of this region.' Criterion iv: 'Through the nature and quality of its architecture and of its outstanding quality as a public open space, the Grand-Place illustrates in an exceptional way the evolution and achievements of a highly successful mercantile city of northern Europe at the height of its prosperity.'

Around the Grand Place is a larger protected zone, the so-called 'buffer zone'. Although buffer zones are not part of the nominated property, any modifications to the buffer zone subsequent to inscription of a property on the World Heritage List should be approved by the World Heritage Committee. In the nomination document for the Grand Place there is no specific information about the requirements of its buffer zone. The generic Operational Guidelines for the Implementation of the World Heritage Convention (UNESCO 2013) define a buffer zone as

> an area surrounding the nominated property which has complementary legal and/or customary restrictions placed on its use and development to give an added layer of protection to the property. This should include the immediate setting of the nominated property, important views and other areas or attributes that are functionally important as a support to the property and its protection.
>
> (UNESCO 2008, 26–7)

The Grand Place has a buffer zone of 21 hectares (the World Heritage Site itself is only 1.5 hectares in size) (Figure 6.2). It consists of twenty-six housing blocks with the long, narrow land parcels that were typical of cities during the Middle Ages. In this district, the old urban structure with small and winding streets is preserved. The share of safeguarded buildings matches the richness of the architectural heritage. Data from the monitoring of this district (IBSA 1999–2012) reveal that between 1999 and 2012 the total number of protected monuments grew from 135 to 320.

The Grand Place itself is well maintained, but in contrast some streets of the buffer zone (such as Hoedenmakersstraat, Schildknaapstraat and many side streets of the Grasmarkt) exhibit extreme degrees of vacancy. It is remarkable that most of the buildings in these streets are protected monuments (Figure 6.3). Although the intrinsic heritage values of the Grand Place in Brussels are well known and internationally recognised, this does not seem to be sufficient to prevent or to solve problems relating to vacancy. A strange phenomenon emerges as the well maintained central market square is threatened by its own hinterland zone. This results in a privileged island in a decaying zone full of vacancy and degradation.

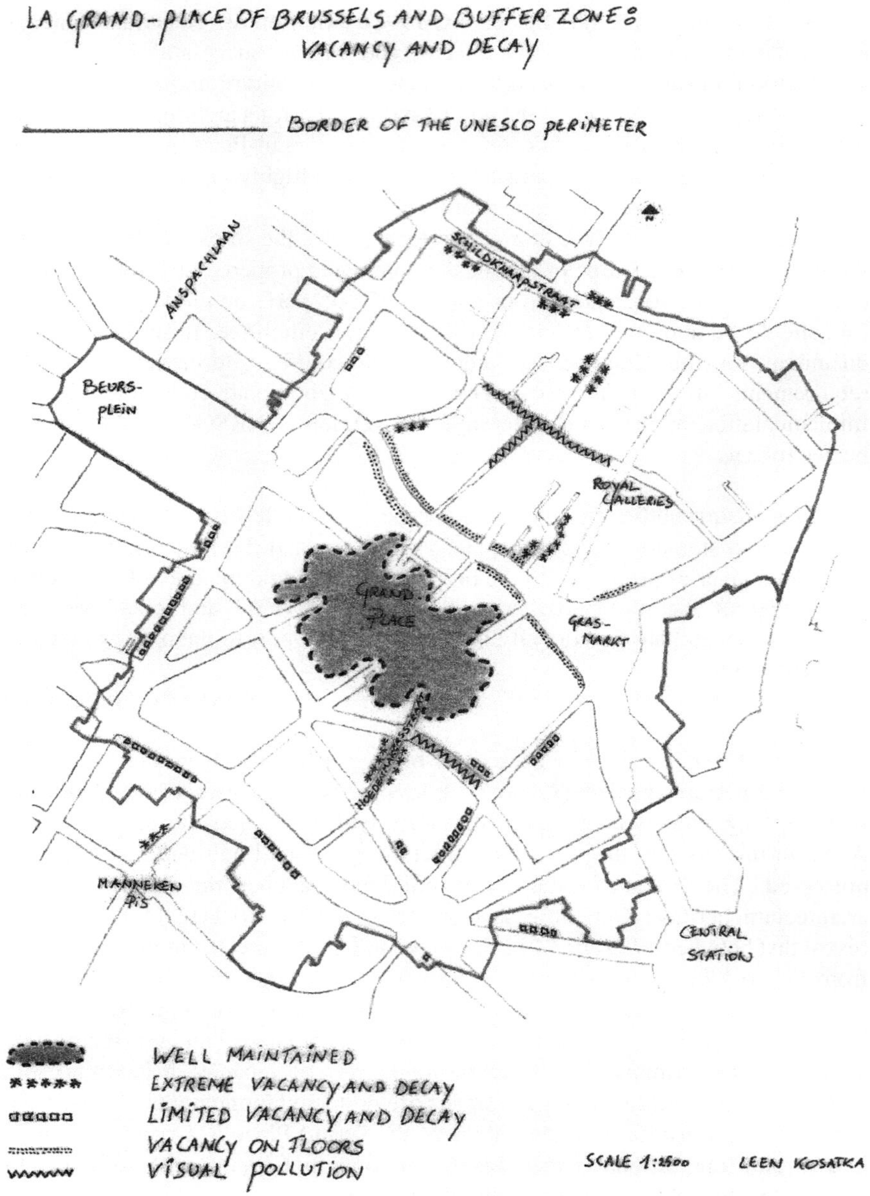
LA GRAND-PLACE OF BRUSSELS AND BUFFER ZONE:
VACANCY AND DECAY
BORDER OF THE UNESCO PERIMETER
ANSPACHLAAN
SCHILDKNAAPSTRAAT
BEURS-PLEIN
ROYAL GALLERIES
GRAND PLACE
GRAS-MARKT
MANNEKEN PIS
CENTRAL STATION
WELL MAINTAINED
EXTREME VACANCY AND DECAY
LIMITED VACANCY AND DECAY
VACANCY ON FLOORS
VISUAL POLLUTION
SCALE 1:2500
LEEN KOSATKA

Figure 6.2 The Grand Place, Brussels: the boundaries of the World Heritage Site and its buffer zone

Drawn by L. Kosatka.

Figure 6.3 Extreme degree of vacancy and poor building condition in the buffer zone of the Grand Place, Brussels (Hoedenmakersstraat)

Photo: L. Kosatka.

Demographic data

Vacancy and degradation depend on many different social, indeed cultural, and economic factors. IBSA data indicated that only 13.40 per cent of the dwellings in the buffer zone were owner-occupied. This is much lower than the 41.45 per cent average of the Brussels region as a whole. The average monthly rent (€583 in 2010) also was lower than in the other districts of Brussels. In the period 2007–2010, the number of grants or subsidies for renovations and upgrading of housing per 1,000 households was 1.31 per cent (1.05 per cent for façade renovation) in the World Heritage zone compared to the average of 2.30 per cent (0.76 per cent for façade renovation) in the Brussels region. Although there were many empty buildings, the buffer zone had a high population density and showed a positive migration index of 11.36 (2001–2006) that was higher than that in the other districts of Brussels (average of 4.39 during the same period). This means that despite what might appear from the vacancy problems, the area still attracts inhabitants. The buffer zone, however, as well as other districts, is characterised by an emigration intensity of 119.16 per cent (2001–2006). This can result in a lack of commitment to and engagement with their cultural heritage. In combination with the large amount of traders, this could be an explanation for the limited social inclusion. More recent demographical data are not yet available to assess how this trend is evolving.

Sustainable aspects in practice

The main focus of this research particularly assesses the relation between the people and the heritage dimensions of sustainable development, viewed from a heritage basis but against the background of the holistic vision that is indispensable for the creation of a set of indicators. In the management of cultural heritage, increasing interest is being attached to social participation (Avrami 2009) but when cultural heritage sites are also part of an active and living community this aspect is even more important. Therefore the goal of the survey and interviews was to obtain in-depth information to understand the users' experiences. Due to the absence of recent statistical data on vacancy, this report is mainly based on qualitative observation and the perceptions of the users of this district, which given the aim of this research is perhaps even more important than statistical data.

The heritage dimension (Figure 6.4a)

In the heritage dimension ways of valorising the cultural heritage are examined. This concerns the management of the site so that an optimal appreciation is achieved and the sustainability of heritage values is assured. Four factors were assessed because they are linked to the ability of a site to convey significance: (a) accessibility (physical and psychological); (b) knowledge building; (c) spatial aesthetics; and (d) immaterial cultural heritage.

(a) *Accessibility* describes the degree to which the site is physically accessible and opened up for the public and especially the host community, which in turn depends on communicating information and initiatives of heritage education. Because accessibility and opening-up are linked, they are categorised in one aspect. Both have an important inclusivity element. Almost all the residents and tourists questioned found the physical accessibility of the site very good and use public transport for their mobility. The town centre with pedestrian zones, the short distance to the central station of Brussels and the presence of a metro station, as well as the low cost of public transport, were appreciated. A negative point for cyclists and disabled people were the uncomfortable, cobblestoned streets.

As one inhabitant of the zone pointed out: 'This zone is accessible because I can do nice walks and there is only little traffic.' Another participant related the accessibility to: 'Well organised public transport in this zone.' Only one participant was not satisfied with the distance to public transport and notes: 'For less mobile and elderly persons public transport is located too far away from the zone.' Parking was perceived negatively due to the limited space and high cost. It is worth highlighting that the city of Brussels undertook many efforts to improve the inclusiveness of the cultural heritage for disabled people. A few persons underscored the lack of parking in the area. In particular, Beursplein and Anspachlaan, situated at the boundary of the World Heritage zone, were disliked by an interviewee because of the heavy traffic. (Scale score: 8/10)

Examination of the opening-up aspect showed that most of the users were informed about the history of the site by literature and narratives. But only a few of them could really list specific historical facts. One participating tourist admitted: 'I do not know the history of the Grand Place and its former function. I didn't immerse myself in it because of my short visit.' Especially striking is the fact that little reference to digital media was reported; only a few respondents had used the webcam and the QR codes. Half of the users pointed out that there was hardly any information about cultural heritage. There was a lack of information panels, and also the markers identifying the protection status were absent, so it was not clear that these buildings are a part of World Heritage. (Scale score: 6/10)

Total score: 7/10 (weighting factor 50/50).

(b) *Knowledge building* tries to answer questions about the extent to which scientific knowledge concerning the site is present and whether this knowledge is broadened and deepened. A lot of scientific research about this WHS has been carried out and important studies published. The Historic Buildings and Landscapes Office of the Brussels region published a brochure on the occasion of the exhibition 'La Grand-Place and Buffer Zone, a World Heritage Site' in the Sint-Goriks Halls in 2000. The City of Brussels presented the study *Evolution du bati dans l'ilot sacré* where each

(a)

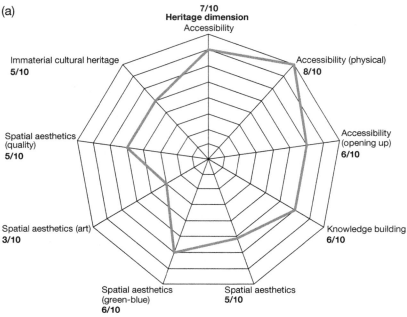

(b)

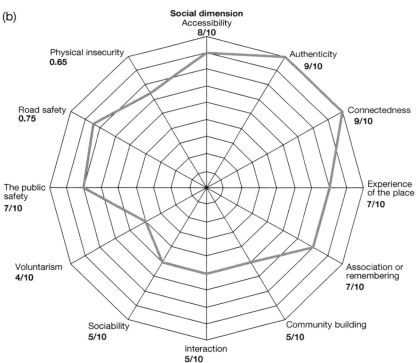

(c)

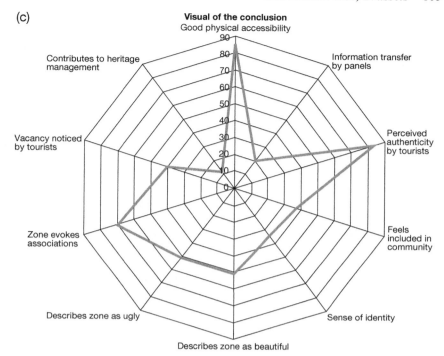

Figure 6.4 a–c Analysis of the survey questionnaires: (a) heritage dimension, (b) social dimension, (c) summary

Graphs: L. Kosatka.

housing block of the entire buffer zone was examined. The 'Historical and Architectural Study of the Houses of the Grand-Place' of the Cultural Heritage Cell of the city of Brussels and the book *La Grand-Place de Bruxelles* by Isabelle De Pange give a complete historical review of the Grand Place.

Slightly more than half of the residents possessed knowledge of the history of the World Heritage Site of the Grand Place. The respondents noticed for example: 'The history of the guild … the legend of the architect … the function as a market and the presence of craftsmen.' Most often guided tours and books were mentioned as educational elements. It is surprising that hardly any reference was made to websites, exhibitions or television programmes. Only the website of the City of Brussels was well-known. One participating tourist was aware of the fact that the Grand Place was bombed by the French and rebuilt. He added: 'I received this information by visiting an exhibition in the museum of the city located on the Grand Place.'

Total score: 6/10.

(c) *Spatial aesthetics* focuses on the aesthetic quality of the site as a total concept. It includes the integration of the green-blue networks, the integration of art which is emphasised by the Vienna Memorandum, Article 23 (UNESCO 2005) as a catalyst of urban renewal, and overall aesthetic quality including image quality, legibility of the site, harmony of the total concept, quality of restoration, and multi-sensorial aspects. Half of the users (inhabitants and tourists) referred to the lack of green and water infrastructure. One resident noted: 'A water source or drinking fountains would give this city more charm.' (Scale score: 6/10). Only a few tourists mentioned art as the driver for a visit to this WHS. The city's official mascot, the seventeenth-century bronze statue of *Manneken Pis*, by Jerome Duquesn, is the only remarkable art piece in this neighbourhood. Participating inhabitants mentioned as disturbing 'poorly maintained streets ... bad smell of waste ... dilapidated houses and noise during the night'. (Scale score: 3/10).

All the respondents were asked to circle a list of adjectives that are best suited to the WHS and the buffer zone. Almost all the tourists marked 'beautiful' and only half of the inhabitants find the site 'beautiful'. All the respondents admit that the central market is their favoured place. A few times a participant notes: 'I don't like the lack of uniformity in this zone caused by the billboards.' (Scale score: 5/10)

Total score: 5/10 (weighting factor: 25/25/50).

(d) *Immaterial cultural heritage* refers to the traditions and life expressions of a culture such as oral history, stories, music, rituals or festivals. Referring to the UNESCO Convention (2003), intangible cultural heritage is considered as a mainspring of cultural diversity and a guarantee of sustainable development. The Convention also takes account of the anecdotes and memories which are linked to the site. It is interesting to note that elderly people especially have come to know the history of this cultural heritage by way of oral tradition. As an older inhabitant mentioned during the interview: 'I know the history and function of the World Heritage zone from stories that my husband, originally from Brussels, told me.' Another participant pointed out: 'The music of Brussels, more specifically "Jazz", is a source of information about the zone.' Only a few inhabitants associated the site with intangible aspects, as a former site of executions, for example the execution of the counts of Egmont and Horne, or as a political and administrative centre for the celebration of royal visits. An important folkloric manifestation is the annual procession in which 1,400 people take part, which is connected to the legend of the Church on the Zavel (De Pange 2011, 28–9). For the past five years this event has been very successful as a tourist attraction because the stories are explained in three languages.

Total score: 5/10.

The social dimension (Figure 6.4b)

The four social aspects relevant to both the people and heritage that were researched are: (e) sense of place; (f) community building; (g) voluntarism; and (h) public safety. Such factors are described in the working document prepared by the UNESCO Secretariat based on expert contributions (UNESCO 2011).

(e) *Sense of place* is a term derived from environmental psychology which has flourished since the end of the 1990s, especially in the English heritage world (Stubbs 2004, 289–92). It has also been described as *genius loci*, as the meaning created by people for a certain place, or as the identification factor of a place and its inhabitants. Cultural heritage sites are frequently pre-eminently places where a sense of place emerges explicitly. Therefore this aspect can be defined as the degree to which the place provokes a certain notion of particularity and solidarity with the past (Hawke 2011, 32–40). Sense of place is assessed in the World Heritage zone by three sub-aspects: the first concerns authenticity, an essential qualifying factor of cultural heritage and a combination of material and immaterial aspects that addresses the plurality of values and cultural diversity of the site (Jokilehto 2006). WHSs are considered to be of outstanding value because in addition to the specific criteria, they also meet the integrity and authenticity conditions that refer to the ability of a site to convey significance. The second aspect concerns connectedness, a sense of identity or pride. Sense of place also involves the experience of the place. In this sub-aspect especially, the disturbing effect of vacancy is evaluated. It has been pointed out that the most common reason for an intention to revisit a site, and the strongest indicator of satisfaction after a visit, is its perceived attractiveness (Um et al. 2006). The final aspect, association or remembering, is advocated by the Australian Burra Charter (Icomos Australia 2013, Article 24.1): 'Significant associations between people and a place should be respected, retained and not obscured.'

For the assessment of sense of place it is essential to take the residential status of the interviewed into account (Hay 1998). It is important to remark that all the inhabitants had lived in this area for many years. The inhabitants were questioned about all three sub-aspects, while the interviews with the tourists only look into the experience and associations with the cultural heritage. As might be expected on a WHS, the first and the second aspect, authenticity and connectedness, are very explicit. Almost all the interviewed residents were fully aware of the historic and unique character and the authenticity of their living environment, and they were proud to live and work in this WHS. One participating inhabitant was proud to live in the World Heritage zone because the zone is an important place for history and for culture. Another interviewee mentioned 'the architectural diversity' as a reason to feel proud. That it was 'an educational zone' and 'a place where I can enjoy' were also noted by the interviewees. (Scale score: 9/10 for both sub-aspects)

Most of the interviewees admitted that the cultural heritage enhances the personal experience and understanding of the values of this site. But the negative perception of vacancy and degradation was more pervasive among the inhabitants than with the tourists. This is because the length of stay is shorter for tourists and many of them do not visit the buffer zone (Scale score: 7/10). In contrast with the buffer zone, the Grand Place also acts as a remembering place that evoked associations from two-thirds of the inhabitants and tourists, and they were attracted to this place because of its beauty. One inhabitant said: 'The Grand Place reminds me of the history of Belgium.' Another inhabitant was more specific: 'The Grand Place makes me think of the formation of Brussels and of the people of Belgium.' A few interviewees mentioned 'childhood and school trips' as associations with this place. (Scale score: 7/10)

Total score: 8/10 (weighting factor 25/25/25/25).

(f) *Community building* refers to the degree to which a site is able to create a balanced, coherent and well functioning community. This aspect discusses integration and sociability (Vandevyvere 2010, 231–3). About one-third of the inhabitants of the WHS don't have Belgian nationality, and 85 per cent are aged between 18 and 64 years, with an average age of 39 (IBSA 2011) and an activity level of 65 per cent (IBSA 2009).

Integration refers to the social inclusiveness of the site. Is the site characterised by a social mix of both inhabitants and users? Social peace is necessary for human development, helping to build social cohesion (Inglehart et al. 2008). Answers to the Rosenberg question (1956) – 'Generally speaking, would you say that most people can be trusted or that you need to be very careful in dealing with people?' – revealed that half of the residents trusted most people, and felt part of society. One-third of residents admitted that the overflow of tourists and the bilingualism was the reason for this lack of trust, and only a few had no opinion about this aspect. 'This moralistic trust is an indirect measure of our cultural values and the cultural attitudes of societies toward cooperation' (UNESCO 2011). An inhabitant noted 'the multicultural open atmosphere' as the reason why he felt included in the community. 'It is a place where I feel easily at home' he says. Another interviewee mentioned 'Good contact with other people, the church and associations'. One person belonged to the social association 'De Nerothekers', a Flemish Brussels guild. Another belonged to a social group attached to the Brussels deanery. (Scale score: 5/10)

Sociability or social inclusion draws attention to the degree in which the built environment can encourage social life, facilitate small meetings (Soenen 2006) and provoke social interaction. 'A good city is like a good party: guests stay because they are enjoying themselves' (Gehl 2010, 147). The organisation of the public space which is important for interaction is not well organised, there are no benches that offer people the chance to enjoy common city space.

Also physical degradation has a negative impact on sociability. One tourist remarked on 'the lack of typical cultural activities by people of Brussels'. One person mentioned 'a coffee to go and sit on benches'. (Scale score: 5/10)

Total score: 5/10 (weighting factor 50/50).

(g) *Voluntarism* refers to the 'generic' category of Michael Stubbs' framework (2004, 302). This aspect is related to participation in cultural- and heritage-related activities as mentioned in the working document (UNESCO 2011). It measures the degree to which users are convinced of the overriding importance of sustainable development for the care of heritage and vice versa. The main focus lies on the intrinsic motivation to invest more time and energy in this issue than is strictly necessary (Verhelst 2014). The effects of participation also result in the reinforcement of social capital (Hawke 2011, 37–8). Whilst people are proud to live and work in this World Heritage zone, still no one feels involved in the preservation of the cultural heritage or takes a close interest in the sustainable development of this area. There is hardly any spontaneous stewardship; only 10 per cent of the residents said they contribute to the management of the site. A member of the social group 'The Royal Theatre Toone' pointed out the *estaminets* (small cafés) and the puppet theatre as features to bring people together and make people aware of the heritage. And an inhabitant said: 'I contribute to the management of the World Heritage by my work in the museum.' An inhabitant and trader answered: 'I take care of the World Heritage by organising an exhibition.'

Total score: 4/10.

(h) *Public safety* plays an important role in the attractiveness of the area. Safety is one of people's basic needs. Referring to the hierarchy of walking needs in the neighbourhood as defined by Alfonzo (2005), safety is an important condition for improving the well-being of a neighbourhood. This aspect can be split up in to two sub-aspects, road safety and physical security, under which all other security aspects such as crime, social control and public safety are subsumed and measured. In general, road safety is ensured by the speed limit of 30km/h and the fact that half of the streets of the centre are car-free pedestrian zones. Only 30 per cent of users reported being disturbed by the pressure of traffic. (Scale score: 7.5/10)

On the other hand, a third of the residents drew attention to the insecurity of the site and regarded this neighbourhood as unsafe. A clear distinction between insecurity and the feeling of insecurity is necessary. Mincke (2010, 11) states that

> [i]nsecurity is an objective situation of a risk of victimisation, whereas the feeling of insecurity is a subjective perception of this risk. The factors at the origin of the feeling of insecurity are very diverse and are not

automatically linked to the commission of offences: poverty, degraded environment, social exclusion, etc.

Over a ten-year period the total number of crimes fell by 3.8 per cent (Lleshi 2014). This observation conflicts with the residents' perception of an increase in violence and crime. One inhabitant said: 'At night there should be more police in the zone to control the big fight.' One person explained his unsafe feeling as follows: 'A person was stabbed in my street and there are threats of immigrant neighbours.' 'Uncertainty' and 'delinquency' were words often used by the participating inhabitants and employees of the zone. (Scale score: 6.5/10)

Total score: 7/10 (weighting factor 50/50).

Conclusions from the interviews (Figure 6.4c)

The interviews reveal the critical points that characterise the problems and the relationships between different aspects. In regard to the heritage-based dimension it is remarkable that there is an opposition between good physical accessibility and bad psychological accessibility. The users also get little incentive to increase their knowledge of the cultural heritage on show. The aesthetic quality of the buffer zone of the Grand Place is often simultaneously described as beautiful as well as ugly. Also, the way of dealing with immaterial cultural heritage aspects needs a focus of attention. The low scores for the opening-up of information and the immaterial heritage offer opportunities to define and give a more precise solution to the profile of this zone and thus give further effect to the pre-established objectives and actions of the WHS management plan for the area.

The buffer zone of the WHS ranks very low on many social aspects. Although the information accessibility and the communication should be better, the WHS was experienced by all respondents as an authentic zone. The historic baroque buildings contributed to this experience. This is expressed in a high score for the sense of place. The correlation between social inclusion and perception of degradation and vacancy results in a decreased sense of identity. The interviews reveal that community building and voluntarism stand out as particularly negative. These aspects are typical of dense historic city centres with a high migration rate and a loss of social fabric under the influence of the touristic dynamic.

The openness to an integral approach to sustainable development that is expressed by voluntarism, which is strongly related to the sense of place, is a special challenge for future development.

Reflections

The people dimension will be a particularly important criterion for evaluating the management of WHSs over the coming years. International interest in sustainable heritage development is still growing. The recent Communication from the European Commission to the European Parliament, European Council, and its

Economic/Social and Regions committees – 'Towards an Integrated Approach to Cultural Heritage for Europe' – calls for stronger cooperation at EU level to share ideas and best practice, which can feed into national heritage policies and governance (EC 2014). Europe's cultural heritage, both tangible and intangible, is 'an irreplaceable repository of knowledge and a valuable resource for economic growth, employment and social cohesion'.

The preservation of World Heritage zones inclusive of their buffer zones without taking into account social aspects is in contradiction with the principles of sustainable development of cultural heritage sites. The case study of the buffer zone of the WHS of the Grand Place in Brussels shows that there is a broad tension between sustainable development and the preservation of the WHS. Although we are in the heart of the city of Brussels, we get the impression of being in a museum with very good historical buildings but a centre in which it is difficult to live. The very large number of protected buildings does not prevent a high degree of degradation and vacancy. It is striking that the worst decay is found in buildings that are not on the World Heritage List, but yet are protected or safeguarded by national or local measures. These are buildings that stand within the buffer zone, and have a high art-historical value.

This research reveals that intrinsic and extrinsic values are in conflict with each other. A strong focus on the art-historical value of these protected buildings without a broader approach to the implications for the society creates a bizarre and unsustainable situation. The degree of vacancy and degradation is inextricably linked with the other aspects of the society, but they leave their mark on the social value of historical sites; the effects of mass tourism (such as waste, noise or nuisance) also have major impacts on the site and its inhabitants.

In assessing the question of how sustainable development and cultural heritage are interconnected, it is important to realise that sustainable cultural development and management rely on four pillars: the three pillars of People, Planet and Profit, which have traditionally been defined as the pillars of sustainable development, and the Patrimony – or heritage – pillar. It is absolutely essential that these four pillars be of equal value, and moreover that there be a constant interaction between them.

The question arises, however, of whether UNESCO regards the patrimony pillar to be equivalent to the other three. Precisely because of the outstanding universal value of its World Heritage Site, in Brussels the patrimony pillar has been disconnected from the other pillars of sustainability, even though constant interaction between these pillars is a precondition for sustainable heritage management.

From the case study it became clear that both residents and tourists are rarely well-informed about the heritage. The interviews reveal that this heritage needs to be appreciated by society to help preserve it for future generations. This requires a greater involvement and more participation of existing social groups in the heritage. In the buffer zone of the Grand Place WHS, the relationship between society and World Heritage can first be enhanced by providing better information about that heritage. Moreover, creating in this area a consultative forum or 'heritage house', in which all social groups of the area are represented, could increase involvement and public participation in the heritage. Through a consultative forum, themes like vacancy, decay, reallocation and restoration could be considered from different points of view. For the future, it is clear that the social pillar, in addition to the other pillars of sustainable development, becomes an important task in the evaluation of the management of WHSs. Therefore, as well as acknowledging a site's outstanding universal value, it is an equally important task for UNESCO to bring together the various stakeholders in a public forum.

References

Alfonzo, M. 2005. To walk or not to walk? The hierarchy of walking needs. *Environment and Behavior* 37, 808–36.

Ashworth, D. and Howard, P. (eds) 1999. *European Heritage Planning and Management*, Exeter: Intellect Books, s. l., 8–10.

Avrami, E. 2009. Heritage, values and sustainability. In Richmond, A. and Bracker, A. (eds), *Conservation: Principles, Dilemmas and Uncomfortable Truths*, London: Heineman, 177–83.

Avrami, E., Mason, R. and de la Torre, M. (eds) 2000. *Values and Heritage Conservation: Research Report*, Los Angeles: Getty Conservation Institute, www.getty.edu/conservation/resources/ (1 May 2013).

Banzhaf, E., Kindler, A. and Haases, D. 2007. Monitoring and modelling indicators for urban shrinkage. *EARSeLe Proceedings* 6, 101–14.

Bell, S. and Morse, S. 2010. *Sustainability Indicators: Measuring the Immeasurable?* London: Earthscan.

EC (European Commission) 2014. Towards an integrated approach to cultural heritage for Europe, Communication COM(2014) 477 final. http://ec.europa.eu/culture/library/publications/2014-heritage-communication_en.pdf (27 November 2014).

Gehl, J., 2010. *Cities for People*, Washington, DC: Island Press.

Hawke, S. 2011. Local residents exploring heritage in the North Pennines of England: sense of place and social sustainability. *International Journal of Heritage and Sustainable Development* 1, 32–40.

Hay, R. 1998. Sense of place in developmental context. *Journal of Environmental Psychology* 18, 5–29.

IBSA 1999–2012. L'Institut Bruxellois de Statistique et d'Analyse. http://brussels.irisnet.be/about-the-region/ministry-of-the-brussels-capital region/secretariat-general/institut-bruxellois-de-statistique-et-danalyse ibsa?set_language=en (1 May 2013).

Icomos Australia 2013. The Burra Charter: Australia ICOMOS Charter for Places of Cultural Significance 2013. http://australia.icomos.org/wp-content/uploads/The-Burra-Charter-2013-Adopted-31.10.2013.pdf (1 May 2013).

Inglehart, R., Foa, R., Peterson, C. and Welzel, C. 2008. Development, freedom, and rising happiness: a global perspective. *Perspectives on Psychological Science* 3(4), 264–85.

Jokilehto, J. 2006. Considerations on authenticity and integrity in world heritage context. *City and Time* 2(1). www.ct.ceci-br.org (1 May 2013).

Lleshi, B. 2014. Criminaliteit in Brussel: perceptie en werkelijkheid, www.knack.be/nieuws/belgie/criminaliteit-in-brussel-perceptie-en werkelijkheid/article-opinion-123240.html (27 November 2014).

Low, S. 2010. Social sustainability: people, history, and values. In Fairclough, G., Harrison, R., Jameson, J. H. and Schofield, J. (eds), *The Heritage Reader*, London: Routledge, 392–404.

Mincke, C. 2010. Insecurity and the feeling of insecurity. *Brussels – What the Security Monitor Tells Us*, issue 39.

de Pange, I. 2011. *La Grand-Place de Bruxelles*. Brochure-guide, Brussels: Editions Aparté.

Rosenberg, M. J. 1956. Cognitive structure and attitudinal affect. *Journal of Abnormal and Social Psychology* 53, 367–72.

Soenen, R. 2006. *Het kleine ontmoeten. Over het sociale karakter van de stad*, Antwerp.

Stubbs, M. 2004. Heritage-sustainability: developing a methodology for the sustainable appraisal of the historic environment. *Planning, Practice and Research* 19(3), 285–305.

Um, S., Chon, K. and Ro, Y. 2006. Antecedents of revisit intention. *Annals of Tourism Research* 33(4), 1141–58.

UNESCO 2003. Convention of the Safeguarding of the Intangible Cultural Heritage (MISC/2003/CLT/CH/14), art. 2; http://portal.unesco.org/en/ev.phpurl_id=17716&url_do=do_topic&url_section=201.html (17 December 2013).

UNESCO 2005. Vienna Memorandum on 'World Heritage and Contemporary Architecture – Managing the Historic Urban Landscape' (WHC-05/15.GA/INF.7), http://whc.unesco.org/archive/2005/whc05-15ga-inf7e.pdf (17 December 2013).

UNESCO 2008. World Heritage Papers 25 – World Heritage and Buffer Zones, http://whc.unesco.org/en/events/473/ (17 December 2013).

UNESCO 2011. Towards a UNESCO culture and development indicators suite, www.unesco.org/fileadmin/MULTIMEDIA/HQ/CLT/creativity/pdf/culture_and_development_indicators/C+D per cent20Indicator per cent20Bibliography.pdf (17 December 2013).

UNESCO 2012. *Proceedings of the Consultative Expert Meeting on World Heritage and Sustainable development, OuroPreto (Brazil), 5–8 February 2012*, http://whc.unesco.org/en/events/794/ (17 December 2013).

UNESCO 2013. Operational Guidelines for the Implementation of the World Heritage Convention, http://whc.unesco.org/archive/opguide13-en.docx (17 December 2013).

UWC 1998. UNESCO World Heritage Centre, http://whc.unesco.org/en/list/857 (17 December 2013).

UZMPB 2012. UNESCO Zone Management Plan Brussels, www.brussels.be/dwnld/23275391/volumepercent201_FR_2012-09.pdf (17/12/2013).

Vandevyvere, H. 2010. Strategieën voor een verhoogde implementatie van duurzaam bouwen in Vlaanderen. Toepassing op het schaalniveau van het stadsfragment, Ph.D., K.U. Leuven, Leuven, Belgium.

Verhelst, W. 2014. Duurzaamheidsevaluaties van erfgoedsites, Unpublished master's thesis. Promotor: M. Leus, U. Antwerpen, Antwerp, Belgium.

Part II

Construction, recovery, resilience

Heritage is by definition a product of the passage of time. Its material dimensions were created in the past and have travelled through time, changing and being modified in the process, to our world. But today is not an end-destination; the journey continues, as does the constant of change and modification. Nor is that change only or even predominantly concerned with the material and the tangible. The biggest changes, as always, are cultural and cognitive. They include changes in the way people perceive their heritage, in what they hold dear or what they wish to forget, and in what they are allowed to remember. There are always changes too in what they wish to mark as lessons for the next generations, and in what they think needs to give way to make room for new developments and changes in their perceived 'needs', to return to Brundtland's definition.

The chapters in this second part of the book are still mainly focused (like Part I's chapters) on heritage as place, and on the landscapes and townscapes of everyday life, but they also explore some of the ways in which the definitions, limits and values of heritage evolve alongside culture and socio-political change. Europe, perhaps the world, seems to be at a stage where history is central to people's consciousness; nothing must be forgotten or lost, perhaps because confidence in a better future is low. This widespread interest in the past is evidenced in almost all of the chapters in both parts of this book, and seems to be as much a product of our times as nationalism (for example) was of Central Europe in the nineteenth century, or feudalism was in Western Europe in the eleventh century. The idea of heritage, indeed perhaps the need to see the world *as* heritage, is a historically specific phenomenon; earlier generations approached the past/future interface through different rhetoric. It is also culturally determined. As times change, whilst culture changes, so does 'heritage', and thus the inter-generational onward transfer that lies at the heart of the sustainability ideal becomes even more complicated. This second half of the book offers stories and examples of how in recent decades heritage has been changed, or is in the process of being changed, in a continual process of cultural renewal and adaptation that mirrors the familiar methods of conversion and adaptive reuse – recycling by any other word – that has come to characterise heritage conservation in the past half century. Adapting attitudes, and 'needs', to new circumstances, adjusting behaviour and relationships with other people and with the non-human world, being resilient and transilient through both big and tiny step-changes, are important aspects of sustainability. These heritage-based examples offer insights into what can be achieved.

7 Language revitalisation, sonic activism and cultural sustainability

Voicing linguistic heritage on Jersey

Henry Johnson

Introduction

A pop-folk band is playing on the cliffs of the north coast of the island of Jersey as part of a video it is making that will be released on YouTube (Badlabecques 2012b). The lead singer mixes Jèrriais, the indigenous and severely endangered language of Jersey, with English lyrics, and a person dressed as a giant puffin holds signboards showing the English translation of the Jèrriais lyrics. The song, called 'Little Green Shoots', is about the local environment, and the setting of the video is a contested site being proposed for a new housing development; the financial proceeds from the video and iTunes downloads were planned to be donated to the campaign to save Plémont, the headland at the centre of the campaign. What is particularly interesting about this politically driven protest song is that the band used an island language – Jèrriais – that most people on Jersey did not understand. What is the reason for such a performance? Who are the performers? Why sing pop-folk music in a language that is not well known? It is with questions such as these that this chapter contributes to the discourse on cultural sustainability, in this case in connection with language revitalisation, sonic activism and cultural heritage sustainability.

The band performing for the video is Badlabecques ('Chatterboxes'), who sing primarily in Jèrriais as a way of helping to promote Jersey's indigenous language. Having been formed in 2012, originally as part of a project to record songs in Jèrriais for use in schools, Badlabecques' distinct association with such language heritage mirrors the band's other local connections in terms of what and where it performs. That is, Badlabecques not only voices part of the island's linguistic and musical heritage through its upbeat versions of 'traditional' songs using Jèrriais, but it also performs in contexts that are heritage sites as a way of promoting the language. In this context, Jèrriais is viewed as part of the island's heritage, but it has entered a new stage of its existence in that it is no longer a living language that is part of the everyday lives of most islanders. In connection with the context of the *Little Green Shoots* video, lead singer of the band, Kit Ashton, notes that the song is about 'hope'.

There used to be a beacon at Plémont, and the song focuses on this as a metaphor for hope – that taking this unique chance to undo the mistakes of the past will also show how Jersey's public does really value and respect nature, and our legacy for future generations – the 'Little Green Shoots' of tomorrow's community.

(Kit Ashton, in National Trust for Jersey 2012)

This statement encapsulates much about Badlabecques' *raison d'être*: being established as a result of intervention by linguistic activists, performing in contexts that link the band to emblems of island heritage, and singing in a language that most people on Jersey do not understand.

The theoretical orientation of this chapter draws from research on heritage, endangered languages and ethnomusicology. In a context where around half of the world's 6,000 languages are in danger (UNESCO 2002a), language is heritage; it 'embodies the symbolic value of cultural identities and constitutes a fundamental reference for structuring society' (UNESCO 2002b). In particular, a link between regional and minority languages in connection with the heritage industry has been noted by, for example, Barthel-Bouchier (2013), who was influenced by the work of the linguist Louis Jean Calvet. The study of Jèrriais as an endangered language has been included in several studies, notably in connection with Jersey's linguistic heritage and language revitalisation (e.g. Jones 2000; 2001; Sallabank 2011; 2013). Counter to the reduction in numbers of native speakers, with the help of language educators (and especially of the L'Office du Jèrriais, the 'Jèrriais Office', see later), an increase in signage and other icons of Jersey's linguistic past has been evident over the last few years (Johnson 2010). This has included the use of Jèrriais as a second or third language (i.e. with English and/or French) on noticeboards, and even on Jersey banknotes. Just as heritage represents the cultural capital of one part of local identity politics (Riganti 2010, 229), for Badlabecques, the band is blending several aspects of local intangible heritage, including language and song, which in turn moves heritage into new creative forms of expression in the modern age, and for new audiences. If heritage can be said to be 'created through a process of exhibition' as a 'mode of cultural production in the present that has recourse to the past' (Kirshenblatt-Gimblett 1995, 369), in the case of Badlabecques the exhibition consists of upbeat versions of traditional songs framed by heritage sites or similar backdrops (Figure 7.1).

The transformation of folk music in new contexts has been explored in ethnomusicology in the work of scholars such as Bohlman (1988), Ramnarine (2003), Rosenberg (1993), Russell and Atkinson (2004) and Sweers (2005), who focus mainly on the use or transformation of traditional songs in popular music settings. Sweers, for instance, discusses what she calls 'electric folk music', and for Ramnarine, the focus has been on music that is 'far removed from the traditional model of folk music as orally transmitted traditions located in rural contexts' (2003, 14). These and other scholars emphasise music as the source of transformation, whereas for Badlabecques the focus is on language. Such interconnections have been offered in related studies, such as those by Grant

Figure 7.1 Badlabecques performing at the Jersey Arts Centre, February 2013
Photo: Dan Garrido; courtesy of Kit Ashton.

(2010; 2011; 2012a,b; 2014) and Johnson (2005; 2008), and this chapter offers one band as a case study that foregrounds a subcultural sound (Slobin 1993) and that brings an almost hidden yet symbolic aspect of Jersey's heritage into a broader island awareness as a result of intervention (cf. Finnegan 1989).

The discussion is in three main parts. Following this short introduction, the first part of the discussion explores local identity in connection with speaking heritage; the second part introduces the idea of intervention as a revitalisation process by re-energising linguistic heritage; and the final part focuses on the recent establishment of the pop-folk band in connection with cultural creativity and singing heritage in the context of intervention and a broader goal of cultural sustainability.

Speaking heritage

Jersey has an unusual political identity. It is a British Crown Dependency, known politically as the Bailiwick of Jersey, and neither a part of the United Kingdom nor a member of the European Union. The territory was a part of the Duchy of Normandy at the time when its duke, William (1028–87), invaded England in 1066 and made himself the first Norman king of England; thereafter the king of England and the duke of Normandy were the same person until in 1204, when he lost mainland Normandy to the king of France, Philippe Auguste (1165–1223). The Channel Islands, of which Jersey is a part alongside the Bailiwick of Guernsey (that is, the islands of Guernsey, Alderney and Sark), remained loyal to their old Norman duke (i.e. the king of England), did not become part of the French king's territory and were allowed legal autonomy as English Crown possessions. To this day, Jersey has its own government (known as the States of Jersey), prints its own currency, and has its own laws.

Even in this context of the transmission of Norman cultural heritage through the English crown, Jersey along with the other Channel Islands maintained very strong cultural links to its Norman mainland, which is about 23 km away, whereas its British (i.e. Great Britain) mainland is about 137 km distant (States of Jersey Statistics Unit 2012, iii). As part of this cultural heritage, the Norman language was particularly influential in the Channel Islands, and over many centuries several distinct languages and dialects were formed on the different islands (Sallabank 2011). Known in Jersey as Jèrriais (and sometimes as Jersey Norman French or patois), the language evolved some variety even in an area of just 117 km² (Spence 1993; States of Jersey Statistics Unit 2012, iii), not only *vis-à-vis* other members of the language group such as those on Guernsey, Sark or Normandy but also within the island itself where distinct versions of Jèrriais can be found (Le Maistre 1966). However, a more recent decline in native speakers has influenced the adoption of a predominant dialect that is used in education.

Over the centuries, and especially during the British militarisation of the Channel Islands as protection against possible attack from France, English gradually became the dominant language. In Jersey, which was until the twentieth century an island with many trilingual speakers (i.e. Jèrriais, French and English), French was the legal language of the island (i.e. Jersey Legal French), French (often called 'good French' – see Spence 1960) may have been known, and Jèrriais may have been spoken. In 1960, for example, it was estimated that at least 10,000 islanders would still use or know some Jèrriais (Spence 1960). Just a few decades later, the island census of 2001 noted that 2,874 people knew the language (3.2 per cent of the population; States of Jersey Statistics Unit 2002); and a survey in 2012 noted that there are probably less than 100 fluent speakers of Jèrriais left on the island, in a total population close to 100,000 (States of Jersey Statistics Unit 2012, 56).

Jèrriais is today seen as a part of Jersey's cultural heritage. The fact that the language has undergone rapid decline has helped add to this status, and even the island's government has acknowledged its importance as part of the island's identity (States of Jersey 2014). Moreover, as noted by Jersey's Education, Sport and Culture Committee (later the Department of Education, Sport and Culture):

> Jersey almost lost its language in the 20th century. ... In the 21st century strenuous efforts are being made to re-establish it. *Le Don Balleine*, funded by the States, is leading a programme in schools teaching Jèrriais. *L'Assembliée d'Jèrriais* promotes the language generally. Language brings distinctiveness, a sense of localness and a whole new set of skills all of which are important qualities in attracting the creative economy. It is fundamental to the Island's identity. This objective is to work with these organisations to help in the revival and status of the language.
>
> (States of Jersey 2005a)

In the twentieth century, Jersey's indigenous language moved from mainstream to marginal, from a living language to a severely endangered language, and from everyday culture to cultural heritage. In the setting of discussing cultural sustainability and the transmission of cultural heritage, one might wonder about the call to revive Jèrriais. How is Jèrriais being revived? What does such an intervention mean for the island's heritage and identity? Can a severely endangered language be revived? The next two parts of this chapter address such questions, particularly in relation to the voicing of linguistic heritage on Jersey not only through speech but simultaneously through song.

Re-energising linguistic heritage

Jèrriais has long been acknowledged to be in decline (Jones 2001). As a reaction to the diminishing number of fluent speakers of the language, particularly in the twentieth century, several cultural and heritage organisations were established as a way of helping to sustain Jèrriais as a spoken language on the island. These organisations are varied in terms of their role, and include L'Assembliée d'Jèrriais (est. 1951), Le Don Balleine Trust (est. 1951), La Section dé la Langue Jèrriaise (est. 1996) of La Société Jersiaise, and L'Office du Jèrriais (est. 1998). There is also Lé Congrès des Parlers Normands et Jèrriais, which is an umbrella organisation representing all of the above. Formal contexts where Jèrriais can be heard or read are La Fête Nouormande (also known as La Fête des Rouaisouns), an annual Norman cultural festival (Johnson 2008), the *Jersey Evening Post*, which has a regular Jèrriais column, BBC Radio Jersey, which has a weekly Jèrriais programme (*Lettre Jèrriaise*), and the Jersey Eisteddfod, an annual competition that includes a section for speech and performance in Jèrriais. These contexts are rich with sonic activism in the form of language and song, although with Jèrriais presented in framed settings and thus as an emblem of cultural heritage rather than as an everyday form of communication (cf. Williams 1985).

More broadly in terms of Jersey's contemporary political milieu, the island is a member of the British–Irish Council, which 'comprises representatives of the Irish and British governments and of the devolved institutions in Northern Ireland, Scotland and Wales, together with representatives of the Isle of Man, Guernsey and Jersey' (British–Irish Council 2014). The promotion of Jèrriais forms part of the Council's work on indigenous, minority and lesser-used languages. Unlike Welsh, Gaelic Scots, Ulster Scots, Cornish and Manx, however, all of which are also part of the Council's jurisdiction, Jèrriais is not recognised in the European Charter for Regional and Minority Languages.

Of the cultural organisations noted earlier in this part of the chapter, one that is especially active is L'Office du Jèrriais. It promotes Jèrriais at all levels of education (primary, secondary and adult), as well as promoting the language through consultation and linguistic activism. While Jèrriais classes for adults have been run since 1967 (Jones and Singh 2005, 119; States of Jersey 2005b), a Jersey Language Teaching Coordinator was appointed in 1998, and the following year 170 primary school students were learning the language on a voluntary basis (States of Jersey 2005b; 2010). L'Office du Jèrriais is run by Le Don Balleine Trust, which receives funding for L'Office du Jèrriais from the States of Jersey through the Department of Education, Sport and Culture. By 2011 there were twenty-four primary schools and seven secondary schools (with around 170 students each year) in the voluntary teaching programme, as well as four types of classes for adult learners (around 25–30 students each year). A Jèrriais qualification equivalent to a General Certificate of Secondary Education has been introduced, with several secondary school students taking the option, although to date no students have passed the examination. In 2012, the teaching of Jèrriais in schools took a new path. As well as the language being introduced in a compulsory programme on Jersey Studies, which comprises six Jèrriais classes (one per week) in 'Year 4' (8 and 9 year olds) at primary level, voluntary after-school tuition was restructured so that four primary schools now acted as *pallions* ('a place to meet and talk').

As Jèrriais continued its decline in terms of the number of fluent speakers, by the twenty-first century the state of the language began to take on currency by Jersey's government in educational and heritage contexts. This was particularly evident in one of the objectives in its Cultural Strategy: 'To investigate the feasibility of adopting Jèrriais as the Island's official minority language and to work with the *Société Jersiaise*, *Le Don Balleine* and *L'Assembliée d'Jèrriais* to revive the language of Jèrriais' (States of Jersey 2005a; see also Riddell 2007). While the government has yet to formally adopt a political framework for Jèrriais as an official language for Jersey, or to implement a substantial and compulsory part of language acquisition of Jèrriais in school education, the language's status as island heritage and its links to island identity have been firmly established. Through the activism of L'Office du Jèrriais, amongst other language-centred organisations, Jèrriais is increasingly seen on signage, bank notes and in education; and it is heard in staged performances at heritage festivals and at a competition. As discussed in the next part of this chapter, Jèrriais and its culturally creative element of song are especially linked to heritage places on the island, and even contemporary transformations of 'traditional' songs, along with some new contributions to the song repertoire, are performed primarily in ways that highlight the island's emblematic history.

Singing heritage

Traditional songs in Jèrriais are mainly heard at 'framed' cultural heritage locations, and are usually performed by staff at L'Office du Jèrriais, their students and members of La Section dé la Langue Jèrriaise. Such heritage sites include La Fête Nouormande ('Norman Fête'), La Séthée d'Nièr Beurre ('Black Butter Evening') and La Faîs'sie d'Cidre ('Cider Festival'), and the Jèrriais songs add a sense of tradition to the events. The first of these, La Fête Nouormande, is an annual festival that celebrates Norman heritage, especially through speech and song. Even though only established in 1998, it is now an important part of the local Norman calendar, its venue rotating annually between Jersey, Guernsey and mainland Normandy (Johnson 2005; 2008). It stands out as a venue for the performance of songs in Jèrriais (Figure 7.2). Another event where Jèrriais is sometimes sung is at the annual Eisteddfod, in a section called Les Sethées

Figure 7.2 Badlabecques performing at La Fête Nouormande in Jersey, in collaboration with Norman-language speakers from Jersey, Guernsey and Normandy, June 2014

Photo: Henry Johnson.

Jèrriaises ('Jèrriais Evening'). The organisation called L'Assembliée d'Jèrriais is also involved in Jèrriais song at its Easter and Christmas services (Lé Service Annuel de L'Assembliée d'Jèrriais), where hymns are sung in the language. Jèrriais speakers/singers also perform Christmas carols annually on the main street of Jersey's capital, St Helier.

The above-mentioned settings are hyper-traditional, framed performance sites, where not only are songs performed, but also language and local identity. The performers of the songs are often learners or teachers of Jèrriais, or active in one of the organisations that strive to maintain the language. In terms of such re-contextualisation and cultural transformation, local heritage in the form of song might be described as existing in a process of continual change and invention. Just as Hobsbawm and Ranger (1983) noted that cultural phenomena giving a first impression of being well established and passed down through long historical durations to the present day are often invented traditions, many songs in Jèrriais are also part of an invented tradition, part of a flexible repertoire that foregrounds language over music. While some songs have gained a distinct place in a modern-day repertoire of traditional songs through events such as those mentioned above, it is actually the language that is usually the focus during performances, and especially in songs that have been translated from another language or have been written for a specific event. Here, such songs might be described as living heritage – continually evolving pieces that emphasise language over music as a result of sonic activism (Johnson 2012).

There is little documentation on the history of performance practice of songs using Jèrriais over the centuries, but in 1957 and 1960 the folk-song collector Peter Kennedy (1922–2006) travelled to Jersey and made some recordings of songs that used Jèrriais. These were later released on several recordings and transcribed into staff notation (Kennedy n.d. a; b; c; 1975a; b, 246–92). Kennedy's fieldwork included interviewing several key informants, and his publications included transcriptions in staff notation of the songs, as well as information on their background and performance practice. Some of the songs have a mixture of Jèrriais and French, and several are known in the same or similar form on mainland France (Johnson 2008). Kennedy compared the songs he found on Jersey with three main types of other songs: (1) Norman songs; (2) songs of western France; and (3) French songs in general (Kennedy 1975b, 249). What is interesting about the recordings, which are from a limited number of informants, is that during my own fieldwork on Jersey in 1989–90, my informants knew of only a few of the ones included in Kennedy's work (Johnson 2008, 78–9). One might deduce from this that songs in Jèrriais are nebulous in terms of being part of an established repertoire, and that cultural bearers will have varying notions of what constitutes being 'traditional'.

In 2012, ten folk songs using Jèrriais were re-contextualised and culturally transformed as a result of direct cultural heritage intervention by language officers and educators at L'Office du Jèrriais. The aim was to make them more accessible to a wider audience and consequently help to promote the language. Here, intervention is in the form of linguistic activism through language promotion in education and cultural heritage maintenance, transmission and production. In the same year, Kit Ashton, who had recently returned to the island as a professional musician, was commissioned by L'Office du Jèrriais to arrange a selection of songs in Jèrriais and record them in an upbeat style for use in school Jèrriais classes (Figure 7.3). As part of this process, the band called Badlabecques was formed.

While Badlabecques recorded songs for the school resource *Jèrri chîn' et là* ('Jersey Here and There') (L'Office du Jèrriais 2012), it also started to give public performances. As its repertoire and reputation grew, it decided to make an album. Before the end of 2012, Badlabecques released *Hécque Badlabecques!* ('Long Live the Chatterboxes'), a ten-track album, also available as an online download, including six of the songs on *Jèrri chîn' et là* (Badlabecques 2012a). Since mid-2012, Badlabecques has given numerous performances around the island, and made a number of media appearances promoting the band, its album and its linguistic aims. It has also performed in Sark (another of the Channel Islands) and in France. In connection with language promotion, 50 per cent of the income of album sales goes to community projects, 25 per cent to L'Assembliée d'Jèrriais to help promote Jèrriais, and 25 per cent to La Motte Street Studios to help support local musicians (Badlabecques 2013b). The band helps to promote Jèrriais in a community way, with its amateur yet high quality recordings made with language revitalisation at the core. The other main recording output from the band was a selection of ten Christmas carols (well known translations of English carols, as

Figure 7.3 Kit Ashton of Badlabecques participating in a primary school class in Jèrriais organised by L'Office du Jèrriais, June 2014

Photo: Henry Johnson.

well as some lesser known French and Jersey carols), released as a free downloadable album, *Eune Bordée d'Noué* ('A Christmas Party'), towards the end of 2013 (Badlabecques 2013a). There are plans for a further album when funding has been secured.

Hécque Badlabecques! includes an eclectic selection of songs (see Table 7.1). There are traditional songs with unknown origin, songs with a known composer, and more recently-composed songs. What is important in this collection is that it is intended to be a cultural representation of Jèrriais through song. While some of the songs are better known than others, the process of assembling songs for the album reveals the way that the cultural sustainability of Jèrriais is linked directly to the notion of living between the past and the future. That is, cultural heritage transmission is represented in diverse ways, including through a process of creating cultural heritage in the present day. Each track on the album is performed in an upbeat way, and the instrumentation includes instruments typically used in popular music, with the addition of an accordion and violin, which are often used in pop-folk styles. The songs represent a repertoire that is currently known on the island, or, rather, more recently constructed at sites such as those mentioned above that frame Jèrriais through re-contextualised performance.

Whilst the album represents island heritage in one way, in another way it is a transformed and new heritage. The songs are from various sources, but at the staged settings noted above most are heard more usually as vocals or vocals with accordion accompaniment and sung by an older generation of performers. What

Table 7.1 Song list on the album *Hécque Badlabecques!*

Track	Title	Translation	Composer
1	'Tandi qué bouôn mathinnyi bait'	'A drink before setting sail'	Words by A. A. Le Gros (1840–77); Music by Alfred Amy (1867–1936)
2	'J'ai pèrdu ma femme'	'I lost my wife'	Traditional Jersey folksong
3	'Man bieu p'tit Jèrri'	'Beautiful Jersey'	Based on the English original, words and music by Lindsay Lennox (d. 1906); Jèrriais words by Frank Le Maistre (1910–2002)
4	'Jean Gros Jean'	'John, Fat John'	Anon. Traditional Jersey folksong
5	'L'île Dé Jèrri'	'The island of Jersey'	Jèrriais words by unknown author, based on the English original, words and music by George Ware (1829–85)
6	'Chant d'Jèrri'	'Island song'	Words by Geraint Jennings; Music by Daniel Bourdelès
7	'Belle rose'	'Beautiful rose'	Anon. Traditional Jersey folksong
8	'Lé rapinneux'	'The money grabber'	Words by A. A. Le Gros (1840–77); Music by Kit Ashton
9	'Rigodon d'chorchel'lie'	'The wizzard's rigadoon'	Words by Frank Le Maistre (1910–2002); Music by Daniel Bourdelès
10	'Man bieu p'tit Jèrri'	'Beautiful Jersey'	Based on the original version in English with words and music by Lindsay Lennox (d. 1906); Jèrriais words by Frank Le Maistre (1910–2002)

the band has done on its album is to re-contextualise the songs from a traditional into a neo-traditional (i.e. pop-folk) musical style. With this album, as well as with the video *Little Green Shoots* (see above), the band has extended heritage and created culture by producing instrumental arrangements of traditional songs, incorporating creative elements from popular and folk music styles that extend or vary traditional song structures, and composing new songs that mix languages. The songs on the album are part of a process of (re-)creating culture. That is, they are new renditions of musical and linguistic heritage through the medium of pop-folk music and are intended for a new audience. The one main caveat in this process of music appreciation, or local music consumerism, is that one must wonder who would actually understand the lyrics of the songs in the first place. The members of the band are not native Jèrriais speakers, and most have only connected or reconnected with the language as a result of joining the band. While the music can certainly be appreciated in its own right, for most of the new listeners the lyrics are most likely to be a linguistic emblem of Jersey of bygone days. Nevertheless, the group's objective has been to promote the language over its accompanying music, so the more exposure the Jersey public gets to the pop-folk versions of the songs in Jèrriais, then the more the band is fulfilling its primary purpose.

A study of one of the tracks on the album helps illustrate the type of musical and linguistic transformations that have taken place. 'Belle Rose' is the title of a song that was collected on Jersey in 1957 by Peter Kennedy. His informant for this song was Adolphus Le Ruez, a man of an older generation who sometimes mixed Jèrriais and French in a process of language code-mixing. The Jèrriais lyrics (with English translation) of the first two verses, as found in Badlabecques (2012a), are as follows:

Jèrriais version	*English translation*
J'ai tchilyi la belle rose,	I've plucked the beautiful rose
J'ai tchilyi la belle rose,	I've plucked the beautiful rose
Tchi pendait au blianc rôsyi,	Which hung from the white rose bush
Belle rose,	Beautiful rose
Tchi pendait au blianc rôsyi,	Which hung from the white rose bush
Belle rose, rose au blianc.	Beautiful rose, rose of white
Jé l'apportis à ma méthe,	I brought it to my mother
Jé l'apportis à ma méthe,	I brought it to my mother
Entre Saint Jean et Saint Ouën,	Between Saint Ouën and Saint John
Belle rose,	Beautiful rose
Entre Saint Jean et Saint Ouën,	Between Saint Ouën and Saint John
Belle rose, rose au blianc.	Beautiful rose, rose of white

Even though the song has been included on Badlabecques' album as a Jèrriais song, it is also known in a number of French and French Canadian versions. Indeed,

> [w]e know of 149 extant versions, of which fifty-nine were collected in Canada and eighty-two in France. The earliest reference goes back to 1633. It tells a charming story which cannot be understood outside its historical context, since it refers to a medieval custom in which a young girl or woman gathered flowers to signal her choice of a lover.
>
> (Laforte 2006, 6)

What this extract reveals is the distinct localisation of heritage in the Jersey context. The Jèrriais version includes references to local places, as shown in the second verse above with references to two of the island's twelve parishes (Saint Jean and Saint Ouën [St John and St Ouën]), and the French versions include French place names such as Paris and Rouen (*J'ai cueilli la belle rose* 2014; Kennedy 1975c). Such place name references offer locations that Jèrriais learners can easily recognise, and help with the learning process and comprehension of the lyrics. Hence, such a song functions as an ideal tool to help facilitate language acquisition. The song may well be considered a part of Jersey's heritage, regardless of its origins, but with Badlabecques' arrangement, the song has been transformed in several ways. Not only does it include 'non-traditonal' keyboard, drums, guitar and backing vocals, but also a way of creating heritage from the island's past.

Conclusion

As a linguistic case study, this chapter has shown that a need for cultural heritage sustainability on Jersey is manifest in the contemporary creative music practices of a pop-folk band. Through migration and external influences, the common language of Jersey has changed over the past few centuries, and dramatically during the twentieth century. The increased dominance of English has been met with the establishment of cultural heritage organisations and, more recently, language educators and activists who view Jèrriais as an emblem of island heritage and a part of culture that should be sustained. In this context, Jèrriais is a part of island culture, and the notion of development is linked to English as the language that has marginalised the island's traditional lingua franca. As the island develops, it is both looking outward to English as the dominant language, and inward to Jèrriais as a significant aspect of the island's cultural heritage.

It is at this juncture that the notion of sustainable development is important to consider, not only for Jersey, but also for the many other marginalised and endangered languages the world over. Working from the viewpoint that governments should be protecting endangered languages, the question is how might governments do this in the context of change and development. The key point here is that language carries cultural heritage, and it offers a way of understanding cultural location. This case study has shown some of the ways that Jersey has responded to the dominance of English and the decline of its indigenous language, and helps show language as heritage practice in action where new traditional and local culture is created as a result of sonic activism.

For Badlabecques, culturally transformed versions of traditional songs have been produced in a context of living between the past and the future, and have the aim of helping to promote and revitalise part of Jersey's linguistic and musical heritage (that is, Jèrriais itself, as a severely endangered language, and local folk songs). The band's intervention is a form of cultural sustainability. What is distinct about the activities of Badlabecques is that their contribution to language promotion also creates culture. The band may adapt songs for a popular music medium, but at the same time it contributes to the maintenance of linguistic heritage, although in a transformed way. Put another way, linguistic heritage in song is traditional and living as a result of different kinds of framed performance contexts: 'traditional' as found in cultural heritage sites and organisations, and 'contemporary' as found in the medium of pop-folk as a result of major cultural, musical and sonic transformation.

Cultural heritage sustainability in practice is evident in Badlabecques' performances and recordings. Through linguistic intervention by language educators and musicians, local heritage has been reproduced in the form of pop-folk music that has helped to sustain not only traditional folk songs, but also a severely endangered language. For Badlabecques, what makes the band especially interesting in heritage studies is that the group is branding itself as being linked to Jersey in terms of its traditional culture, particularly its Norman heritage. The band performs mainly at heritage sites that have local, historical culture at the core, and its purpose of singing in and promoting Jèrriais immediately links the band to a minority yet highly symbolic aspect of local culture. Because the audience who understands the song lyrics is very small, and possibly of a generation that might not ordinarily listen to pop-folk, Badlabecques might be described as de-centring pop music – music that is in a pop music style, but not for the masses.

In conclusion, Badlabecques are voicing linguistic heritage on Jersey in several ways: through song lyrics in Jèrriais as a way of promoting the sustainability of the language; through music that has been popularised in terms of its sounds; and through the band's association with a network of heritage sites and venues, where the idea of transmitting cultural heritage is foregrounded as a way of celebrating Jersey's past through present-day linguistic and musical cultural transformations.

Acknowledgements

The help of Badlabecques, and in particular Kit Ashton, and L'Office du Jèrriais in providing information and sources is gratefully acknowledged.

References

Badlabecques 2012a. *Héque Badlabecques!* Music Core.
Badlabecques 2012b. *Little Green Shoots.* YouTube. At: www.youtube.com/watch?v= BMfY9hwg6lw (accessed 10 March 2014).
Badlabecques 2013a. *Eune Bordée d'Noué.* At: http://badlabecques.bandcamp.com/album/ eune-bord-e-dnou (accessed 14 March 2014).
Badlabecques 2013b. Badlabecques album to carry mark of local provenance. At: www. badlabecques.net/2013/09/28/badlabecques-album (accessed 14 March 2014).
Barthel-Bouchier, D. 2013. *Cultural Heritage and the Challenge of Sustainability*, Walnut Creek, CA: Left Coast Press.
Bohlman, P. 1988. *The Study of Folk Music in the Modern World*, Bloomington: Indiana University Press.
British–Irish Council. 2014. About. At: www.britishirishcouncil.org/about (accessed 18 September 2014).
Finnegan, R. 1989. *Hidden Musicians: Music-Making in an English Town*, Cambridge: Cambridge University Press.
Grant, C. 2010. The links between safeguarding language and safeguarding musical heritage. *International Journal of Intangible Heritage* 5, 45–59.
Grant, C. 2011. Key factors in the sustainability of languages and music: a comparative study. *Musicology Australia* 33(1), 95–113.
Grant, C. 2012a. Analogies and links between cultural and biological diversity. *Journal of Cultural Heritage Management and Sustainable Development* 2(2), 153–63.
Grant, C. 2012b. Rethinking safeguarding: objections and responses to protecting and promoting endangered musical heritage. *Ethnomusicology Forum* 21(1), 31–51.
Grant, C. 2014. *Music Endangerment: How Language Maintenance Can Help*, Oxford: Oxford University Press.
Hobsbawm, E. and Ranger, T. (eds) 1983. *The Invention of Tradition*, Cambridge: Cambridge University Press.

J'ai cueilli la belle rose. 2014. At: http://gauterdo.com/ref/jj/j.ai.cueilli.la.belle.rose.html (accessed 14 March 2014).

Johnson, H. 2005. Maintaining and creating heritage: music and language on Jersey. In *Refereed Papers from the First International Small Island Cultures Conference*, ed. M. Evans, Sydney: Small Island Cultures Research Initiative, 73–84.

Johnson, H. 2008. Localising Jersey through song: Jèrriais, heritage and island identity in a festival context. *Shima: The International Journal of Research into Islands Cultures* 2(1), 73–98.

Johnson, H. 2010. Branding Jèrri: art, image, and identity in contexts that celebrate Jersey's Norman heritage. In A. Gridehøj (ed.), *Refereed Papers from the Sixth International Small Island Cultures Conference, Guernsey, June 2010*. At: http://sicri-network.org/ISIC6/e.%20ISIC6P%20Johnson.pdf (accessed 25 January 2015). Sydney: Small Island Cultures Research Initiative, 13–24.

Johnson, H. 2012. 'The group from the west': Song, endangered language and sonic activism on Guernsey. *Journal of Marine and Island Cultures* 1, 99–112.

Jones, M. 2000. Swimming against the tide: language planning on Jersey. *Language Problems and Language Planning* 24(2), 167–96.

Jones, M. 2001. *Jersey Norman French: A Linguistic Study of an Obsolescent Dialect*, Oxford: Blackwell.

Jones, M. and Singh, I. 2005. *Exploring Language Change*, London: Routledge.

Kennedy, P. n.d. a. *Au Bord D' une Fontaine: Songs from the Channel Islands*, FTX-012.

Kennedy, P. n.d. b. *Tra-Di-Ra-Di-Ra: Folkmusic and Customs of Jersey*, FTX-244.

Kennedy, P. n.d. c. *Vive La Vie. Song: Dance and Customs of Jersey*, FTX-214.

Kennedy, P. 1975a. *Au Logis de Mon Pére*, Folktracks FSB-60-012.

Kennedy, P. 1975b. *Folksongs of Britain and Ireland*, London: Cassell.

Kennedy, P. 1975c. *La Collection Jeriaise*, Folktracks FSC-60-614.

Kirshenblatt-Gimblett, B. 1995. Theorizing heritage. *Ethnomusicology* 39(3), 367–80.

Laforte, C. 2006. French songs in North American oral tradition. *Canadian Folk Music/Musique Folklorique Canadienne* 40(4), 1–11.

Le Maistre, F. 1966. *Dictionnaire Jersiais-Français*, Jersey: Le Don Balleine.

L'Office du Jèrriais 2012. *Jèrri chîn' et là*, St Helier: The States of Jersey.

National Trust for Jersey 2012. Singing to safeguard Plémont. Plémont press release. At: www.nationaltrust.je/latest-news/plemont-press-release-25-11-2012 (accessed 14 March 2014).

Ramnarine, T. 2003. *Ilmatar's Inspirations: Nationalism, globalization, and the Changing Soundscapes of Finnish Folk Music*, Chicago: University of Chicago Press.

Riddell, A. 2007. Jersey: the development of an island cultural strategy. *Shima: The International Journal of Research into Island Cultures* 1, 72–87.

Riganti, P. 2010. Cultural capital, local identities and ethnic diversity: a study of Amsterdam cultural tourism trends. In *The Sustainability of Cultural Diversity: Nations, Cities and Organizations*, eds M. Janssens, M. Bechtoldt, A. De Ruijter, D. Pinelli, G. Prarolo and V. Stenius, Cheltenham: Edward Elgar, 224–44.

Rosenberg, N. 1993. *Transforming Tradition: Folk Music Revivals Examined*, Champaign: University of Illinois Press.

Russell, I. and Atkinson, D. (eds) 2004. *Folk Song: Tradition, Revival, and Re-creation*, Aberdeen: The Elphinstone Institute, University of Aberdeen.

Sallabank, J. 2011. Norman languages of the Channel Islands: current situation, language maintenance and revitalisation. *Shima: The International Journal of Research into Island Cultures* 5, 16–41.

Sallabank, J. 2013. *Attitudes to Endangered Languages: Identities and Policies*, Cambridge: Cambridge University Press.

Slobin, M. 1993. *Subcultural Sounds: Micromusics of the West*, Lebanon, NH: University Press of New England.

Spence, N. 1960. *A Glossary of Jersey-French*, Oxford: Blackwell.

Spence, N. 1993. *A Brief History of Jerriais*, St Helier: Le Don Balleine Trust.

States of Jersey 2005a. Development of a Cultural Strategy for the island. Lodged on 19 July 2005 by the Education, Sport and Culture Committee, States Greffe At: www.statesassembly.gov.je (accessed 15 May 2012).

States of Jersey 2005b. *Jèrriais: Provision in Jersey Schools*. Written report presented to the States on 9 August 2005 by the Education, Sport and Culture Committee, States Greffe. At: www.statesassembly.gov.je (accessed 15 May 2012).

States of Jersey 2010. Education and Home Affairs Panel hearing: Cultural Strategy review, 5 October. At: www.statesassembly.gov.je (accessed 15 May 2012).

States of Jersey 2014. Jersey's traditional language – Jèrriais. At: www.gov.je/Leisure/Jersey/Pages/Language.aspx (accessed 22 January 2014).

States of Jersey Statistics Unit 2002. *Report on the 2001 Census*, St Helier: States of Jersey Statistics Unit.

States of Jersey Statistics Unit 2012. *Jersey in Figures, 2012*, St Helier: States of Jersey Statistics Unit.

Sweers, B. 2005. *Electric Folk: The Changing Face of English Traditional Music*, Oxford: Oxford University Press.

UNESCO 2002a. *Atlas of the World's Languages in Danger*. At: www.unesco.org/culture/languages-atlas/index.php?hl=en&page=atlasmap (accessed 15 May 2012).

UNESCO 2002b. United Nations Year for Cultural Heritage. At: http://unesdoc.unesco.org/images/0012/001271/127155eo.pdf (accessed 12 March 2014).

Williams, B. 1985. *Ethics and the Limits of Philosophy*, London: Fontana Press/Collins.

8 Heritage resurrection

German heritage in the Southern Baltic cities

Mariusz Czepczyński and Michał Czepczyński

Cultural memory and interpretations of the past

National and local society can be understood as a community connected by memories and obliviousness (Renan 1995). Aggregations of people united by historical experience, perhaps accompanied by others who identify themselves with the chosen aspect of the past, create a unique 'memorial community'. Each community needs certain emotional binders, incorporated into its symbols, narrations, and institutions. Interpretation of the past has always been politically conditioned, and societies have developed traditions and heritages to help define a sense of group identity. Since history is no longer always seen as linear, individuals and groups face disjuncture and narrative gaps, which must be ignored or bridged. This has required the assembling of heritages and traditions from a variety of spatial and cultural sources, and the linking together of events from many different centuries. All those assemblies and collections rely on social memory in a group in a given time–space context.

Social memory explores a connection between social identity and historical memory. It asks how and why diverse people come to think of themselves as members of a group with shared (though not necessarily agreed upon) pasts. While the term 'collective memory' places the emphasis on the internalisation of group identity, 'social memory' usually calls attention to the social contexts in which people shape their identities and debate their conflicting perception of the past (French 1995, 9). Personal memory is enhanced by collective memory, and heightened by media, education and public discourses, while social memory shapes our perception of ourselves as part of the groups in which we define ourselves by sharing the same history. 'Vast and seemingly impersonal historical and/or economic "forces" have always been the aggregate products of the choices that were made by individuals' (Rykwert 2000, 9). Each social group has constructed its cultural memories out of specific tracks of remembrance, oblivion and narratives, which are *believabilia* rather than actual *memorabilia* (de Certeau 1985). Facts and events that we remember, recall and believe develop into the meanings and significance of cultural features. When considering the production of personal, collective, cultural and social memory we need to see 'a complex process of cultural production and consumption that acknowledges the persistence of cultural traditions as well as the ingenuity of memory makers and the subversive interests of memory consumers' (Kansteiner 2002, 179).

In an effort to bridge the gap between 'social' and 'cultural' memory, 'communicative' memory will transform itself into 'cultural' memory. Memory is not just an individual, private experience but is also part of the collective domain.

> Cultural memory exists in two modes: first in the mode of potentiality of the archives whose accumulated texts, images, and rules of the conduct act as a total horizon, and second in the mode of actuality, whereby each contemporary context puts the objectivised meaning into its own perspective, giving its own relevance.
>
> (Assmann and Czaplicka 1995, 130)

Memory is a phenomenon that is directly related to the present; our perception of the past is always influenced by the present, which means that it is always changing. Cultural memory is seldom a coherent, homogeneous and unitary symbolic narration. It has rather a heterogeneous mosaic structure, and some of its components and texts spread with different speed and directions via different media. Other scholars opt for an 'epidemiological' approach in memory studies, where individuals and groups are 'infected' by somebody else's memories (Hirst and Manier 2008). Specific social and cultural conditions, especially during major political transformations, are more 'infectious' and more people are more receptive to certain 'memory infections'.

Distinguishing between memory and history is crucial in understanding a phenomenon of cultural memory. With the realisation that 'history' is only one version of the past, people became more concerned to use cultural heritage to help them shape a collective, national and place-based identity. Nora (1989) pioneered academic thinking about connecting memory to physical, tangible locations, termed *lieux de mémoire*, as a new form of interpretation of a 'history of second degree'. Memory goes beyond just tangible and visual aspects, thereby making it flexible and in flux. Every memory we try to reproduce becomes – as Terdiman (1993) states – a 'present past'. It is this impractical desire to recall what is gone forever that brings to the surface a feeling of nostalgia, noticeable in many aspects of daily life but most specifically in cultural products. In many societies, especially in nation states and other passionate political organisations, it has been usual for one historical narration to seek domination over all other possible interpretations of the past. Single meta-narrations, however, can be, and recently often are, replaced by a polyphonic memory, consisting of a few corresponding and supplementary interpretations and memory traditions (Traba 2006). Memory, as representation of the past, is an important political resource: 'if one controls people's memories, one controls their dynamism [...] . [it] is vital to have possession of this memory, to control it, administer it, tell it what it must contain' (Foucault 1975, 25–6). Power over historical memory can be an important tool of historical policy, used to legitimise present actions. George Orwell's novel *Nineteen Eighty-Four* (1949) rightfully points out that he who controls the past commands the future; he who commands the future controls the past.

Heritage as a social process

History and heritage (heritage being what we opt to select from the past) are used everywhere to shape emblematic place-identities and to support particular political ideologies (Graham 1998). Memories, identities and cultural codings do not remain stable, but are continually reflected upon and negotiated. Heritage contains traces of past activities, and people select stories they tell, memories and histories they evoke, interpretative narratives they weave, all to facilitate their activities in the present. What to inherit and what not to keep is an indicator of social aspirations and desired cultural identities. This reformulation is aimed at local societies and at investors and tourists to show both where we are coming *from*, or rather where we like to see ourselves coming from, and where we are going *to*.

Cultural heritage can also be interpreted as a legacy of physical and mental artefacts; tangible and intangible attributes of a group or society that are inherited from past generations, maintained in the present and bestowed for the benefit of future generations. These include social values and traditions, customs and practices, aesthetic and spiritual beliefs, artistic expression, language and other aspects of human activity. Heritage and its significance always represent cultural, economic, political, ethnic, religious and philosophical values, but also the fears, hopes and expectations of a particular group of people. Heritage is always socially constructed, whether by intent or default. Only accepted and assimilated succession becomes real heritage, which is always connected with both culture and history, two multifaceted and challenging concepts. It is always only a fraction of the total stock bequeathed by the past generations, the fraction that is recognised, appreciated and accepted by their heirs, used for contemporary economic, cultural or political purposes (Kieniewicz 2002). If culture is a communication system based on symbols and meanings generated by the previous generations, it also aims to unite a group and distinguish it from others. Cultural heritage is thus a substantial part of the past, providing a 'cultural glue' that sustains social links with the group and ensures its identity.

Inheritance can be analysed on a combination of levels, including personal, institutional, social, regional, national, and global or civilisational levels. Frameworks of heritage can be also specified in a range of contexts, including the historical, social and spatial. Historical context here refers not only to the past of the place, but also to the past of the social group and often to the descendants' personal history. Social background varies according to ethnic and national milieux, but also according to gender, age, social class and family upbringing. Spatial context or sense of place seems to provide the perfect compromise, and acts as a unifying platform for historical and social perspectives. A sense of place based on heritage also shows the importance of space and personal landscape. For many, spatial identity or a heritage-focused sense of place can be the easiest way to define self-identity (Czepczyński 2008).

One of the crucial aspects of heritage is the relation between the legacy of the past and those who inherit it. Personal heritage choices are conditioned by a variety of circumstances, including family background, education, occupation, or home. There is no obligation of choice according to birth, family, religion, nationality or ethnicity, although those identities strongly influence and perhaps constrain the decision. Cultural heritage is generally accessible to everybody, though certain assimilation procedures are necessary to tailor the available heritage stock to the existing, socially and personally conditioned, demands of heritage. Heritage can be easily lost, forgotten or eliminated; it can also, even after centuries of non-existence, be brought back to life (Kieniewicz 2002). The assimilation of inheritance depends mainly on the decoding and accommodating decisions and actions of the heirs. Assimilation involves not only material artefacts – objects, buildings and places – but also myths, lifestyles and values – all of what can be called culture. The choices often take an eclectic form, since heritage allows a polysemic set of meanings, perpetually transformed and altered with the passing of generations.

Liminality of heritages

History is transferred and transformed through and by memory practices and inheritance processes. There are two main traditions in memory research: one focused on 'who' remembers, the other more concerned with 'what' is to be remembered. Both are closely connected and essential to understand and interpret the process of memorising and recalling the past (Ricoeur 2004, 3–4). There were two processes of memorising, related to words in ancient Greek – *mnēmē* and *anamnēsis* – to mark, on the one hand, a memory as something that comes passively, unintentionally, and on the other (*anamnēsis*) standing for the recollection as a result of searching, remembering and recalling. Remembrance, then, means both having a memory and searching for it. This cognitive and pragmatic dualism is reflected in memory's claim to be 'true', which has to be confronted with historical and more objective sources (Ricoeur 2004). Heritage policy reflects the process of *anamnēsis*, where landscape features are being searched for, remembered and related to past events. The place–memory discourse becomes more noteworthy in transitional societies, when a changing political and social system implies a changing reminiscence and recollection of the past. The most popular way to deal with redundant memories is to recall only the features of the past which go well with current systems, but not those which work against the new structure.

Interpretations of the past commonly change gradually, as a form of cultural-historical evolution. In some circumstances, however, cultural memory is re-interpreted in a more revolutionary manner as a crossing of cultural borders or *limes*; a liminal act that is accompanied by ambiguity, openness and indeterminacy. In this period of transition (liminality), during which our normal limits to thought, self-understanding and behaviour are relaxed, opening the way to something new, one's sense of identity dissolves, bringing about disorientation. It is a limbo, an ambiguous period characterised by humility, seclusion, tests and haziness. Arnold van Gennep's (1960) threefold structure of *rites of passage* can be interpreted as:

- A pre-liminal phase (separation), based on sorting out the 'good' from the 'bad'; defining and new coding begin an epistemological transformation, with cultural cleansing also a part of this phase;
- A liminal phase (transition), most typically characterised by a *ménage* of meanings and representations; the old is re-interpreted and de-contextualised, while the new is constructed, both physically and mentally;
- A post-liminal phase (reincorporation), the final rite; the division between 'old' and 'new' becomes insignificant and eventually disappears, the 'old' merging and becoming assimilated into contemporary social, cultural and economic life (Czepczyński 2008).

The evolution of heritage concepts and consensus in the cities and regions of the Southern Baltic through the twentieth and (so far) twenty-first centuries can be presented as a classic example of liminality in heritage construction. German-originated heritage structures have crossed borders that are both 'real' – geographic and political – and cognitive. The remainder of this chapter offers this as a case study.

Borders and limits in South Baltic heritage

From the thirteenth century, Germans and German culture had dominated the whole of the coast of the Southern Baltic from Lübeck to Reval (Tallinn). In the past 100 years, many deeply liminal economic, social, cultural and political shifts have transformed the region and its cities. In 1919 Germany lost parts of its Prussian provinces to Poland and Lithuania, only to take them back in 1938–9, but to lose them again in 1945 at the end of the Second World War. In the few years that followed, state borders were significantly redrawn under the terms of the post-war Potsdam Agreement and two large swathes of land were re-assigned. East and West Prussia, Silesia and a significant part of Pomerania ceased to be parts of Germany, and important industrial and cultural centres like Danzig, Königsberg and Stettin became part of Poland and the Soviet Union, being renamed, respectively, Gdańsk, Kaliningrad and Szczecin.

The redrawing of borders has not been uncommon in the history of Europe. For centuries states had been winning and losing different areas. Most people were bound to the land rather than to the state, so if regimes changed, people tended to stay in their own territories. In the wake of the Second World War, in the late 1940s, however, not only did national borders change drastically, but there was the enforced migration and resettlement, of often millions of people. Apart from the human costs, cultural landscapes constructed over hundreds of years lost their builders. New inhabitants had to start their lives in new, alien, sometimes hostile, surroundings. The integration of the new regions into new states required a tremendous amount of effort. The authorities were faced with the problem of adaptation. It was not enough to build transport routes, efficient administration or industry. New place-identities and a new society were also required but could not be so rapidly created. New inhabitants had to begin to identify themselves with the new lands, government and owners had to build new legitimisation. All these things required action in cultural narrations and landscapes. New myths and symbols had to be created or adapted. The annexation of new lands needed justification. It was not simply a question of 'spoils of war', but part of a wider ideological concept of historic conflict between Germans and Slavs. The taking-over of these lands needed the construction of new legitimacy.

Liminal transformations of cultural, social and spatial memories become in this period a fundamental political project. Both communist and nationalistic leaders became memory makers, fully understanding the significance of culture, heritage and symbols. Symbolic violence is in some senses much more powerful than physical violence in that it is embedded in the very modes of action and structures of cognition of individuals, and imposes the vision of the legitimacy of social order. The symbolic layer of landscape may be a battlefield in political conflict (Nijakowski 2006), and victory in the symbolic dimension can translate into control over landscape and thus the legitimisation of power. Landscapes can be seen to be a social, cultural and political product of creative destruction. The key is hidden in the term 'creative destruction', which proposes a situation whereby creating something new entails destroying the old one. Thus, old layers were thought to need to be erased to make way for new symbols and texts. Herscher (2000) combined the words *war* and *architecture* to create the term *warchitecture*, claiming that there was no aim to destroy an enemy's identity but only to strengthen the identity of the destroyers. New identity was deemed possible only on the rubble of former identities, the significant symbols of former citizens; destruction of the old means building the new.

Landscape 'cleansing'

After the Second World War a battle for the cultural landscape and heritage of the Southern Baltic began. Every sign of former German inhabitation first had to be removed, erased or covered. Special laws forbade the use and even presence of German names, symbols (also commercial) and inscriptions. Even such seemingly unimportant things as ashtrays or beer mugs in restaurants had to be 'de-Germanised', and all the city information signs had to be changed, with words like *Toiletten*, *Restaurant*, *Post*, or *Achtung* being made to disappear from public view (Rutowska 2000). All the German monuments, especially war memorials and statues – and not only those equestrian statues of the Kaiser that could be found in all the cities discussed here, but also statues of Gutenberg (in Gdańsk) and Kant (in Kaliningrad) – were being removed and melted down or smashed as early as the summer of 1945. German-language epitaphs and inscriptions, and even cemeteries, were destroyed, either through neglect and a lack of renovation, or by deliberate demolition. Other important changes were in vocabulary. German toponyms for streets, squares, districts and even whole cities (Kaliningrad becoming Königsberg, for example) were replaced by Polish and Russian ones. What is interesting is that it was not always only or simply a matter of translation. Danzig became Gdańsk for example, but Danzigerstrasse in Stettin, historically the route to Danzig, was not translated to Gdańska Street in Szczecin, which today is in a different part of the city, but to Miłosławska Street; thus it is no longer a memento of the historic route but rather a tribute to the city of Gdańsk.

Additionally, historical architecture that was considered as being 'German architecture' was demolished. Königsberg suffered most in the process of *warchitecture*, and not only during the three-month siege but also after its fall, when the city was 'largely bulldozed in a virtual eradication of German-ness, which must be seen in the context of the bitter post-war Europe and the absence of any Soviet cultural identification with the city' (Tunbridge 1998, 246–7). Witnesses recall the explosions through the summer nights of 1945, and as late as 1968 the ruins of another 'Germanic' building – the urban castle of Königsberg – were blown up to make way for the (never completed) 'House of the Soviets'.

German monuments were sacrificed without regret. Nobody felt obliged to take care of the symbols or heritage of former enemies. Even the intelligentsia saw no reason to protect the remains of German culture. The eminent Polish art historian Stanislaw Lorenz said: 'there is no reason to regret or duty to protect the monuments of German pride' (Zybura 1999, authors' translation). The scale and character of the experience of the 1940s, and the trauma deriving from the war need to be recalled, however. By 1950, Germans and German culture were not associated with Goethe's poems or Kant's philosophy, but with genocide, suffering and the chimneys of Auschwitz. There was a widespread belief that Germans and their culture fully deserved such a fate. It represented a symbolic – and aggressive – punishment.

Expunging the signs of former inhabitants was only a first step, however. They had to be replaced by new symbols and new myths. The recognition that traditions which 'appear or claim to be old are often quite recent in origin and sometimes invented' (Hobsbawm 1983, 1), especially in the context of new or re-stated nationalism, is relevant here. The construction of such 'invented traditions' is complex of actions on symbolic or ritual levels, at some level always referencing a past real or imagined, which imply some norms and behaviour believed to be desired by the community as a whole. The role of 'invented tradition' is to create or enhance the unity of a society, to legitimise institutions and power and to disseminate specific values, beliefs and behaviours. In the cities of the Southern Baltic after 1945, 'invented traditions' played a big part in the process of adaptation to new situations. Reference to the past is particularly noticeable in Poland, where the myth of 'recovered territories' has been related to Slavic medieval history. Children could read in their schoolbooks about the perennial conflict between Slavs and Germans. In one schoolbook from the communist era we can read: 'We know that houses and tribes struggled with each other. We know also, that Germans are our worst and oldest enemies' (Mazur 1995, 109, authors' translation). Polish 'ownership' of the territory of modern Poland was reinforced by reference to the tenth-century Piast dynasty and their ninth-century semi-legendary predecessors. Such mixtures of nationalism and communism were used repeatedly by communist-period authorities. The presence of claims to 'Slavic heritage' and war heroes can be clearly seen in the names of streets and squares and of public buildings such as cinemas. Moreover, the relationship of the names and location of streets was not coincidental; streets with names associated with the history of medieval Polish–German conflicts, for example, are situated on the way to the German border like symbolic sentinels, standing on the front line of the cultural landscape (Twardochleb 1995).

The 'dematerialisation' of tangible 'German' heritage was accompanied, however, by the loss or obliteration (both intended and unintended) of alien and unwanted intangible heritages. Local, historical names, stories and languages were enciphered and/or forgotten, and regional traditions, rituals, cuisine and heroes disappeared together with the expelled German population. New inhabitants, with their own codes, languages, stories, beliefs – in other words, broadly speaking, 'cultures' – had to be settled in unfamiliar, often foreign and strange environments, surrounded by signs and settings that were to one degree or another not understandable. It took at least a generation in the Baltic coast cities for the process of assimilation and inheritance to begin properly. Furthermore, despite great political and social effort, the 'German cultural layer' remained under the freshly added landscape layers. When plaster fell off old buildings, for example, people could see again inscriptions in German. New generations, knowing war only from books and movies, and starting to look for their local identity, began to treat the Southern Baltic not as enemy territory but as homeland. They started rediscovering history and landscape narratives, and they were ready to adapt to the remains of other cultures. During communist times, however, it was not easy to kindle new narratives. Socialism's society should be monophonic, with space only for one ideology, one interpretation of history. Education was centralised and focused on a central-orientated vision of history and culture.

Risen from the ashes

The gradual ending of the Cold War, however, produced a once-'unimaginable resurrection' of former German heritages (Tunbridge 1998, 247). Communism began its collapse in Poland and Central Europe, and within a few years in the USSR too. That was not only a great political and historical moment, but a very important turning point for culture and heritage, both in Poland and the former Soviet bloc, and in the former Soviet Union itself. The changes had tremendous impact, particularly on the former German territories (Sakson 1996). The reunification of Germany in 1990 also led to the final recognition, in a formal German–Polish border treaty, of the post-1945 Polish–German frontier, so that Poles could finally and legally feel ownership of those lands. Before then, many German atlases described the Polish 'Western Lands' and the Kaliningrad region as being 'under temporary Polish administration' (Kamusella 2010). There was also an increasing investment in the border zones as they ceased to be seen as defended lines, and elsewhere, growing sovereignty of local and regional governments allowed the development of local and regional policies. Increasing standards of living facilitated opportunities for civil activity and disobedience, and new opportunities opened up for minority groups to make articulate demands about minority memories, which evoked a growth of *lieux mémoire*. Such changes made it possible to redefine not only local identity but also attitudes to German heritage. It was noticed that 'new local identity' was of a different type, no longer based on folklore and folk culture, but on local identification with big cities as cultural centres (Sakson 1996). The (re-)assimilation of German heritage was a part of the process of creating these new local identities.

A crucial role was played by significant memory makers, including journalists and politicians. In 1990 the former dissident and eminent Polish journalist Jan Józef Lipski published in *Gazeta Wyborcza* an essay about the remains of German culture in Poland. He claimed that Poland is now a major archive or depository of a huge output of German material culture. Being a depository is a type of duty, and brings responsibilities – including responsibilities to protect monuments from destruction, and perhaps to restore them, preferably in cooperation with Germans, as a way of reconciliation (Lipski 1990). A few years later, in 1996, Donald Tusk (later to be Poland's prime minister from 2007 to 2014, and now president of the European Council), published *Był sobie Gdańsk* (which might be translated as 'Once There Was a City Called Gdańsk'), a sentimental and nostalgic photo album, a collection of pictures from pre-war Gdańsk. The book became a bestseller, since thousands wanted to see, experience and inherit the unknown past of the city, and it spawned a sequel, *Wydarzyło się w Gdańsku 1901–2000* ('It Happened in Gdańsk'), which clearly implies unity between German and Polish times – 'one city', 'one history'. The implication of a heritage continuity has been successful and popular belief in 'one city' has continued to develop. Dozens of other cities, towns and even rural communes followed the Gdańsk model and published pre-war photographs, postcards, guide books and cook books to bridge the heritage gap (Figure 8.1).

In many municipalities, both cities and smaller communes, 'heritage' became a key strategic issue, incorporated in legal development documents, as vital elements of local identity and in municipal development plans. There are many example of heritage presented as continuity, such as the Gdańsk *wiki*, 'Gedanopedia', presenting over 4,000 entries from Polish and German history and presence of the city (www.gedanopedia.pl). Another popular link with the past can be seen on city trams: each new tram carries the name of a more or less famous Gdansker, and most of them are of German origin, such as von Conradi, Clüver, Süchten and Butenandt.

Gdańsk always had a good tradition and reason for quite easily assimilating the Germanic past into contemporary Polish narratives. The city was part of the Kingdom of Poland until 1793, and between the two twentieth-century wars it kept the status of a 'free city', with a small, but significant Polish and other Slavic (Kaszubian) population, unlike Stettin or Königsberg. The pro-heritage trend was first visible in the late 1940s, when the communist government decided to 'rebuild' the historical centre in a more or less Renaissance and Gothic style. The process of 'historisation' of the Gdańsk urban landscape continued through to the 1980s and 1990s with strong support from historians, architects and the media, as well as the city's inhabitants, who opted for a continuation of the reconstruction of the

Figure 8.1 Kaliningrad shop window decorated with pre-war pictures of the former Kant Street (now Leninskiy Prospect) in 2008

Photo: Mariusz Czepczyński.

city centre. In 1997 Stągiewna Street was reconstructed according to pre-war photographs, with even neo-Gothic and neo-Renaissance façades being copied. A similar process was followed, although a few years later, in Szczecin, where the Old City has been 'rebuilt'; in Kaliningrad, a 'heritage' fishermen's village has been 'reconstructed' to seek to bring new middle-class inhabitants to the city centre. In addition, EU structural funds generously support protection and development of cultural heritages, both tangible and intangible.

German heritage has thus ceased to be bashfully hidden, but on the contrary to be proudly emphasised (Figure 8.2). It is starting to be considered as an inseparable part of local history and identity. What is more, the heritage of former inhabitants is starting to be recognised as the nation's own. At the end of the twentieth century local media in Szczecin organised a poll to identify the 'Szczeciner of the Century'. First place went to Piotr Zaremba, first (Polish) mayor of post-war Szczecin in 1945. But second place went to Hermann Haken, the mayor of Stettin at the turn of the twentieth century, and his successor Friedrich Ackermann took third place. Both Haken and Ackermann had a tremendous impact on the landscape of Stettin/ Szczecin, introducing and developing characteristic urban and architectural structures to the city. Both have been commemorated in street names and suchlike, Haken at a big roundabout on the route to the border crossing and Ackermann in

Figure 8.2 Carefully renewed pre-war German shop advertisements on Janaz Kolna Street (former Schichaugasse) in Gdańsk in 2014

Photo: Mariusz Czepczyński.

the city centre square. But recognition of these great names did not necessarily mean acceptance in cultural landscape terms. Three years after the poll, during the renovation in 2003 of the museum on the riverside promenade Wały Chrobrego (named after the first king of Poland crowned in 1025), an inscription was revealed under later plaster of the street's former name, Hakenterrase. For pre-war Stettin and post-war Szczecin, the promenade had been an important landmark, a symbol of the city. This discovery aroused a discussion about what to do with the inscription. Some suggested it should be preserved as a period symbol and a connection between 'old' Stettin and 'new' Szczecin. Others said that there was no place for German inscriptions in a Polish city.

German heritage is being adapted as their own by new owners, and by a more active local society prepared to defend it. After the war many of Szczecin's monuments were treated as trophies, and despite the fact that according to the treaties Szczecin would be a part of Poland, moved into other places and museums in Central Poland, mostly Warsaw (Zybura 1999). Local history lovers began tracking local monuments; one of them – a statue of Bartolomeo Colleonie – was found in the courtyard of the Warsaw Art School, and in 2001 Szczeciners, in an action started by the local newspaper, demanded its return. What is particularly interesting is the strong reaction it triggered in Warsaw. There was no desire by decision-makers there to return it. In *Polityka*, a major weekly opinion-former, Piotr Sarzyński published an essay attacking and questioning the 'authenticity' of local identity (Sarzyński 2001). This Warsaw-centric text incensed Szczeciners, and the editors received a mass of letters in which they defended their identity and 'their' statue of Colleonie (If it was ours before the war, it should stay here in our city', *Aura Colleoniego* 2002) and the rector of the Warsaw School of Art agreed to give back the statue on the condition of keeping a copy. Public fundraising amongst Szczeciners gathered 450,000 zlotys (about 125,000 euro), and in 2002 the original statue of Bartolomeo Colleonie was returned to Szczecin.

The search for a *genius loci* became an important local development matter. The growing belief that there is something left from the former inhabitants, and the former glory of the city, town or region, and that its spirit can be transferred and/or inherited by the present population, becomes an important factor. The *genius loci* can be traced in a number of locations and events, and heritage markers include manhole covers bearing the words *Kanalisation Danzig* and old *Kolonialwaren* ('colonial goods') shop signs, and can be hidden in any 'historical' villa, house, gate, wall, bunker or cobblestone street. The other aspect of resurrected cultural memory can be seen at flea markets and antique shops. Local, pre-war artefacts, including ashtrays, glasses, clothes hangers, postcards, maps, mugs and other bibelots and trinkets inscribed in one way or another with the words *Stettin, Danzig* or *Königsberg* are in demand, and often cost three times as much as they would in Berlin.

Kaliningrad is struggling more to re-establish both its economy and its identity on a durable basis. Cut off from the rest of Russia by independent Lithuania and Poland, there is nevertheless a surprising appropriation by many, mostly younger, city residents of what hitherto was an alien and misplaced heritage. By the 1990s, Immanuel Kant's tomb next to the cathedral ruins had become a shrine upon which flowers were regularly laid, with quotations in both German and Russian from Kant and other literary figures appearing on roadside plaques. A replica of a lost statue of Kant was installed by the university, which in 2005 was renamed Immanuel Kant Baltic University (Figure 8.3).

By that time, the cityscape was dominated by a typical northern German rebuilt Gothic cathedral, together with the unfinished House of Soviets on the site of the old royal castle. Newly discovered Gothic crypts have provoked another wave of public discourse on the past and future of the city's heritage. Kant's tomb is the most popular, traditional background for wedding photographs (in most other Russian cities it is Lenin's monument). Thus the process of re-evaluation has evolved into a more general appreciation of German relics in the townscape, and this remains the clearest marker of a sense of place, one very different from Russia proper. Even the until-recently forbidden German name of the city is coming back into use, especially by the younger generation, who call their city 'Koenig'; some add 'Königsberg' to their car licence plates, and the largest bus transport company of the region is called 'Koenig-trans-auto'.

Figure 8.3 Replica of the Kant statue in front of the Kant University in Kaliningrad in
    2008

Photo: Mariusz Czepczyński.

Conclusion

The rise of cultural memory in recent decades that this chapter has described as
exemplified by the old German cities of the Southern Baltic in present-day Poland
and Kaliningrad is typical not only of these regions. We can see similar tendencies
in other parts of Poland, and in many other places, especially in Central and
Eastern Europe. Looking back to the values of heritage landscape is much safer

than looking forward to an uncertain future (Ashworth and Tunbridge 1999). In turbulent and insecure times, when everything changes fast, the old splendour can be like an anchor or a lighthouse that stabilises people in place and time, and which reminds them of their identity and origin. A post-liminal *anamnēsis* is based on recollection and search for the cultural memory of a place rather than of social and family memory. All this 're-remembered' history, these artefacts, traditions and people reappear and re-enter the social and cultural life of the new Southern Baltic middle classes. After the decades of ignorance, decease and/or oblivion, the ghosts of the German past, or, perhaps, the *genii loci*, have been resurrected, to make a bridge from the old European, secure, rich and attractive past of the cities to the contemporary, new European expectations and hopes. The *believabilia* become solid foundations for future generations.

Heritage can be seen as a feature and function of a city, as well as a development option, but it requires a choice of what heritage. What is considered cultural heritage by one generation may be rejected by the next, but revived by a succeeding generation. One generation's trash becomes the other generation's treasure. Heritage is connected with continuity and is voluntary; it is something passed down the generations. Perhaps a medical analogy will fit best. If we think about a transplant, we have a donor and a recipient, and we have an organ, but the donor (usually) has no opportunity to choose the recipient. The transplant is rather the result of twists of fate, so 'cultural transplant' could actually describe the ongoing process of heritage resurrection or transplantation in the Southern Baltic.

References

Ashworth, G. J. and Tunbridge, J. E. 1999. Old cities, new pasts: heritage planning in selected cities of Central Europe. *GeoJournal* 49, 105–16.

Assmann, J. and Czaplicka, J. 1995. Collective memory and cultural identity, *New German Critique* no. 65, 125–33.

Aura Colleoniego 2002. *Gazeta Wyborcza Szczecin* no. 205.

Certeau, M. de 1985. Practices of space. In M. Blonski (ed.), *On Signs*, Baltimore, MD: Johns Hopkins University Press, 122–45.

Czepczyński, M. 2008. *Cultural Landscape of Post-Socialist Cities. Representation of Powers and Needs*, Aldershot: Ashgate.

Foucault, M. 1975. *Discipline and Punish: The Birth of the Prison*, New York: Random House.

French, S. A. 1995. What is social memory? *Southern Cultures* 2(1), 9–18.

Gennep, A. van 1960. *The Rites of Passage*. Chicago: Chicago University Press.

Graham, B. 1998. The past in Europe's present: diversity, identity and the construction of place. In B. Graham (ed.), *Modern Europe: Place. Culture. Identity*, London: Arnold, 1–18.

Herscher, A. 2000. Warchitecture. *Assemblage* 41(April), 31.

Hirst, W. and Manier, D. 2008. Towards a psychology of collective memory. *Memory* 16(3), 183–200.

Hobsbawm, E. 1983. Introduction: inventing tradition. In E. Hobsbawm and T. Ranger (eds), *The Invention of Tradition*, Cambridge: Cambridge University Press, 1–14.

Kamusella, T. 2010. The twentieth anniversary of the German-Polish border treaty of 1990: international treaties and the imagining of Poland's post-1945 western border. *Journal of Borderlands Studies* 3–4, 120–46.

Kansteiner, W. 2002. Finding meaning in memory: a methodological critique of collective memory studies. *History and Theory* 41(2), 179–97.

Kieniewicz, J. 2002. Stojąc w drzwiach: odczytywanie dziedzictwa i wybór przynależności. In J. Purchla (ed.), *Europe Środkowa. Nowy wymiar dziedzictwa*, Krakow: Międzynarodowe Centrum Kultury.

Lipski, J. J. 1990. Depozyt. Niemieckie dziedzictwie narodowe w Polsce, *Gazeta Wyborcza*, 1 March 1990.

Mazur, Z. 1995. *Obraz Niemiec w polskich podręcznikach szkolnych do nauczania historii 1945-1989*, Poznań: Instytut Zachodni.

Nijakowski, L. M. 2006. *Domeny symboliczne. Konflikty narodowe i etniczne w wymiarze symbolicznym*, Warsaw: Wydawnictwo Naukowe Scholar.

Nora, P. 1989. Between memory and history: les lieux de mémoire. *Representations* 26, 7–25.

Orwell, G. 1949. *Nineteen Eighty-Four, A Novel*, London: Secker & Warburg.

Renan, E. 1995. 'What is nation?' In O. Dahbour and M. R. Ishay (eds), *The Nationalism Reader*, Amherst, NY: Humanity Books, 143–55.

Ricoeur, P. 2004. *Memory, History, Forgetting*, Chicago: University of Chicago Press.

Rutowska, M. 2000. Elementy polityki wobec niemieckiej spuścizny kulturowej na Ziemiach Zachodnich (1945–1950). In Z. Mazur (ed.), *Wspólne dziedzictwo? Ze studiów nad stosunkiem do spuścizny kulturowej na Ziemiach Zachodnich i Północnych*, Poznań: Instytut Zachodni, 167–201.

Rykwert J. 2000. *The Seduction of Place: The History and Future of the City*, Oxford: Oxford University Press.

Sakson, A. (ed.) 1996. *Pomorze – trudna ojczyzna?: kształtowanie się nowej tożsamości. 1945–1995*, Poznań: Instytut Zachodni.

Sarzyński, P. 2001. Popatrzmy na arcydzieła – niektóre mogą wkrótce zniknąć. *Polityka* no. 31, 54.

Terdiman, R. 1993. *'Historicizing Memory', Present Past: Modernity and the Memory Crisis*, Ithaca, NY: Cornell University Press.

Traba, R. 2006. *Historia – przestrzeń dialogu*, Warsaw: Instytut Studiów Politycznych Polskiej Akademii Nauk.

Tunbridge, J. E. 1998. The question of heritage in European cultural conflict. In B. Graham (ed.), *Modern Europe: Place. Culture. Identity*. London: Arnold, 236–60.

Twardochleb, B. 1995. Polskie Pomorze Zachodnie: od regionu osadników do prywatnej ojczyzny. *Transodra* 10/11, 59.

Zybura, M. 1999. *Pomniki niemieckiej przeszłości: Dziedzictwo kultury niemieckiej na Ziemiach Zachodnich i Północnych Polski*, Warsaw: Centrum Stosunków Międzynarodowych.

9 Sustainability through alteration

Eastern Baltic manors in the Estonian tradition

Tõnu Viik, Linda Kaljundi, Anu Printsmann and Hannes Palang

Introduction

Landscape and sustainability are concepts that many researchers have tried to study, often from landscape ecology, but without total success. Marc Antrop has said outright that 'the concept of sustainable landscapes could be viewed as a utopian goal' (Antrop 2006, 187), the reason being that the very idea of sustainability contradicts with the definition of landscapes, as the latter are in constant change and every new generation creates its own landscape. He suggests that the focus in sustainable landscapes should be on the preservation of what he calls 'inherent' landscape qualities and values: '[a] sustainable preservation of these qualities demands maintaining traditional practices and functions, and keeping the necessary knowledge to do so' (Antrop 2006, 195). From an ecological perspective, Laura Musacchio (2009, 993) has proposed 'six "E's" of landscape sustainability – environment, economic, equity, aesthetics, experience, and ethics' as a conceptual framework for translational landscape research and practice as a scientific basis for landscape sustainability. For her,

> [a] sustainable landscape is not based on a deterministic state or condition that is frozen in geographic space and time, or something likely achieved by practicing a cook-book of practices. It represents a dynamic state of the system with multiple trajectories and outcomes and embodies multi-functionality, provides ecosystems services, and is resilient and adaptive.
>
> (Musacchio 2009, 1007)

Further, Jesper Brandt (Brandt et al. 2012) having explored 'all the classical wisdom of Chinese and western philosophy' argues that an ideological position on the human-nature relation is not a prerequisite for sustainable landscape management; sustainability is multi-functional.

How does cultural sustainability fit into this picture? A culture can be called sustainable when it is capable of absorbing elements of other cultures; that at least is one possible definition of sustainability. Put another way, 'transition to a sustainable future depends on mobilizing social and cultural resources associated with a re-animation of place' (Birkeland 2008, 283). Geographers have identified the time-layered structure of landscapes, each layer bearing its own particular cultural identity or significance; geographers have also called for study of the links between these layers. To put it in the words of the distinguished cultural semiotician Juri Lotman, whose ideas heavily underpin our argument in this chapter, and to whose work we will return, a new culture must describe the previous one in order to understand the earlier layers (Lotman 1992; 2009). Help in this task has been sought from many other disciplines such as philosophy, literature studies and semiotics, to name just a few.

In this chapter, we explore these questions further using phenomenological and semiotic methods, or to be more precise a combination of these methods, in order to better study the sustainability of both culture and landscape. We apply our approach to a specific component of the Estonian cultural landscape, the 'German' rural manors that are a legacy of the German colonisation in the Baltic region dating back to the Middle Ages. In less than a hundred years, Estonian attitudes towards these buildings and their landed estates have shifted (by way of practical use and exemplary showcases) from hatred and resentment of them as symbols of foreign oppression and power to national pride in them as valuable tourist assets (Figure 9.1).

Figure 9.1 Alatskivi Castle, in Eastern Estonia, rebuilt on the site of a medieval manor house in 1880–85 in a Scottish baronial style inspired by Balmoral Castle. Recently renovated, it is now owned by the local community and provides tourism and leisure services

Photo: A. Printsmann.

Marrying phenomenology and semiotics

What makes certain locations, spaces, and territories significant and meaningful? Or to put this question in phenomenological terms, how do we experience places as bearers of meaning, the meaning that defines these places for us? A home, for example, is a spatial location that is significant and meaningful for the people dwelling in it. The significance of a home, however, cannot be reduced to a single intellectual dimension but is characterised by a complexity of rational and emotional meaning-contents that constitute its meaning as an integrated whole. This meaning makes a spatial location significant for its inhabitant. Similarly, a territory or a landscape of larger size such as a market place, a town hall square, a shopping centre, a train station, a suburb, a city, or a whole country, is experienced *as* a place, with a certain significance that defines it.

From the phenomenological point of view, a place or a territory is defined by a specific meaning that is experienced as belonging to the place, and as defining its integrity. This meaning need not be explicit or vocally expressed, and it does not arise from the city as a collection of objects and perceptions, but is, as Merleau-Ponty said of experiencing Paris, a matter of the city's 'whole being … a certain style or a certain significance which Paris possesses' (Merleau-Ponty [1945] 2002, 327–8); it may be latent and diffused throughout the territory, but nevertheless it is something that 'holds the place together' as one meaningful unit, making it different from any other territorial or spatial unit.

It is important in this phenomenological definition to note that a location is experienced 'as' a place. In Husserlian thought, anything that one can be conscious of, any object or spatial unit, is always experienced '*as*' something, 'as a home', for example, as we saw above. The identity of an experienced object is achieved by synthetic acts of consciousness that unite diverse perceptions of separate items, or their aspects, around a single meaning – the interpretative sense (*Sinn der gegenständlichen Auffassung, Auffassungssinn*) (Husserl 2009, 430 [V §20]). This 'interpretative sense' defines the unity to which the particular aspects and details are experienced as belonging. Thus, in our example, the particular acts of looking at the door, then glancing at a kitchen table, then thinking of a book in the library, can be experienced as particular details of a certain place that the subject knows to be her home. The 'interpretive meaning' of the home functions in the same way as the significance of Paris in the example used by Merleau-Ponty – it is the sense that makes the cafés, people's faces, poplars along the quays and the bends of the Seine, stand out against the city's whole being in the same way as certain gestures, a certain voice and a way of walking may be expressions of one and the same person.

This phenomenological insight about meaning can be used to distinguish between space in general and particular places.

> Space has to be seen in distinction to place as a realm without meaning …
> [but] … when humans invest meaning in a portion of space and then become
> attached to it in some way (naming is one such way) it becomes a place.
> (Cresswell 2004, 10)

150   *Tõnu Viik et al.*

Needless to say, the everyday life of human beings is essentially spatial not just in the sense of our bodily dwelling in the world, suggested by Heidegger's notion of being-in-the-world (*In-der-Welt-sein*) and Merleau-Ponty's notion of bodily existence, but also in the sense of living in and constantly experiencing feelings of both belonging to, and alienation from, various places. Places do not just have a meaning that is to be comprehended intellectually; their meaning also has positive or negative emotional impacts on the subject, and it can be restrictive or encouraging of certain practices.

Juri Lotman used the notion of 'cultural space' in the sense defined by Cresswell in discussing meaningful spatial units from the point of view of cultural semiotics (Lotman 1994 [1974]). He argues that space has been experienced from the beginning of human culture as being divided between inner (experienced as 'ours') and outer (experienced as 'alien' or 'foreign'). The inner space of culture – be it cave, house, city square, or the whole city within its walls – has become an object of strong emotional ties and cultural significance. As human culture developed, the binary opposition between the space of culture versus outer alien space developed immense complexity. Thus, for example, the city-space was divided into political, administrative, business, religious, and private places. Even the hut of a Russian peasant included a certain religious place within it – the 'icon corner' (Lotman 1994 [1974], 318–19). What is more, Lotman claims that each cultural space is characterised by a certain normative standard of behaviour and discourse. Being at work or at leisure with friends, being at a ball or at a parade are all cases of inhabiting particular cultural spaces the meanings of which prescribe certain behavioural and linguistic norms for the subjects (ibid., 321).

The cultural codes (secondary modelling systems) of creators of a cultural space and the code of its later inhabitants are not identical, however, as Lotman argued. Very often the differences between codes are substantial, as for example in the case of old churches used as night clubs, or old factory buildings turned into apartment homes. New inhabitants may be willing to employ some of the pre-existing codes, or they might choose not to apply them, and in either case they can be successful or not in their attempt. But there is always a distinction between the 'original' code of the creators of a place's meaning and the code of its current inhabitants. In the case of cultural places, Lotman (1994 [1974], 22–47) suggests that its cultural code expresses itself as a 'style of things'. What is more, what might seem as the original style of a place is usually already a 'creolisation' of several styles functioning simultaneously at the time of the creation of a cultural place. A style as a cultural code is subjected to historical evolution, in the main through gradual development, but Lotman suggests that there can also be instants of 'semiotic explosion', when a semiotic system undergoes a thorough transformation very rapidly (Lotman 2010, 46). Explosions of the semiotic field create new possibilities of meaning-making that were impossible before, and whose appearance was absolutely unpredictable within the old cultural code. A semiotic explosion restructures the cultural code of a place, and consequently also the significance of a place that was created by using it.

Lotman even says that 'the moment of an explosion is not just the point of creating new possibilities, but the moment of creating another reality, of [cultural] change and of the restructuring of [cultural] memory' (ibid., 50). We need to keep in mind, however, that whilst a semiotic explosion changes reality, it does so only *via* perception by the viewers: 'Reality changes depending on our point of view' (ibid., 47). It means that after a semiotic explosion the reality becomes reconceptualised or reinterpreted according to a new cultural code, after which it might be also recreated in a physical and material sense.

Thus a semiotic explosion may be viewed as an event of replacing one set of cultural codes with another, the moment of opening up new interpretive possibilities when the set of preciously efficient cultural codes loses its power. Lotman specifies that such explosions may be initiated by a non-linguistic real event in the physical sense, but if they are to have any semiotic impact, i.e. if they are going to change the ways of interpreting things, then this event has to initiate the transformation of the 'style of things' (ibid., 205–7). In somewhat similar terms, changes in the meaning-constitution of landscapes can occur when a new socio-economic formation tries to re-create landscapes by wiping away the uses and symbolic values of previous formations and replacing them with new ones (Cosgrove 1998). Whilst in the Western world such turnovers are more distant in time, they are much more recent and still highly visible in Eastern Europe, where the political turmoil of the twentieth century has resulted in four still-easily recognisable layers in the landscape (Palang et al. 2006).

Let us summarise our discussion of how we experience places as being meaningful. A particular cultural space is a system of spatially arranged items that are governed by a meaning that defines the things that fit this place and their co-arrangement. It also defines the gaze of human subjects towards them, as well as the norms of their behaviour and their practical encounters with them. The 'style' of things is therefore connected to the cultural code of viewing and engaging with them. This approach is supported by the phenomenological understanding of experiencing objects, according to which experiencing objects always involves a certain 'interpretative meaning' (*Auffassungssinn*) that unites the particular aspects and elements of a scene into a meaningful whole. By altering the interpretative meaning the same constitutive elements will be experienced differently, i.e. as belonging to a different meaningful whole.

As we will see in the remainder of this chapter, the Baltic German manors have gained the status of Estonian heritage objects precisely due to the type of reconstruction of meaning just discussed, in their case one that redefined them in the eyes and minds of the general public. This rearrangement of meaning from being object of national hatred to object of national pride became possible when the new cultural codes were implemented. This process led to the renovation of many of the manors in their 'authentic form' as showcases of Estonian national history, and these places turned out to be sustainable with regard to historical changes. What needs to be noticed, however, is that this type of sustainability derives from cultural change and the creation of the new possibilities of meaning-making, rather than the preservation of the old ones.

In the following sections, we will explore the transformation of meaning of a particular cultural space – the manors ('big' house and rural estates and farms) of the Baltic German landowning classes of nineteenth-century Estonia. We will do this in order to demonstrate the apparent paradox that the present-day sustainability of these manors is being achieved by means of radical alterations to, rather than preservation of, the (heritage) values and meanings that are attributed to them, that is, the replacement of their cultural codes. To start our discussion we look at the German manors in their nineteenth-century context, giving a short history of this phenomenon but concentrating, because cultural codes always belong to specific social groups, on the perception of the German manors held by Estonians. We will then turn (after a brief mention of an intermediary period of forgetting and neglect) to the changes that have arisen from Estonia's new independence. On this journey, we will see several semiotic explosions that have created revised meanings for the German manors which are leading to their preservation rather than extinction.

The Baltic German manors as 'other': the long nineteenth century

Historically, Eastern Baltic manors consisted of many spatial and material objects, buildings and artefacts, as well as the social relations organised around them. In this sense the constituting sense of what a manor is has changed to a great extent. The Estonian word *mõis*, like the word *manor* in English, and its cognates in other European languages such as French, has had many meanings; current usage varies too. Its definitions range from purely legal (one of the building blocks of administration and land control of medieval feudalism), to managerial and economic (the farmed estates that surrounded large aristocratic houses), to meaning just the big houses themselves (and often their adjuncts), and have evolved to highly colloquial or vernacular senses such as meaning someone's 'neighbourhood' or 'territory'. In a region that was industrially little-developed, manors in Estonia held an economically central position until the turn of the twentieth century, very late in wider European terms. Because of the belated modernisation of Baltic society in the late nineteenth century, they also retained for a long time their key and dominant role in arranging social life and welfare.

Any discussion of Estonian perceptions of the manor inevitably has to start with the interplay of positive and negative conceptualisations that characterise the Estonian relationship to this spatial formation. Ever since the appearance of an Estonian nationalist discourse in the 1860s, 'a manor' has been the signifier of 'other' space. And for a long time, 'manor' remained the most significant signifier of 'other' space. The most important explanation for this negative view stems from the subordinate political and social position of the Estonians, which goes back to the medieval colonisation of the Eastern Baltic (present-day Estonia and Latvia, historically Livonia) by German-speaking groups as a result of the so-called 'Northern Crusades' at the turn of the thirteenth century. Control over land, people and privileges gradually accumulated in the hands of the German-speaking secular and clerical elite. While in the Middle Ages no centralisation of power took place in Livonia, from the sixteenth century these lands became the target of the expansion of the neighbouring early modern states. After the Livonian War (1558–83), Livonia was divided between Sweden, Poland and Denmark, and following the Great Northern War (1700–21) became a part of the Russian Empire.

The aspirations of the Russian state to secure the loyalty of the German elites in the lands that had now become the Baltic Provinces of the Russian Empire led to the strengthening of the so-called Baltic *Landesstaat* (a system inherited from the Swedish imperial system that gave great local power and autonomy to the Baltic German nobles). For the German elites, this secured a number of major privileges, a German-speaking local government, and their overwhelming social domination in Livonia as holders of most estates and privileges; additionally many of the social hierarchies that were characteristic of the previous regime were preserved. By the late eighteenth century, the Baltic Germans made up less than 3 per cent of the Estonian population (and less than 7 per cent in Livonia); an even smaller percentage owned the land on which the peasantry (90–95 per cent of the population, largely semi-unfree serfs, and mostly of Estonian and Latvian origin) had to live. Ethnic and social hierarchies thus reinforced each other. While the German term for Estonians was *Undeutsche*, for them social mobility meant Germanisation. The status of the peasants as serfs was another major differentiator between the Eastern Baltic lands and the rest of Europe. Even though serfdom was banned in 1816 and 1819, it was replaced by the corvée (forced labour) that was in many ways more difficult as it reduced both the peasants' control over exploitation and landowners' obligations regarding the social welfare of the peasantry.

While the long resistance to change of the pre-modern, strongly hierarchical social order is one of the reasons behind the negative perception of manors in Estonian culture, it is also relevant that the making of Estonian nationalism coincided with rapid and large-scale social changes. On the one hand, these changes were based on the major social reforms that put an end to the power autonomy of the Baltic *Landesstaat*. The abolition of serfdom had provided the peasantry with a theoretical possibility of buying land, but this became genuinely possible after the reforms that started in 1849, which fundamentally altered the *corvée*-based organisation of agricultural production that was both economically and ethnically outdated. The new laws replaced *corvée* with monetary rent and enabled farmers to buy farms and farmland from the manorial owners, as well as encouraging land consolidation. On the other hand, it is necessary to take into account the introduction of nationalism, one of the major European ideologies of the nineteenth century, to this multi-ethnic frontier of a major empire. Nationalist ideas, further accelerated by the appearance of social rivalry, led to the appearance of Estonian and Latvian national movements. At the same time, the counter-reaction of the German-speaking upper class to the increasing pressure of Russian imperialism resulted in the birth of a specific Baltic German identity. Hand in hand with the modernisation of agricultural production in their estates, this resulted in the last golden age of the German Baltic manors, bearing witness to the building of new mansions. In the architecture of those mansions, the spread of historicism and in particular the revival of Gothic styles, illustrate a wish to build a specifically German identity for the Baltic frontier.

As for the Estonians, social-cultural rivalry with the Baltic Germans appeared, but social hierarchies also began to emerge among the Estonians. The period 1870–1900 was particularly dynamic due to a number of other reasons stemming from a belated, but relatively substantial modernisation, the results of which stretched from urbanisation to changes in daily life, including the restructuring of village society, and the rapid rise of social stratification among the Estonians. Typical of regions where colonial legacies loom large, the socially mobile Estonians imitated as well as challenged the Baltic German upper class.

The imitation of Baltic German manors by the first generations of Estonian farmers is a good example of the imprint of colonialism in Estonian culture – the new Estonian elite, which had gone through a rapid social mobility, defined their new status vis-à-vis the Baltic German manors. On a smaller scale, we can also see numerous signs of imitation amongst socially less advanced Estonian farmers, which stemmed from the centuries-long co-existence. A good example of this is the many plants – e.g. lilac – that domesticated themselves in the gardens of the Estonian peasants in the late nineteenth century.

Despite these developments, the Baltic German manor remained negatively conceptualised in Estonian culture. Almost one in twelve manor houses were burned or looted by peasants and workers during the 1905 Revolution in the Russian Empire (Figure 9.2). This event of major symbolic significance came to

Figure 9.2 The manor house of Haljala (like Järvakandi, listed on Table 9.1) was one of the 160 estate houses burned and looted by peasants and workers during the 1905 Revolution

Source: Courtesy of the Estonian History Museum. Photo: Nikolai Königsfest, 1905.

be conceptualised as a struggle against the Baltic German elites, and during the interwar period was turned into a key moment in Estonian national history. During the Soviet period it was treated as an example of class struggle, and since 1991 the event has faded from active cultural memory.

In the three or four decades leading up to the First World War, cultural representations of the manor houses were equally negative, for example (first and foremost) in fiction, journalism, and history writing. These descriptions were to some extent based on the legacy of the humanist and Enlightenment authors who for the first time introduced the critique of slavery and the ruthless exploitation of the peasantry in this region. The Estonian representations of manors, likewise, centred on the topography of exploitation, violence and colonial humiliation: the fields and barns in which the peasants worked, and the places where corporal punishment of the peasantry was carried out (stables and the like). On the other hand, early Estonian writings also look into the interior of the mansions and highlight the contrast between the luxurious lifestyle of the Baltic Germans and the extreme poverty of the farmers' living conditions.

Between times, 1919–91

The end of the manorial system came with the land reform of 1 January 1919, enacted during the War of Independence after Estonia had declared its independence in February 1918. The reform nationalised land formerly belonging to the German manorial estates and divided this among the peasantry. This also helped to mobilise peasants into the army – they now had a much better understanding of what they were fighting for. The manorial buildings were nationalised, too, with the land, appropriated from those who fought on the *Landeswehr* side. Thereafter, each took a different trajectory through the twentieth century (Table 9.1).

Some were used as hospitals, schools and nurseries. Some were awarded to war heroes. Many of the Baltic Germans left; in many cases the former owners were allowed to stay in the buildings, but their economic base had been removed. After the invasion and annexation of Estonia by the USSR in 1940, and after the end of the Second World War, agriculture was collectivised. The old manors sometimes became headquarters of collective farms, or shops and clubs, and their ideological significance was diminished since Soviet ideology aimed to suppress the very idea of private farms and preferred to emphasise class struggle and anti-German sentiments. In the 1970s and 1980s, however, some of the better-off collective farms, and also some forestry enterprises (in a foretaste of post-1991 changes in attitude) began to bring some manors out of the shadows, restoring them as a resource for conversion to concert halls and museums (see, e.g., Kodres 1997 for more).

Table 9.1 The 'path-trajectories' of eight typical German manor houses in Estonia across the three ideological and societal thresholds of 1919, 1940 and 1991

Estate (manor built)	Estate land nationalised (1919)	All land nationalised (1940)	Return to 1940 ownership (1991)
Palmse (1785)		In decay	Renovations 1970s–1980s	Owned by museum, rooms for hire
Sagadi (1795)		School until 1974	Renovations 1977–1980s	Owned by State Forest Management Centre, museum, hotel
Järvakandi (1820s)	Burnt 1905	In ruins	
Porkuni (1874)	Partly owned until 1939	School for the hearing-impaired since 1924	Recently sold into private ownership
Undla (1877)		Clinic	Nursing home	Currently for sale
Esna (1880)	Owner murdered 1921	Various functions, office for Red Star collective farm	Private ownership, managed by NGOs
Sangaste (1883)	Partly owned until 1939	Sanatorium, Pioneer camp	Hotel, rooms for hire, currently for sale
Alatskivi (1885)		Schoolhouse, border guard station, collective farm centre	Municipality-owned, hotel, workshops

Source: A. Printsmann.

'Ours after all': the re-conceptualisation of the manors – Soviet legacies and post-Soviet trends

It is the contrast of contemporary attitudes towards the German Baltic manors with the judgemental perspectives of the past that provoked us to contextualise the present-day perception of the manors in a historic, social and phenomenological setting. We argue that the manors have been gaining a more and more positive meaning ever since the restoration of Estonian independence in 1991. In the process, or perhaps even as a cause, the elements or components that constitute 'a manor' in Estonian culture have gone through a remarkable change. This is visible in literature – to take only one example, we can look at the works of Tõnu Õnnepalu, one of Estonia's most esteemed and popular writers today. He has produced various works on and around the theme of the German manors (and for some years lived in one, in Esna), a blog (between 2009 and 2010), a novel, *Mandala*, in 2012, and a play, *Sajand* ('Century') premiered in 2013. All stand out as innovative in Estonian culture due to their interest and sympathy towards the

Baltic Germans, and their exploration of new ways to describe the co-existence between the manor and the farmstead.

Another trend that has been reshaping the significance of the manors in Estonian culture and society for the past twenty years concerns, first and foremost, the leisure time and preferences of the new elite – the redesigning of the manor buildings (most notably the mansions) for luxury hotels, restaurants, spa resorts, homes and the like. A slightly alternative, but equally elitist and global pattern of use, is well illustrated by a group of manors owned or formerly owned by one of the wealthiest Estonian businessmen, Hannes Tammjärv, who has used them either for charitable aims (a school), or for centres that have developed 'alternative', semi-cultural, semi-new-age-style ways of spending leisure time for the new Estonian elite (yoga classes, concerts, ecological restaurant, etc.).

To see some of the preconditions of this nonetheless positive re-evaluation of the manors, one should first look back towards the period of Soviet rule in Estonia (1940–1, 1944–91). Seemingly paradoxically, the Soviet period both strengthened the negative stereotyping of the manors and created the material and mental basis for their positive re-conceptualisation. First, the amplification of the negative meaning of 'the German manor' mirrored Soviet ideology and propaganda more widely: the Soviet version of the Estonian past radicalised, albeit no doubt also transformed, many trends that had been prominent in the previous nationalist interpretation of Estonian history. Mostly this concerns the interpretation of Estonian history as an eternal fight against the German conquerors, which was now backed by the generally anti-German attitudes of Soviet historiography, as well as by the leading principle of the Marxist interpretation of history, class struggle.

In addition, it was in the Soviet period that 'our', pronouncedly 'Estonian' space became clearly attached to the antipode of the manor and the mansion, the traditional barn-dwelling. Infinitely reproduced in writing and different forms of visual culture, the most prominent celebration of these dwellings became the Estonian Open Air Museum, which opened in 1957. The prominence of the barn-dwelling as the ideal representative of Estonian rural life differs remarkably from the interwar period, when national heritage production and self-representation preferred to focus on the prehistoric and pre-colonial sites (such as hill forts) as the signs of authentic Estonian-ness. National representations also included the modernised versions of the farm-mansions, but the dwellings of the poorer peasants, reminders of past subordination and humiliation, were not a part of the young nation's self-image.

Nevertheless, as mentioned, the Soviet period also laid the foundations for the revaluation of the manors and especially the mansions as sites of heritage. From the 1970s onwards, the upkeep and renovation of the mansions relied on the economic strength of the Soviet Estonian collective farms, the leaders of which sought new ways of investing their benefits and demonstrating the success of their enterprises. Yet, the extensive renovation projects – the best known examples of which are the iconic mansions of Palmse and Sagadi in Northern Estonia – would not have been possible without the input of art historians, architects and interior designers, among whom at around the same time there had already spread an interest in 'manor culture'. It is thus necessary to recognise several interlinked social, material and intellectual impulses. Additionally, as a number of these renovated mansions (and in most cases it is the mansion, because the majority of the working buildings and infrastructure had already disappeared) became easily reachable as tourist sites, a new and unprecedentedly positive perspective was introduced. Yet, we would like to draw attention to one particular feature of those renovated mansions, which is the remarkable sterility of their interior design. The renovations were designed for festive public use such as concerts and receptions, and reveal hardly any hint of their previous inhabitants, who had indeed vanished already by the mid-century as a result of the resettlement of all Baltic Germans between 1939 and 1944. Hence, while the present interest in the elitist, and at the same time also alternative, appropriations of manors and mansions in particular largely relies on the Soviet legacy, the interest in the domestication of the manor space (as a residential home, or a boutique hotel), and remembering the previous inhabitants of that space points towards a radical change.

Conclusion

Places that lose their functionality can be lost. In the more turbulent landscapes of Eastern Europe during the twentieth century, loss of functionality often coincided with major political overhauls (see Palang et al. 2006). These turns usually also affect the meanings of places. A major question, including in terms of sustainability, is how to handle the past – forget, destroy, or absorb into the new emerging system? These overhauls of significance and meaning act as veils that partly hide the past, or sometimes even act as ruptures that break the link with the past, and research has tried to understand how these veils work (e.g. Palang et al. 2011) – what of the past is being used and what are the roles of culture and sustainability here. As said before, a culture can be called sustainable when it is capable of absorbing the elements of other cultures. So, when Birkeland (2008) claims that cultural sustainability has much to do with re-animating senses of place, the story of the Baltic German manors is well in line with this. Leaving aside the pragmatic use of the buildings, their meaning has changed from negative to positive. From what was once conceived as 'other' (the alien, oppressing place of the colonial masters), the manors, or at least their mansions, have become part of historical Estonian-ness.

This chapter contributes to the understanding of how the overhauls mentioned above work. It has been asked (Palang et al. 2011) whether semiotics could help – this chapter provides one possible answer. We claim that changes in the image of the manors happened by means of a reconstruction of the cultural code for constituting its meaning. The reconstruction of a cultural code can be seen as semiotic explosion in the sense of Lotman: external events initiated the generation of new secondary modelling systems, by means of which Estonian self-identity has been creatively reconstructed. In other words, manipulation of the social memory of Estonians altered the meaning of physical objects, and thus the objects themselves. As a result, what was formerly regarded as the (unwanted) heritage of 'others' became recognised as 'ours', as part of the nation's cultural space and topographic self-identity, and as something sufficiently valued to be worth keeping, renovating and reusing through a process of regeneration.

We claim that the sustainability of these manors has resulted from the reconstitution of their meaning, and would not have been possible without semiotic explosions that refurbished important cultural codes. We might be used to thinking that the sustainability of places (understood as meaningful territorial units with their corresponding landscapes) is dependent on the preservation of 'originally' constituted meanings attached to them, but our case study shows that the process of preserving the manors has in fact followed an opposite route, by way of changing their constituted meaning. In such ways (and because the formation of landscape meaning, as Soini and Birkeland [2014] claim, is indeed complex and transdisciplinary), the phenomenological theory of meaning-making and semiotics can contribute to the better understanding of the role that culture plays in sustainability and landscape. Perhaps, too, an understanding of the processes by which landscape meanings are constructed by various social agents can contribute to making sustainability achievable after all, rather than being only a utopian goal.

Acknowledgements

This work was supported by institutional research funding (IUT 3-2 'Culturescapes in Transformation: Towards an Integrated Theory of Meaning Making' and IUT 18-8 'The Making of Livonia: Actors, Institutions and Networks in the Medieval and Early Modern Baltic Sea Region') of the Estonian Ministry of Education and Research and by the European Union through the European Regional Development Fund (Centre of Excellence in Cultural Theory).

References

Antrop, M. 2006. Sustainable landscapes: contradiction, fiction or Utopia? *Landscape and Urban Planning* 75, 187–97.
Birkeland, I. 2008. Cultural sustainability: industrialism, placelessness and the re-animation of place. *Ethics, Place and Environment* 11(3), 283–97.
Brandt, J., Aagaard Christensen, A., Svenningsen, S. R. and Holmes, E. 2012. Landscape practice and key concepts for landscape sustainability. *Landscape Ecology* 28, 1125–37.
Cosgrove, D. E. 1998 [1984]. *Social Formation and Symbolic Landscape*, Madison: University of Wisconsin Press.
Cresswell, T. 2004. *Place: A Short Introduction*, Malden, MA: Blackwell.
Husserl, E. 2009. *Logische Untersuchungen* [1900–1901; from Husserliana XVIII, 1975 and XIX/1–2, 1984], ed. E. Ströker, 1st edn, Hamburg: Felix Meiner.
Kodres, K. 1997. Restaurierung und das Problem der nationalen Identität: Paradoxa der sowjetischen Kulturpolitik in Estland. *Nordost-Archiv: Zeitschrift für Regionalgeschichte* 1(6), 241–72.

Lotman, J. (Лотман, Ю.М.) 1992. КультураиВзрыв, Семиотика, Гнозис: Прогресс, Москва.

Lotman, J. (Лотман, Ю.М.) 1994 [1974]. Художественный ансамбль как бытовое пространство, в Избранные Статьи в Трех Томах, ed. Л.Н. Киселева, Александра, Таллинн, 3: 316–22.

Lotman, J. 2009 [1992/2004]. *Culture and Explosion.* trans. W. Clark, ed. M. Grishakova, Berlin and New York: Mouton de Gruyter. (First published as Lotman, J. M. 1992. *Kul'tura i vzryv*, Moscow: Gnozis. The 2009 translation is from Lotman, J. M. 2004. Kul'tura i vzryv. In Juri Lotman, *Semiosfera*, 11.148. St Petersburg: Iskusstvo-SPB.)

Lotman, J. (Лотман, Ю.М.) 2010 [1993]. Непредсказуемые Механизмы Культуры, eds. Т. Кузовкина и О.И. Утгоф, Tallinn: Bibliotheca Lotmaniana, Tallinna Ülikooli Kirjastus.

Merleau-Ponty, M. 2002 [1945]. *Phenomenology of Perception*, trans. C. Smith, London: Routledge.

Musacchio, L. R. 2009. The scientific basis for the design of landscape sustainability: a conceptual framework for translational landscape research and practice of designed landscapes and the six Es of landscape sustainability. *Landcape Ecology* 24, 993–1013.

Palang H., Printsmann, A., Konkoly Gyuró, É., Urbanc, M., Skowronek, E. and Woloszyn, W. 2006. The forgotten rural landscapes of Central and Eastern Europe. *Landscape Ecology* 21(3), 347–57.

Palang, H., Spek, T. and Stenseke, M. 2011. Digging in the past: new conceptual models in landscape history and their relevance in peri-urban landscapes. *Landscape and Urban Planning* 100, 344–6.

Soini, K. and Birkeland, I. 2014. Exploring the scientific discourse on cultural sustainability. *Geoforum* 51, 213–23.

10 The potential space for cultural sustainability

Place narratives and place-heritage in Rjukan (Norway)

Inger Birkeland

Introduction

This chapter examines changing cultural attitudes over the past century to Rjukan, a town and municipal centre in the municipality of Tinn located in the region of Telemark in southern Norway (Figure 10.1). Rjukan underwent rapid industrialisation in the early twentieth century, and holds a special place in Norwegian history and identity as the cradle of Norway's industrial adventure. The town was built by Norsk Hydro, which can be described as Norway's first modern industrial company. Industrial development took place here because of the opportunities for hydroelectric power production afforded by the Rjukan waterfall, whose force was captured and channelled to a power station, Vemork, which when opened in 1911 was the largest in the world. Because of technological development, however, and global shifts in the world's economy, particularly since 1945, Rjukan experienced a long and continuing decline in industrial jobs, outmigration, and falling population numbers.

Both Rjukan's industrial development and its post-industrial decline changed the identity of Norway completely, physically in the landscape, and economically, socially and culturally. At the beginning of the twentieth century only 350 people lived in the innermost part of the narrow mountain valley. Twenty years later, the population had risen to 8,500. The physical remains of its industrialisation – dams, pipes and tunnels, power stations and factories, and urban development – exist today and despite change and development are very visible to anyone visiting the area. Some buildings have been reused, such as the Vemork power station which houses the Norwegian Industrial Workers Museum.

De-industrialisation is a phenomenon that has affected many regions in complex ways in the twentieth-century Western world. This chapter deals with the production of heritage related to industrialisation and de-industrialisation, and how the past at Rjukan has been understood and used. A critical examination of this phenomenon is relevant in light of the Norwegian government's proposal in 2014 to nominate the industrial heritage of Notodden and Tinn municipalities for UNESCO's World Heritage (WH) list. The nomination is based on four qualities, or so-called 'outstanding universal values': the facilities for power production, factories and industrial plants that used the power, the transport system, and related place-making activities (urban development or townscapes).

162   *Inger Birkeland*

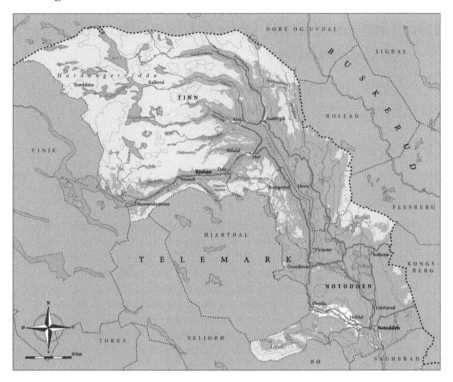

Figure 10.1 Map showing location of Tinn and Notodden municipalities in Telemark in southern Norway

Source: copyright, Geir Tandberg Steigan.

About 18,000 people live within this industrial landscape today, and would be affected strategically by World Heritage status in the future. Tinn municipality aims to use industrial heritage as a tool for local development, and in particular heritage tourism as a strategy to create new jobs and economic growth. Research from other areas indicates that a transition from industrial production to industrial heritage tourism is challenging. Areas of conflict or dispute concern the relationship between conservation and use (Jones and Munday 2001; Holm et al. 2007), social and cultural identity (Dirall 2002; Jansen-Verbeke 1999; Robinson et al. 2012), existing relations of power (Stanton 2005) and development strategy and management issues (Evans 2002; Landorf 2009). As many researchers have indicated, World Heritage status does not necessarily in itself lead to the intended development (Kurin 2004; Pocock 1997; Lowenthal 2008; Kirschenblatt-Gimblett 2006).

Although the WH nomination covers two towns, Rjukan and Notodden, this chapter will focus on Rjukan due to the particular ways that this town's past has been used ideologically. The example of Rjukan is interesting because it illustrates how places may be produced as particular forms of 'place-heritage' through the narratives that are woven around them. Aspects of the heritage-making of Rjukan are discussed by adopting a narrative approach to heritage and a critical approach to uses of place-heritage. Place narratives of Rjukan have been accorded particular and ideological value in modern Norwegian society, and two in particular taken together help to constitute Rjukan's meaning. The first narrative tells a story about Rjukan as the cradle of Norway's industrial adventure, where Rjukan is animated as a place of future and progress, a narrative which includes a vision of a sustainable future. The other depicts Rjukan as a problem associated with de-industrialisation; this is a narrative where a sustainable future is absent. These 'local' narratives have been useful to legitimate and uphold a grand global narrative of Norway as a modern, industrial nation (Birkeland 2014). The present chapter argues that any continuing narrative of Norway as a modern, industrial nation depends on seeing Rjukan as a place of the past, without a future. A heritage process of that type will be detrimental to the people who now live in Rjukan and who want to make a living there, who are searching for other narratives and meanings that can animate Rjukan as a place with visions of a sustainable future.

From a theoretical point of view, this chapter asks how place-heritage and its production is related to sustainability. It begins with a clarification of concepts before moving on to the story of Rjukan's development in the twentieth century, and then to the two narratives of place mentioned above. The final section uses a constructivist approach to challenge the idea of heritage purely as preservation and discusses the future of Rjukan in terms of a cultural sustainability that is related to the idea of *potential space.*

The relationship between 'place-heritage' and cultural sustainability

From a constructivist perspective, heritage is always socially created, interpreted and communicated within particular contexts and from particular perspectives (Smith 2006). Heritage is made in the present as a contemporary product, and is consequently distinct from a historical view of the past (Handler and Linnekin 1984; Hobsbawm and Ranger 1983; Lowenthal 1985). The particular form of heritage that is here called place-heritage is thus also a contemporary process and a cultural phenomenon that in the present time claims some of its legitimacy from the past (Kirshenblatt-Gimblett 2004). Place-heritage then becomes a *meta-cultural* production (Kirshenblatt-Gimblett 1998), because contemporary processes transform the meaning of cultural elements of the past, and invest new values in them.

It was not until de-industrialisation, and a growing interest in the industrial past along with the development of particular ways to understand the Western world's industrial past, that industrial places 'became' heritage. At Rjukan we can see the re-visioning of the town as heritage in the reuse of buildings and the institutionalisation of the industrial past with museums for industrial and labour history. The Norwegian Industrial Workers Museum at Vemork, for example, enjoys national status and solid government funding. This particular museum aims at promoting understanding for and knowledge of the culture of industrial workers, the development of hydroelectric power and the uses of energy for industrial purposes, such as the energy-intensive and electro-chemical industries. At Rjukan, as elsewhere, the loss of industrial production due to relocation of industry has created pain, but this can be eased to some extent by honouring and remaking the past (Cameron 2000). Heritage is thus a way in the present to deal with something of the past that is lost, when one is left with forms that no longer have a function. That 'something of the past' is not only the material artefacts of industrial life, but the cultural meanings related to practices and ways of living associated with the objects.

There is something very paradoxical about the phenomenon of industrial heritage; it is in many ways a contradiction in terms (Storm 2008). Industrial places are often complex, problematic and not pretty. Where some former industrial landscapes in Europe have been transformed into heritage objects through restoration projects, tourism development and urban renewal, others have been completely cleared or simply abandoned to physical decay. De-industrialisation has created many marginalised regions around the world, characterised by job loss and outmigration of the younger generations. Many former industrial areas are ruins or derelict lands (Negri 2011), forgotten in the mental maps of people (Solà-Morales 1995), or understood in terms of absence (Frers 2013) and loss but with a particular aesthetics (Edensor 2005). In contrast to many other types of cultural heritage, former industrial areas are often ignored and overlooked, left as ruins or viewed as ugly, leaving them at risk (Jansen-Verbeke 1999). Paradoxically, other areas like Rjukan are romanticised, with many buildings viewed as aesthetically pleasing, and valued for their nation-building qualities that legitimise industrialist discourse (Birkeland 2008).

A general interpretation is often that mainstream heritage discourse has marginalised industrial society and its heritage because it represents the new and the modern, change, progress, future, and not the pre-industrial past (Alzén 1996). The dominant discourse on heritage has resulted in an idea that heritage is about preserving particular and selected, highly valued objects (Smith 2006), often leading to static and fixed views on heritage, leaving out future and dynamic perspectives, and with little understanding of the shifting contexts and people's attachments, identities and senses of place. Heritage, however, is also related to the future and to visions of sustainable futures. Heritage as social process should link and organise not only temporal aspects concerning the past, present and the future, but also spatial aspects concerning here and there, local and global, place and space. Such processes are not innocent or value-neutral, but are deeply related to the workings of power in society. Heritage processes create a network of places, where places are linked in relationship to each other, and also through an order of scale, which connects social processes at different spatial scales embedded in the time–space compression of globalisation. Such processes affect different places and groups of people differently (Massey 1994), and are very important for the overall sustainability of places. Heritage processes are thus related to power relations, how values and power relations are involved in and affect the construction of place narratives. A selection of elements of the past is made, creating particular place narratives, legitimising particular values and interests. Place-heritage is thus political, where different interest groups and individuals use heritage for different purposes and with varying degrees of hegemony and legitimacy (Smith 2006).

The concept of cultural sustainability developed in this chapter is closely related to a narrative approach to culture, where culture works as a medium for making meanings, including meanings of sustainability. In an overall sense, culture plays a fundamental and necessary role for sustainability (Soini and Birkeland 2014; Birkeland 2014; Birkeland et al. in progress). Meaning-making is organised and patterned, as everything in life and all events in life are organised, and made understandable *as* culture through narratives. A narrative approach to culture shows how sustainability is cultural by being contextual, historically and geographically concrete; everything human beings do is woven into culture in terms of webs of meaning created by human beings (Geertz 1973). Culture appears and is understandable through narrative organisation (Frønes 2001) and cultural sustainability can emerge as a social process through narratives that connect the past with the future, and the local with the global.

The cultural sustainability of a place, or of a group of human beings, is a contemporary process just like other heritage processes, but it does not stop with the present. It includes perspectives, ideas and visions of the future based on the narratives of the past but constructed in the present. Place narratives manage different realities, transformations and differences, and help in the process of place-making. Places appear in this way as imagined communities, as do nations (Anderson 1983). But whilst the purposes of place narratives of cultural sustainability are always in the present, they transform the meaning of the past to create *potential space*, future places. This is relevant to understand how narratives bring places into being as *transitional objects*. 'Potential space' and transitional objects are concepts originally used by the psychiatrist Donald Winnicott (2007) to express the becoming of the child in relation to its environments. Potential space is neither subject nor object, but a perpetual task of keeping different realities separate yet interrelated (Winnicott 2007, 3). Place narratives are related to visions of the future by representing the place concerned as a holding environment, a sort of vision, or narrative, of a future of a place. If the place narratives work well as transitional objects, they act as catalysts of sustainable place-making. If they do not work well, they will be unfit for making possible a potential space for cultural sustainability.

Rjukan from industrial to post-industrial town

Before turning to the history of Rjukan's development, some historical and geographical context will be useful. Rjukan ('Smoky Falls') was the name of a large waterfall in the narrow, sparsely populated (*c.* 350 people) valley of Vestfjord, close to the Hardangervidda mountain plateau in the southern part of Norway (Figure 10.2). This waterfall provided the opportunity for the industrial company Norsk Hydro to produce electricity. Sam Eyde, the industrialist behind Norsk Hydro, had bought the rights to the Rjukan Falls and land in Vestfjord Valley in 1903. Within a ten-year period, electricity generation, industrial facilities

Figure 10.2 The Rjukan Falls
Photo: I. Birkeland.

and a company town was developed. Norsk Hydro had already started test production of chemical saltpetre (potassium nitrate) at the neighbouring town of Notodden using power from the Svelgfos power station; when Vemork power station came into operation at Rjukan in 1911, the company started full-scale production there of saltpetre, as well as of ammonia, hydrogen and heavy water.

In order to handle transportation, Norsk Hydro built a railway from Rjukan to Mæl, from where the trains were transported on special ferries (both steam and diesel powered) across the 30-kilometre-long Lake Tinnsjøen to Tinnoset (Figure 10.3), and on by rail to Notodden, then by ship across Lake Norsjø, and finally by canals to the North Sea. These ferry and railway systems have not been in operation for many years, but exemplify the logic of industrial production in the early twentieth century. Since the production of saltpetre required huge amounts of electrical power, and because of difficulties transmitting electricity over long distances, industrial production had to be located close to that crucial factor, electricity.

The scale of the development was new to Norway. The investments were so large they needed international capital, which Eyde managed to find in Sweden and France. Rjukan as a company town was built very quickly, with little reference to the local agricultural life-modes. With all its installations, dams and tunnels for power production, Rjukan was built entirely by manual labour, known as *rallare*, describing the identity of itinerant labourers. Many thousands of such workers migrated to Notodden and Rjukan from all over Scandinavia.

Figure 10.3 The steam railway ferry D/F *Ammonia* was the third of four ferries used by Norsk Hydro to transport chemicals from Rjukan down the length of the Tinnsjøen to Tinnoset. She worked between 1929 and 1991

Photo: I. Birkeland.

For a decade or more, until the early 1920s, Rjukan experienced rapid growth. By 1920 the population had risen to 8,500 in the town of Rjukan alone and to 12,000 in the whole of Tinn municipality. But since then there has been a prolonged decline with only occasional smaller periods of growth. Norsk Hydro faced many challenges at Rjukan – new production methods led to cheaper and less energy-intensive production and new business opportunities elsewhere, new technology was developed to transport electricity over longer distances without large energy loss, and it became quite costly for Norsk Hydro to produce at Rjukan, as it was no longer necessary to locate industrial production where electricity was produced.

Production nevertheless continued. At the end of World War II the population had fallen to 6,500 inhabitants in Rjukan, but nevertheless the immediate post-war period was a golden period for Norsk Hydro (Hansen 2004). Industrial jobs were generally relatively safe, in a situation where the agricultural sector was less and less important for the national economy and the major cities of Norway grew, with more industrial jobs. In the longer term, however, the situation for Norsk Hydro at Rjukan was unstable. During the 1960s, Norsk Hydro closed down some activities and relocated them southwards to Herøya on the coast, and the company gradually started to look elsewhere in the world for new industrial locations. The workforce was reduced, and during the 1960s many families left Rjukan to settle elsewhere. The population has continued to fall, to just over 6,000 today for the whole municipality. There is probably no other place in Norway that has experienced such a long and steady population decline (Hansen 2004, 19).

The main challenge for the future of the place is to create the conditions for sustainable development in a wide sense and with a long time perspective (Birkeland 2014). Despite this long process of de-industrialisation, the industrial sector in Rjukan is, however, still alive, and continues to play a large role in terms of employment, providing (including construction) almost half of the jobs in Tinn municipality. At the same time, Rjukan is a town with a more diverse economic structure than before, and with a thriving cultural life. With its surrounding area it is undergoing promising social and economic changes associated with tourism and second-home development, and the population has been relatively stable for the past decade.

Two narratives of Rjukan's place-heritage

This section focuses on the two narratives mentioned in the introduction which have given rise to a particular understanding of the place-heritage of Rjukan. The first narrative is related to the depiction of Rjukan as the birthplace of industrial, modern Norway. In large part it derives from a book by Sverre Kjeldstadli from 1943, *Rjukan – et Moderne Eventyr om Industri- og Bondesamfunn* ('Rjukan – A Modern Fairy Tale about Industrial and Farming Communities'). In this narrative Rjukan is associated with industrial life. Furthermore, industrial society is identified as being superior to pre-industrial and agricultural society, and thus Rjukan is seen as the pioneering *locus* of industrialisation. Rjukan is given a special place in the overall narration of modern Norway as a nation built upon industry, technology and progress. This positioning can be found in many other narratives of Rjukan (see for example Kjeldstadli 1994), and builds upon a construction of Rjukan and its landscape with the Rjukan waterfalls and surrounding mountains as a Norway in miniature, a national icon, in the Romantic period (Fjågesund 2007).

Sverre Kjeldstadli's book presented Rjukan's birth and growth using the structure of a fairy-tale. The narrative (chapter titles here are the present author's translations) starts with 'The Rural Communities', a chapter describing pre-industrial life-modes, but then continues with the introduction of industrialisation ('Enter Industrialisation') and is followed by two chapters on the further development of Norsk Hydro's activities in Rjukan ('The Years Went By', 'Much and Many Things Have Changed'). Finally the book ends with a chapter entitled 'And Still the Fairy-tale is Not Over', so that unlike most fairy-tales, the narrative ends without a final resolution. In the fairy-tale genre there is normally a central conflict that creates tension and development in the narrative; here in Kjeldstadli's narrative it is the relationship between agricultural and modern society. The hero figure is the industrialist (Norsk Hydro), showing the way to the future at the expense of the farmer, who is heading backwards rather than forwards through industrial development. At the time when the book was published there were problems for Norsk Hydro at Rjukan, and the future was unclear, making it easy to end the book without an ending of the industrial adventure.

The second narrative appears in the post-war period, where Rjukan is no longer the scene for progress through industrial development. Now Rjukan has been turned into a problem place. There are quite a few books, reports, publications and media stories that focus on the problems of Rjukan stemming from the long period of de-industrialisation (Birkeland 2014). The social and economic needs created by de-industrialisation laid the foundation for the second narrative, which is one of decline (Birkeland 2008). It is associated with the so-called *Rjukansituasjonen*, which refers to the changes in Rjukan's economy caused by rationalisation and new production processes (Dahl 2000, 4). It was a problem situation, because the town was founded by, and dependent on, one company. This name for a particular situation has since been ascribed to many other towns facing similar challenges.

The 'problem narrative' of Rjukan can be dated back to 1968, when Norsk Hydro was allowed by the Norwegian government to transport electricity produced in Rjukan to other places. The event affected the relationship between the municipality of Tinn and the central government/Ministry of Industry for decades. It was a turning point for many local politicians, and a case of alleged injustice done to Rjukan and Tinn municipality by Norsk Hydro, supported by the Norwegian government. The agreed compensation was not paid, it is claimed, and the affair represents a wound that has never healed for many politicians from Tinn, among them some who took part in the original discussions and political processes (Birkeland 2014).

The result of this event was a national focus on mono-cultural industrial towns in need of economic restructuring. Many government-funded investment schemes and development programmes for restructuring of the economy were directed at such industrial towns. Some schemes succeeded, others failed. Furthermore, as mentioned, the *Rjukansituasjonen*, the 'Rjukan situation' became a name for a problem place. The problem narrative has taken on a life on its own and has shaped Rjukan's position in Norwegian society again, this time narrating Rjukan as a place with no future, quite the opposite of the first narrative which narrated Rjukan as *the* place, a place that was a symbol of the future. What is the connection between these two narratives of Rjukan, and whose interests, and what end, do they serve?

The contested nature of place-heritage

At the outset of industrialisation in Rjukan, industrial development was seen as the one and true road to progress and the future. The first narrative, which is told through the structure of the fairy-tale, constructed Rjukan in contrast to the pre-modern and agricultural world, which is represented as a backward, dirty and dark past. In a classic fairy-tale in Norwegian and broader European traditions, there is a hero, there are enemies and there are helpers. The hero overcomes conflicts and challenges and finds creative solutions to problems. The hero is a winner, and because she shares the resources she has available, in return she receives much more. The hero's helpers are disguised as beggars, poor and marginalised beings who test the virtues and values of the hero so that she can become a morally sound person. The fairy-tale provides a model for moral and human development, and Norsk Hydro is constructed in relation to this model.

With the second narrative, the industrial adventure continues for Norsk Hydro, but not for Rjukan. The hero was challenged by the needs of twentieth-century economic development, and instead of accepting the tests and working with the challenges, instead abandoned Rjukan. This is a happy turn for Norsk Hydro, but not for Rjukan, and in this second narrative Rjukan is left with no future. Rjukan is represented as a place of lack, a place with only a past. The term *Rjukansituasjonen* more or less functioned as a social stigma, an unwanted, degrading quality that can be used to characterise a whole group of people (Goffman 2009). It can also be used to characterise and judge a place. The degrading quality is that Rjukan lacks something of value, namely a future based on industrial jobs and economic sustainability. So Rjukan is no longer the image or icon of Norway's future, but is represented as a place with no future.

These narratives have had a great influence on attitudes to Rjukan, and can be viewed as key narratives. Key narratives tell something fundamental about their society, and influence the judgements and actions of individuals, groups and even society as a whole (Frønes 2001). Key narratives are useful for legitimating purposes, i.e. for shaping identity and belonging. The two Rjukan narratives together tell a story of a great industrial town that was born and then died, a story that has played, and still plays, an ideological role in the construction of Norway as a modern, industrial nation (Birkeland 2014). The birth and death of Rjukan is in many ways necessary for legitimating a master narrative of Norway as a modern, industrial nation. How can this be possible? It is possible because of the position

Norsk Hydro has enjoyed and still enjoys in Norwegian society. Norsk Hydro, the company that built Rjukan, has been the mother of many new companies and has enjoyed wide respect in society across social classes. The company has managed to adjust and develop, and for decades has been a respected place to work for those who have wanted to climb to the top in Norwegian society. It has in many ways replaced Rjukan's image as an icon of Norway's industrial adventure. Today, Norsk Hydro is an international company producing aluminium and related products and employs over 13,000 people in over fifty countries. The state of Norway owns 43.8 per cent of the company. The fact that Norsk Hydro left Rjukan to find economic opportunities elsewhere has not harmed its image as a modern hero, but this image has been constructed at the expense of Rjukan's place-heritage.

The potential space of cultural sustainability

How are we to create future narratives for Rjukan, to imagine a future for the town? When places undergo change due to economic restructuring, those who inhabit these places may find that their relationship to the place also changes. Economic restructuring does not only concern economic sustainability, but the cultural sustainability of a place associated with placeless-ness (Birkeland 2008). Loss of jobs, unemployment and the breakdown of social institutions in the community can erode a positive sense of place and weaken or destroy attachment to place. De-industrialisation in Rjukan has not only led to job loss in an economic sense. The place narratives associated with Rjukan's development have led to a sort of placeless-ness that affects the place's cultural sustainability. The interesting issue here lies in the presence and/or absence of perspectives and visions of the future that were created in the two narratives analysed above, and the potential for new place narratives of Rjukan.

Place-heritage, appearing as place narratives, is not an object, but nor is it a subject. Place-heritage as it is understood here exists as something in-between, and in-the-making. The qualities that are attached and ascribed to places can be made visible and shared through place narratives. These qualities are not descriptions of a past, but remade and made meaningful within the perspective of the present and the future. They are also very important for the future, because particular and sustainable (or animated, living) qualities of places are needed in place narratives in order to gain power and inspiration when seeking ways to make places sustainable. Human beings are related to their surroundings in deep and complex ways, and personal narratives will in many ways be identical or closely related to place narratives. Personal narratives are also related to the presence or absence of visions of a future in a place narrative. Place refers here to *sense of place*, to the subjective and emotional attachment people have learnt and developed as part of culture, through those cultural meanings that are associated with place (Cresswell 2004; Birkeland 2014).

This means that place-heritage appears less as heritage object or subject, but as a medium through which place-making happens. Place narratives bear in this way much resemblance to the workings of heritage as assemblage (McDonald 2009), where heritage acts as a mediator that changes and reassembles places, shaping towns, places and those who live in places. Place narratives have potentially the power to transform our relationships to place, and thus renew and transform place-heritage. If we are interested in changing our relationships to place, we must, according to Margaret Somerville (2008), change those narratives that are written about place. Our relationships to places – and consequential transformations of place-heritage – are constituted through the narratives (and other representations) that we make about them.

De-industrialisation at Rjukan does not necessarily mean that the cultural meaning of industrial society is lost. It may be that the main challenge is to give meaning to, or animate, the cultural values and meanings of past industrial society, while at the same time creating new forms of economic sustainability in the present and in the future. The opportunity of doing that represents the potential space for cultural sustainability. With reference to Rjukan, the sources for creating new place narratives must come from something new, not only from the two narratives depicting the birth and death of a great industrial town, although the new may 'simply' come from seeing these two narratives together, in a new light. Or the new may come from the challenges of unsustainable development, that are becoming more and more overwhelming and which threaten the world's future sustainability with gross social, cultural and ecological imbalances. In this perspective, what will it, or what should it, imply to 'preserve' industrial heritage? Should it imply the continued 'heroisation' of companies like Norsk Hydro and unsustainable industrial development? One hundred years ago, industrial development was *the* way forward for any society in the Western world. Today we know that industrial development, whilst a source of great wealth and social development, improved living conditions and better social institutions, has also been the means for pollution and environmental degradation, increasing inequalities between the North and the South, environmental injustice, resource depletion and the most significant contributions to global warming. Industrial development is both a blessing and a curse, a double-edged sword on which we today, in the twenty-first century, are dependent for the overall economic sustainability of the world. What can we learn from Rjukan from this perspective?

Conclusion

The heritage process can be understood as a post-industrial mode of creativity that refuses to see post-industrial place-making in terms of lack, loss and absence. Instead of constructing heritage as a retreat from the uncertainties of the present, a more dynamic and process-oriented perspective on heritage would focus on the future. Heritage is not the preservation of a fixed past, because the identities of people, groups and places are not stable, secure or bounded but constantly in the making, and unbounded in relation to other people, groups and places. The discourse on heritage preservation is first and foremost a reaction to the risk of loss and absence, and one which keeps heritage users in an artificial bind between seeing heritage as either presence or absence. In this sense, cultural sustainability as a potential space provides important new perspectives, but also corrections, to the discourse on heritage preservation, a dominant discourse in heritage management.

This chapter has analysed the narration of the birth and death of the great industrial town, Rjukan, and has shown that place narratives have consequences for cultural sustainability. Industrialisation, which is as much a cultural phenomenon as it is a social and economic one, was the basis for the growth and development of many places like Rjukan in the Western world. Many of the world's industrial places have been struggling like Rjukan with a global shift in economic development, with de-industrialisation as a consequence. For a particular place, these consequences are many-faceted. In terms of the built environment, the challenge of de-industrialisation has been that of form being left without function, giving way to seeing the forms of the past as heritage, as Rjukan's industrial heritage is now being nominated for UNESCO's World Heritage list. Place-heritage thus concerns the way the past is used in the present, with the prospect of creating a sustainable future. The challenge is cultural as well as social and economic, and is embedded in particular narratives of the past that are created in the present. The key to a sustainable future lies in the social processes of the present.

Place narratives are not neutral and romanticised stories of a past. Place narratives feed into place-heritage in ideological ways. Rjukan's 'journey' from birthplace and icon of Norway's future to a place associated with lack of jobs, lack of people, lack of industry, and by negative implication, lack of future, is also a story of the creation of potential for the future. This 'potential space' can be the basis for cultural sustainability in Rjukan, by means of a process that negotiates the past and the future, but is written in the present. Heritage processes help to preserve particular aspects of the past, but such processes are always selective. The issue is whose narratives are preserved, used and re-used. Place narratives are always in the present, but they transform the meaning of the past by creating the future as a potential space. It is never anything other than a potential space, a space in the making. The potential space for narrating Rjukan as a place with a future will need to move beyond an understanding of heritage as presence or absence. In this sense, we can understand potential space as a hermeneutic device for transforming human relationships to place. Sustainable place-making links the past, which is an absent industrial presence, with a future, which is a post-industrial creative process.

References

Alzén, A. 1996. *Fabriken som Kulturarv: Frågan om ndustrilandskapets Bevarande i Norrköping 1950–1985*, Stockholm: B. Östlings Bokförlag Symposion.
Anderson, B. 1983. *Imagined Communities: Reflections on the Origin and Spread of Nationalism*, London: Verso.
Birkeland, I. 2008. Cultural Sustainability: Industrialism, Placeless-ness and the Re-animation of Place. *Ethics, Place and Environment* 11(3), 283–97.
Birkeland, I. 2014. *Kulturelle Hjørnesteiner*, Kristiansand: Cappelen Damm Akademisk.

Birkeland, I., Horlings, I., Soini, K., Olafsdottir, G. and Stylianou-Lambert, T. (In progress). Culture and Sustainability: A Theoretical Framework. Submitted to *Global Environmental Change* 2014.

Cameron, C. 2000. Emergent Industrial Heritage: The Politics of Selection. *Museum Anthropology* 23(3), 58–73.

Cresswell, T. 2004. *Place: A Short Introduction*, Oxford: Blackwell.

Dahl, H. 1981, 1983, 2000. *Rjukan 1–3*, Rjukan: Tinn Kommune.

Dirall, C. 2002. Heritage Railways as Museums: Occupation and Landscape. *Japan Railway and Transport Review* 30. Available at www.jrtr.net/jrtr30/pdf/f04_div.pdf

Edensor, T. 2005. *Industrial Ruins: Space, Aesthetics and Materiality*, Oxford: Berg.

Evans, G. 2002. Living in a World Heritage City: Stakeholders in the Dialectic of the Universal and the Particular. *International Journal of Heritage Studies* 8(2), 117–35.

Fjågesund, P. 2007. From Sacred Scenery to Nuclear Nightmare: Rjukan and Its Myths. In K. K. Poulsen (ed.), *Northbound: Travels, Encounters, and Constructions 1700–1830*, Aarhus, Denmark: Aarhus University Press, 377–97.

Frers, L. 2013. The Matter of Absence. *Cultural Geographies*. Published online, 13 February 2013.

Frønes, I. 2001. *Handling, Kultur og Mening*, Bergen: Fagbokforlaget.

Geertz, C. 1973. *The Interpretation of Cultures: Selected Essays*, New York: Basic Books.

Goffman, E. 2009. *Stigma*, Fredriksberg: Samfundslitteratur.

Handler, R. and Linnekin, J. 1984. Tradition, Genuine or Spurious. *The Journal of American Folklore* 97(385), 273–290.

Hansen, J. C. 2004. Ungdoms Forhold til Sted: Er Rjukan et Blivende Sted? In N. G. Berg, B. Dale, H. K. Lysgård and A. Løfgren (eds), *Mennesker, Steder og Regionale Endringer*, Trondheim: Tapir, 112–28.

Hobsbawm, E. and Ranger, T. 1983. *The Invention of Tradition*, Cambridge: Cambridge University Press.

Holm, F. E., Daugstad, K. and Frisvoll, S. 2007. Verdensarven etter Festen. *Plan* nos. 3–4, 56–61.

Jansen-Verbeke, M. 1999. Industrial Heritage: A Nexus for Sustainable Tourism Development. *Tourism Geographies* 1(1), 70–8.

Jones, C. and Munday, M. 2001. Blaenavon and United Nations World Heritage Site Status: Is Conservation of Industrial Heritage a Road to Economic Development? *Regional Studies* 35(6), 585–90.

Kirshenblatt-Gimblett, B. 1998. *Destination Culture: Tourism, Museums and Heritage*, Berkeley: University of California Press.

Kirshenblatt-Gimblett, B. 2004. Intangible Heritage as Metacultural Production. *Museum International* 56(1–2), 52–65.

Kirschenblatt-Gimblett, B. 2006. World Heritage and Cultural Economics. In I. Karp, C. A. Kratz, L. Szwaja and T. Ybarra-Frausto, with G. Buntinx, B. Kirshenblatt-Gimblett and C. Rassool (eds), *Museum Frictions: Public Cultures/Global Transformations*, Durham, NC: Duke University Press, 161–202.

Kjeldstadli, S. 1943. *Rjukan, et Moderne Eventyr om Industri- og Bondesamfunn*, Oslo: Cappelen.

Kjeldstadli, K. 1994. Eksemplet Rjukan – et Signalement av et Ensidig Industristed. *Telemark Historie: Tidsskrift for Telemark Historielag* no. 15, 45–56.

Kurin, R. 2004. Safeguarding Intangible Cultural Heritage in the 2003 UNESCO Convention: A Critical Appraisal. *Museum International* 56(1–2), 221–2.

Landorf, C. 2009. A Framework for Sustainable Heritage Management: A Study of UK Industrial Heritage Sites. *International Journal of Heritage Studies* 15(6), 494–510.

Lowenthal, D. 1985. *The Past is a Foreign Country*, Cambridge: Cambridge University Press.

Lowenthal, D. 2008. Authenticities Past and Present. *CRM: The Journal of Heritage Stewardship*. Available at http://crmjournal.cr.nps.gov/02_viewpoint_sub.cfm?issue=Volume%205%20Number%201%20Winter%202008&page=1&seq=1 (accessed 17 September 2009).

Massey, D. 1994. *Space, Place and Gender*, Cambridge: Polity Press.

McDonald, S. 2009. Reassembling Nuremberg, Reassembling Heritage. *Journal of Cultural Economy* 2(1–2), 117–34.

Negri, M. 2011. Introduction. In T. L. Soininen (ed.), *Reusing the Industrial Past by the Tammerkoski Rapids: Discussions on the Value of Industrial Heritage*, Tampere, Finland: City of Tampere/Pirkanaa Provincial Museum, 5–8.

Pocock, D. 1997. Some Reflections on World Heritage. *Area* 29(3), 260–8.

Robinson, M., Bourdeau, L. and Barbas, M. G. (eds) 2012. *On the List: World Heritage Tourism and Identity*, Aldershot: Ashgate.

Smith, L. J. 2006. *The Uses of Heritage*, London: Routledge.

Soini, K. and Birkeland, I. 2014. Exploring the Scientific Discourse on Cultural Sustainability. *Geoforum* 51(1), 213–23.

Solà-Morales, I. de 1995. Terrain Vague. In C. Davidson (ed.), *Anyplace*, Cambridge, MA: MIT Press, 118–23.

Somerville, M. 2008. A Place Pedagogy for Global Contemporaneity. *Journal of Educational Philosophy and Theory* 42(3), 326–44. DOI: 10.1111/j.1469-5812.2008.00423.x.

Stanton, C. 2005. Serving Up Culture: Heritage and its Discontents at an Industrial History Site. *International Journal of Heritage Studies* 11(5), 415–31.

Storm, A. 2008. Hope and Rust: Reinterpreting the Industrial Place in the late 20th Century. Ph.D. thesis, Division of History of Science and Technology, KTH, Stockholm.

Winnicott, D. W. 2007 [1971]. *Playing and Reality*, London: Tavistock.

11 Politics, tourism and cultural sustainability

The construction of heritage in Cyprus

Theopisti Stylianou-Lambert, Nikolaos Boukas and Alexandra Bounia

Introduction

Museums are in the business of preserving, exhibiting and interpreting heritage and are thus in a powerful position to encapsulate and promote official and trusted cultural narratives. They are seen as *official* because museums claim to represent states, nations and/or communities, and are *trusted* because visitors tend to assume that the narratives offered by museums are well researched and objective. These official and trusted cultural narratives, however, are rarely absolute, unchanging or unbiased. On the contrary, what is considered 'cultural heritage' is constantly (re)constructed and (re)negotiated because mutable practical, professional, cultural and political reasons dictate what kind of cultural heritage is visible, or not, and to whom. Second, we cannot ignore the fact that museums are the product of the actions of multiple stakeholders who generally have different interests and motivations. As a result, the museological construction of heritage is to a large degree shaped by these stakeholders and their perceptions about what constitutes 'their' heritage worth preserving and exhibiting. Finally, heritage is bound to the complexities of place and time and therefore the elements that structure it change according to geographical and temporal coordinates. As these coordinates shift, so does the emphasis placed on certain aspects of heritage.

We now turn our attention to our case study and set our geographical coordinates to the small Mediterranean island of Cyprus. In every country, there are undoubtedly many forces that influence the creation and function of museums, such as politics, tourism, private collections and interests, cultural policies and funding, corporate social responsibility programmes, religious groups and various communities. In the case of Cyprus, for this book we have chosen to emphasise the first two of those forces, because politics and tourism are more forceful than others, at least under the current circumstances. Cyprus has a long, turbulent history and is currently involved in political conflict between its two main ethnic communities (i.e. Greek Cypriots and Turkish Cypriots). At the same time, it has a highly developed tourism industry. We will attempt to show that these two forces have influenced the construction of heritage in Cyprus and the narratives presented in Cypriot museums. Furthermore, we will explore the relationship between heritage construction in museums and cultural sustainability. We argue that the place-specific forces of political conflict and tourism play a particularly important role in heritage construction and in the understanding and implementation of cultural sustainability.

Although the discussion that follows concerns Cyprus, it has a wider relevance, because other new nation states that live amidst political conflict, or postcolonial countries that depend on tourism for their survival, face similar issues. As the Cypriot anthropologist and documentary film-maker Peter Loizos has pointed out,

> [i]n any typical year since 1945, between one quarter and one third of the UN's members have experienced internal conflicts involving either attempts to take over a state, to escape from it, or to obtain greater freedom within it.
>
> (Loizos 1998, 36)

As we will see in the case of Cyprus, these internal conflicts (peaceful or not) influence what aspects of a community's heritage is used and how. Furthermore, many postcolonial countries share Cyprus' challenges when it comes to encapsulating and promoting a country's cultural heritage to tourists from all over the world.

Museums, cultural sustainability and the preservation paradigm

As places where heritage is being preserved for future generations, museums play an important role in sustaining culture. The term 'cultural sustainability' is still an evolving one, and its use in any context needs to be clearly framed in order to be better understood and further examined. For the purposes of this chapter we will define 'cultural sustainability' as 'the consideration, preservation and presentation of tangible and intangible heritage, artistic production, as well as the knowledge and skills of various social groups, communities and nations' (Stylianou-Lambert et al. 2014, 4). It is important to keep in mind that social, economic and environmental factors are interconnected with culture, and furthermore, that culture is both time-specific and place-specific. The history and geography of a place thus influence to a large degree its heritage, and how it is envisioned. Finally, certain individuals and groups have the tools and power to promote their cultural artefacts and values more forcefully than others. As a result, some forms of heritage become more visible than others.

When considering the role of museums in cultural sustainability certain parameters and considerations become important. These include heritage preservation, the passing on of cultural skills and knowledge, issues of memory and identity, the development of new audiences and achievement of greater inclusion, the representation of cultural diversity and the fostering of intercultural dialogue, as well as the encouragement of creativity, innovation and artistic vitality (Stylianou-Lambert et al. 2014). All these parameters can be aspects of cultural sustainability. Museum professionals and policy makers, however, may choose to place their emphasis on certain aspects more than others. For example, some museums might place their emphasis on preservation, an activity considered a core one for museums. On the other hand, museums can envision cultural sustainability in broader terms and also emphasise the development of new audiences, the encouragement of creativity and innovation as well as artistic vitality. Thus, cultural sustainability can be understood in narrower or broader terms.

Furthermore, each parameter itself can be approached in more conservative or more liberal ways, or might be more object-oriented or more people-oriented. For example, educational activities can be designed to transfer specific knowledge that revolves around exhibited objects to a specific audience such as schoolchildren, families, or adult visitors. Alternatively, educational activities can be more sensitive to the interests of specific communities, and promote multiple stories and understandings instead of a single, authoritative, curatorial voice.

Cultural sustainability may be envisioned and implemented in very different ways. Current academic literature favours more people-oriented approaches. Indicative of this is the discussion about a paradigm shift from the expertise-led and object-oriented *preservation paradigm* to the inclusive and people-oriented *new heritage paradigm*. When it comes to heritage preservation and museum management, depending on the overall philosophy of the policy maker or museum professional, cultural policies and museum practices can be more object-oriented or more people-oriented. Using the Faro Convention (Council of Europe 2005) as a frame, a comparison of the concept of new heritage with the older preservation paradigm of heritage might conclude that:

> [o]n the one hand, heritage policy might be based on a relatively small, highly managed and publicly subsidised heritage based on traditional approaches such as national criteria, expert assessment, a concern with authenticity and fabric and selective designation (heritage as constraint, heritage as commodity). On the other hand is the new type of heritage that the Faro Convention promotes – a broad, living heritage aligned with sense of place, landscape, sustainability and comprehensiveness, and context, but which might not allow us to 'keep' everything physically.
>
> (Fairclough 2009, 35)

The preservation paradigm sees heritage as the things we have inherited and wish to pass on to future generations because they are special. Experts identify what is considered worth preserving while politicians and decision makers put in place legislations and mechanisms that seek to protect, restore and preserve these selected aspects of material and immaterial culture (Fairclough 2009). This process leaves an open question regarding whether or not these expert decisions are representative of society's cultural perceptions (Rizzo and Throsby 2006). On the other hand, the new heritage paradigm sees heritage as everything we have inherited, is concerned with the everyday life, localness and the common construction of heritage as well as integrating the past with the present and future. In general, heritage is seen as action, process and a resource to be used by people instead of an object or an asset in need of protection (Fairclough 2009). The emphasis on people rather than objects also implies more bottom-up approaches to cultural policy. This paradigm shift is useful in our discussion of heritage construction and the forces that influence it.

Current theories in museum and tourism studies support more people-oriented approaches within a broader understanding of cultural sustainability. Museums are nowadays called to place more emphasis on the experience of the visitor instead of on the objects themselves, to encourage personal interpretations rather than to predetermine educational outcomes, and to be more inclusive, more sensitive to alternative narratives and voices, and more instrumental in public dialogue and reconciliation efforts. A more people-oriented approach means that museums place their emphasis on how the past can be seen through the lens of the present and the future, while recognising that the past is subject to manipulation and that we are usually talking about various versions of it. In effect, we are talking about *pasts* and not *the* past. Furthermore, emerging tourism theories echo developments in museum studies. They emphasise the need to take into account the tourists' cultural needs and to offer a tourist experience that is holistic and exciting, and that does not cultivate stereotypes or perpetuate misunderstandings. They also point towards the development of a new kind of tourism that aims for quality and not quantity, one that seeks to offer 'authentic individual experiences' instead of mass-produced ones.

The following two sections will in turn explore the construction of heritage in Cyprus, under the influence of colonialism, politics and the development of nationalism by the two main ethnic communities of the island, and then discuss the relationship between heritage construction and tourism, as well as the expectations of tourists for an 'authentic cultural experience'.

Politics and cultural identity

What museums collect, preserve and exhibit are the tangible links between the past, present and future, forming one of the cores of cultural sustainability. Apart from being agents of cultural sustainability, museums are also part of a cultural system which selectively renders visible certain aspects of a culture while obscuring others. Like any cultural system or economy, different stakeholders operate within various complex power structures. These stakeholders indicate what they deem to be important to be preserved for future generations as the material and immaterial proof of a country's heritage. In this way, a sense of heritage is constructed and used in the present to advocate national, local and individual identities. Instead of using particular museums as case studies, this chapter investigates the range and types of different kinds of state museums (for example, art, history, archaeological) available at a particular time and place.

Cyprus is home to two main ethnic communities, Greek (mainly Christian) Cypriots and Turkish (mainly Muslim) Cypriots, which are concentrated respectively in the southern and northern parts of the island. The two parts are separated by a *de facto* state border (see Figure 11.1) that is not internationally recognised in law. Cultural heritage is so entangled with politics and perceptions

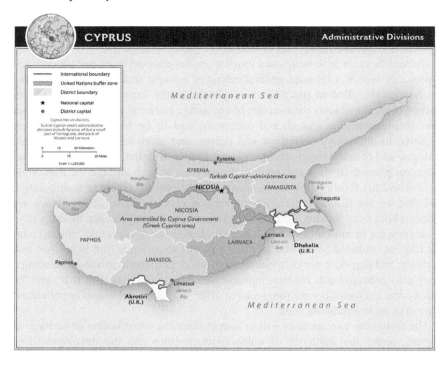

Figure 11.1 Map of Cyprus

Source: CIA, public domain image.

of national identity that it is very difficult to separate it from Cyprus' current political problems. Indeed, what is considered to be cultural heritage, and therefore worth preserving and promoting, often depends on political decisions. Consequently, in Cyprus it is exceptionally obvious that 'heritage' is a time- and place-related social and cultural construct (Rizzo and Throsby 2006).

Heritage construction in Cyprus has been a long process, and has been defined in close relationship to the island's history. Having for centuries been under a succession of foreign 'rulers', Cyprus saw its heritage selectively constructed, according to what was considered important to the colonial rulers, most recently by the British between 1878 and 1960, in the period when modern concepts of 'heritage' began to be formulated. Foreign expeditions revealed ancient Greek treasures that were subsequently exhibited in foreign and local museums as the highlight of Cyprus' past. On the other hand, the communities of the island during a similar time period started developing their own self-awareness of their heritage. The Greek Cypriot community was much larger and in a more advantageous position than the Turkish Cypriot community because of higher educational levels and strong links with Greece. As a consequence, it was the first to start developing its own identity and heritage. Of course, the need for a strong self-identity grew as resistance to British colonial rule grew, and eventually took the form of an emphasis on the island's ancient Greek heritage that took precedence over all other periods of history. This resulted in the establishment of a number of 'archaeological' museums focusing on the long Greek presence on the island and thus orientated towards Mycenean and classical antiquity (Leriou 2007) (Figure 11.2). The Turkish Cypriot community on the other hand, did not have the advantageous position of the Greek Cypriots and tried instead to embrace the heritage that was left behind, i.e. from the medieval past, which was cosmopolitan (and not Greek), multi-religious and closer to the Ottoman rule of the island. Both communities established museums as their sense of nationalism grew, but they embraced different aspects of cultural heritage, whichever was closest to their sense of ethno-national identity.

We focus here on national museums because national museums play a crucial role in (re)inforcing national memory and identity. The influence of politics on national museums in Cyprus is evident when we examine the kinds of national museum established by the two main ethnic communities of the island. The two communities chose to create different kinds of museums based on what they valued as *their* cultural heritage. The Greek Cypriot authorities currently run nineteen museums. The majority (ten) are 'archaeological' in the sense of being focused on classical antiquity, the remainder being ethnographic (four), historical (three) and art (two) museums. The emphasis that the Greek Cypriot government and other bodies place on classical archaeology is justified within the discourse of Hellenism. On the other hand, the Turkish Cypriot authorities place more emphasis

Figure 11.2 The façade of the Cyprus Museum, which was the first archaeological museum founded in Cyprus, in 1888. The photograph was taken in 1956

Source: Department of Antiquities, Cyprus.

on the historical aspect rather than the archaeological one. Of the eighteen museums of the Turkish Cypriot authorities, six are history museums, four are icon museums and four are ethnographic museums. Its main museums focus on aspects of the island's Ottoman past, claiming, in this sense, their share of it (Bounia and Stylianou-Lambert 2011).

Curiously, the Greek Cypriot authorities (mainly Orthodox Christian) have not established any state Byzantine museums, while the Turkish Cypriot authorities (mainly Muslim) have established and run four icon museums. There are about fourteen Byzantine museums in the southern (Greek Cypriot) part of the island, but they are not state-run; instead the majority of Byzantine museums (ten) are run by the Church of Cyprus while the other four are smaller community initiatives. The icon museums in the northern part of the island are viewed by the Turkish Cypriot authorities as a demonstration of respect for Orthodox Christian heritage, although for the Greek Cypriot authorities they are seen as a proof of the continual destruction of Christian heritage (for more on this debate see Stylianou-Lambert and Bounia 2014). Nevertheless, the Byzantine era falls under the medieval past of Cyprus which is embraced by the Turkish Cypriot community, and as such icon museums might be another argument for Cyprus' multicultural past.

It is very difficult to generalise when it comes to such a diverse array of museums of different sizes and kinds. Nevertheless, it is safe to assume that Cypriot state museums are on the whole more object-oriented and follow the older preservation model of heritage instead of the 'new' heritage (as described by Fairclough 2009). State museums follow the traditional process where experts and politicians identify what is regarded as worth preserving and decision makers put in place the necessary form of funding for preservation of the identified buildings and artefacts. Attempts are made to support communities and municipalities financially to develop their own museums; these are, however, case by case initiatives, with no clear cultural policy framework (Gordon 2004).

Today, in Cyprus' state museums some voices are heard louder than others. For example, there are very few (positive) representations of the Turkish Cypriot community in Greek Cypriot state museums, and *vice versa*. Furthermore, there is almost no representation of the other three ethnic and religious communities of the island – Maronites, Armenians and Latins – in any of the museums located in southern Cyprus. In effect, state and church museums in the southern part of the island give a unified message of an (ethno-)national identity that is predominantly Greek Orthodox Christian. On the other hand, Turkish Cypriot museums emphasise the Turkish Cypriot community's long presence on the island as well as the multicultural history of the island.

The preservation model is not only followed by state museums but also seems to be prevalent among museum employees in Cyprus working in state, municipal or private museums. A recent study asked personnel of all museums in the southern part of the island to state what they believed to be the main purpose of a museum. Three-quarters (75 per cent) of the participants indicated that the main purpose of a museum should be the preservation of the national and local cultural heritage, 12 per cent the education of the public, 4 per cent the promotion of historical and social dialogue, 4 per cent the study of the collection, and 2 per cent public entertainment (Visual Sociology and Museum Studies Lab 2013). Thus, the perceptions of museum personnel in Cyprus are closer to the preservation paradigm since preservation is by far their first priority. These perceptions unavoidably influence the functions and practices of museums, as well as how cultural sustainability is understood. Overall, it seems that cultural sustainability in Cyprus is narrowly understood as the preservation of selected cultural heritage.

Tourism and authenticity

Just as with the process of creating a national narrative, the tourism industry demands straightforward, simplified 'cultural selling points' that can be attractive and catchy. We now turn our attention to how tourism has also played a role in constructing heritage in Cyprus.

The link between tourism and cultural heritage is deep and strong. Cultural heritage is one of the prime attractions of a destination and one of the main ambassadors of a place. Under the scope of development, this link can become significantly important. Indeed, as widely argued, there is a beneficial relationship between culture and tourism (e.g. Hughes and Allen 2005). Culture provides resources for the growth of cultural tourism, which in turn reinforces the tourism industry. Revenues from the tourism industry allow cultural assets to be sustained where otherwise they may deteriorate.

From a more anthropological viewpoint, this relationship between cultural heritage and tourism has significant impact on the heritage formation and identification of the host destination. The shift from Fordist (mass production and consumption of standardised tourist packages) to post-Fordist ideas (characterised by technological advancement and enlarged, multifaceted needs of demand) brought alterations to consumption patterns, including those of heritage consumption (Apostolakis 2003). The '"McDonaldization of tourism consumption" characterised by a form of mass customisation presenting to tourists flexible products, based on efficient calculable holidays' (Shaw and Williams 2004, 133) also facilitated the differentiation of consumption patterns. Cultural heritage tourism increasingly grows in importance as tourists seem to move away from 'sun-and-sea' vacations and seek more sophisticated types, characterised by differentiation, uniqueness and exclusivity (Apostolakis 2003). In the context of tourism, however, it is difficult to fully understand which types of cultural heritage are genuinely authentic and which are (re)constructed for the purpose of satisfying visitors' demands (Smith 2003). This becomes more apparent in today's globalised world. As natural and cultural heritage assets are transformed into tourist products, important questions are raised regarding the authenticity of a destination's cultural heritage.

Authenticity is without a doubt a significant characteristic of heritage tourism. As sites housing authentic objects, museums play an important role in providing authentic experiences. Heritage assets are not simply viewed as contemporaneous productions, but are signifiers that are linked to the past and other ages (as Taylor 2001 reminds us). Authenticity in this view is tightly connected to the idea of the 'traditional'. Yet, it is necessary to recall (e.g. Sharpley 1994) that even though the word 'authenticity' appears to describe something that is genuine and real (and perhaps even unique), there are issues that need more elaboration. For instance, something that is not real for one person could be a noteworthy holistic experience for another.

Similarly, the sociologist Erik Cohen (1988) argues that some cultural products developed for tourists may exhibit 'emergent authenticity' and be accepted as 'authentic' by both tourists and cultural producers alike. It has been suggested that tourists seek authenticity but might not be able to distinguish between 'real' and 'staged' events produced by the host community (MacCannell 1973), or that authenticity is used as a promotional device (Waitt 2000) – what is real is open to interpretation, since marketeers decide what will be authentic and what not. All representations of the past are selective of course, and heritage, as an interpretation of the past, is perhaps especially open to appropriation by sectoral (or commercial) interests within society. Additionally, many tourists want authenticity but not necessarily reality. In their travels, tourists may have stereotypical or romantic images about the destination: 'people embark on heritage tourism motivated by their intrinsic feelings of nostalgia, social distinction and the need for an "authentic" experience' (Apostolakis 2003, 800). In this regard, tourism highly influences the formation and (re)construction of heritage mostly for the purposes of competitiveness, development and economic growth. It is also obvious that because of this contribution, cultural policies are shaped and updated in order to incorporate more the preferences and wants of the tourism demand(s).

It can be claimed that through the prism of tourism it is evident that cultural heritage elements (whether historic buildings, museums or other things) add positively to cultural capital, and hence are of great importance for cultural policy:

> [w]hilst the provision of cultural tourism attractions may be just one aspect of a national or regional cultural policy, it has become important, especially with the growth of leisure travel, a development that effectively makes the objects of cultural policy (museums, galleries, festivals etc.) also the objects of the tourist's desires, and hence a vehicle for economic development and regeneration.
>
> (Butcher 2005, 22)

It is thus perhaps understandable why contemporary cultural policies, shaped to a degree through tourism, tend to be object-oriented. There is, however, a tendency to move towards a more humanistic approach to cultural policy making that also incorporates the visitors' expectations, knowledge and experience enrichment (Boukas 2013; 2014). Thus, it is concluded that the 'new heritage' approach is evident in the theory of the contemporary cultural tourism industry.

It is also evident that tourism and politics are interconnected. The ways that heritage items are chosen, assembled and presented to visitors have political effects as well as causes, and these effects do not only consider the presented item *per se*, but also the interpretation given to it by people within a historical, cultural and social context (Kelly 2005). To highlight this interconnection, Ireland offers an example that raises the key question of whether or not heritage representation differs for the self or the other, for the citizen or the tourist:

> Ireland is only one such space in an increasing number of global zones of conflict where concepts of 'heritage and national cultural identity' have become fragmented, blurred and often violently challenged. As tourism increasingly seeks out cultural products, the politics of heritage representation for-self, versus for-others, becomes more and more loaded.
>
> (Kelly 2005, 36)

In the case of Cyprus, representations of the island in museums and tourism campaigns go hand in hand. Tourism tactics often mirror political decisions by emphasising specific aspects of a cultural landscape. In the case of the southern part of Cyprus, the emphasis is placed on the projection of a Greek-related national and tourism identity. The majority of state museums in the southern part of the island exhibit items related to its classical era, and the Cyprus Tourism Organisation (CTO) highlights these items and related archaeological locations in tourism marketing campaigns and promotional material. For example, the CTO promotes Cyprus as the sunny and friendly island of Figure 11.3, that immediately connects

Figure 11.3 'Can't wait to see you again', a Cyprus Tourism Organisation billboard at the entrance to Larnaca Airport, 2010

Source: Cyprus Tourism Organisation.

the island with its ancient Greek past. Indicative of this is the use in the CTO's logo of a statue of the ancient Greek goddess of love, Aphrodite, which is on display at the Cyprus Museum.

Despite the increasing number of tourists that come to the island, the preservation paradigm still prevails. Even though Cypriot society is much more open in comparison to the past (and tourism as an activity has over the years contributed to this change), museums continue to place their emphasis on selected cultural items and objects that communicate the meaning of an interpreted past to the visitors, based on the preservation paradigm. Of course, one aspect that adds to this situation is the fact that for more than fifty years the main focus of tourist development of the island was concentrated mostly on mass tourism elements (tourism oriented to sea and sun) rather than cultural ones (Boukas and Ziakas 2013). Visits to cultural places were mostly additional activities to a mainly 'sun, sea and sand' experience, rather than part of a culturally oriented trip. In this respect, policy did not pay the appropriate attention to visitors' needs, treating them as passive mass tourists rather than as individual visitors with autonomous behaviour, and a genuine interest in the cultural elements of the island. As such, to a large degree, the choice of the representation of Cypriot heritage in museums is a result of culture and tourism policy makers in many cases neglecting the tourists' need to know and understand Cypriot history in a more holistic and genuine way. Notwithstanding the current impetus of cultural tourism, the tourist system operating within the island is still, therefore, based on mass tourism elements and standards.

Nevertheless, the transition towards the new heritage paradigm is more evident today than in the past. Within an internationalised and globalised world, and the several global forces that prevail, tourism in Cyprus faces problems that, overall, highlight the need for diversification to other specialised activities (Boukas and Ziakas 2014), including cultural heritage ones. In this respect, visits to museums as part of an overall cultural tourist itinerary are vital for the overall growth of the island. As such, it is not only desirable for museums to turn towards new heritage in order to provide more vibrant, vivid and holistic experiences for visitors, but it is also essential for the holistic differentiation of the existing tourism product-service mix.

Conclusion

The construction of heritage in Cyprus has been the outcome of a process which is historically understandable and which has been based on decisions made with political and tourism-related national priorities in mind. The force of politics is shaped by Cyprus' past and by the continuing struggle to define its current identity; the force of tourism is inextricably linked to Cyprus' economic development and its future. Echoing the subtitle of this book, Cyprus lives between its past and its future, and this is reflected in its museum narratives.

As mentioned earlier in this chapter, the role of museums in cultural sustainability can take different forms. Without repeating them, these range from preserving objects, skills and knowledge, through issues of memory and identity, inclusion, diversity and dialogue, to creativity, innovation and artistic vitality (Stylianou-Lambert et al. 2014). Cypriot state museums seem to emphasise only two of these parameters: heritage preservation and memory/identity. The kind of heritage preserved and promoted depends on the ideological direction of each of the two main ethnic communities of the island. Political differences seem to lead to different types of museums in the two communities on the island, and to different emphases being placed on different periods of the island's history and heritage. At the same time, mass tourism reinforces stereotypical aspects of the selected heritage. This selective approach shapes memory and national identities for locals as well as tourists.

Seeking the *preservation* of a *selective* body of heritage constitutes a narrow understanding of cultural sustainability. The search for new audiences and for greater inclusion, the discovery and celebration of cultural diversity, the promotion of intercultural dialogue, and the encouragement and support of creative, innovative and artistic vitality, all of which sit at the heart of cultural sustainability and the new heritage paradigm, have mainly been ignored, overlooked or underestimated. Furthermore, the functions of preservation and education are understood in a traditional way in the sense that they aim to reinforce a simple, even singular, ethno-national identity instead of providing a space for discussion and intercultural understanding. A broader and more liberal understanding of cultural sustainability is needed.

Overall, there is no doubt that the directions pointed to by museum studies and tourism literature are useful in marking future directions for museums. Indeed, a move towards more people-oriented approaches and a consideration of all the parameters of cultural sustainability will benefit Cyprus on two levels. On a macro-level, this move will aid sustainable development and society in general by passing on to future generations a living, inclusive and more socially relevant sense of heritage, as well as ease political conflict through mutual understanding. On a micro-level, museums will be able to offer more inclusive and useful (re)construction of the past that would satisfy the needs of cultural tourists for authentic experiences.

Cyprus, like many other countries amidst political conflict, is likely to continue to follow the preservation paradigm, even though it is widely understood that the shift to more people-oriented approaches and a broader understanding of cultural sustainability is more consistent with recent theory and involves more inclusive and democratic practices. But this is not surprising. History has shown that when the national identity of a nation is newly formed or on unstable ground, a nation usually tries to avoid polyphony and instead uses heritage to construct a solid common past that will, it is imagined, unite its people (Aronsson 2011). For as long as Cyprus is involved in political conflict, it seems that the priority will be placed on top-down, object-oriented approaches and predetermined, strong museum narratives. So can a relatively newly-formed nation state such as Cyprus, with an unstable and contested national identity, change and move towards the 'new heritage' paradigm? Is change possible?

The answer to this question is not an easy one and we will not attempt to supply it here. As we have seen, politics and tourism are very powerful forces that dictate to a large degree what is highlighted as the cultural heritage of Cyprus. Whilst politics and tourism in Cyprus push for more top-down and object-oriented approaches, market and commercial forces, foreign influences (including those of the European Union) push for more bottom-up and people-oriented approaches. This is a struggle between different stakeholders with different priorities, and the future is uncertain. But before any change is possible, cultural policy makers as well as museum professionals first need to answer these questions: Whose culture is preserved and exhibited, for whom, and how do these practices influence national, local and personal identities? What is being omitted or obscured and why? Is change desirable, and why? If yes, what direction should change take? What strategies and policies are needed to achieve change?

Acknowledgements

A small part of this chapter was published in the *International Journal of Cultural Politics* (2014). We would like to thank the participants of the COST Action *IS 1007: Investigating Cultural Sustainability* for the interesting discussions and their useful feedback.

References

Apostolakis, A. 2003. The convergence process in heritage tourism. *Annals of Tourism Research* 30(4), 795–812.

Aronsson, P. 2011. Explaining national museums: exploring comparative approaches to the study of national museums. In S. Knell, P. Aronsson and A. B. Amundsen (eds), *National Museums: New Studies from Around the World*, Abingdon: Routledge, 29–54.

Boukas, N. 2013. Youth visitors' satisfaction in Greek cultural heritage destinations: the case of Delphi. *Tourism Planning and Development* 10(3), 285–306.

Boukas, N. 2014. Segmenting youth tourists to cultural heritage destinations: motivational determinants and experiential characteristics. *International Journal of Leisure and Tourism Marketing* 4(1), 63–89.

Boukas, N. and Ziakas, V. 2013. Impacts of the global economic crisis on Cyprus tourism and policy responses. *International Journal of Tourism Research* 15(4), 329–45.

Boukas, N. and Ziakas, V. 2014. A chaos theory perspective of destination crisis and sustainable tourism development in islands: the case of Cyprus. *Tourism Planning and Development* 11(2), 191–209.

Bounia, A. and Stylianou-Lambert, T. 2011. National museums in Cyprus: a story of heritage and conflict. In S. Knell and G. Elgenius (eds), *Building National Museums in Europe 1750–2010*, Conference proceedings from EuNaMus, European National Museums, Linköping, Sweden: Linköping University Electronic Press, 201–44.

Butcher, J. 2005. Cultural politics, cultural policy and cultural tourism. In M. Robinson and A. Phipps (eds), *Cultural Tourism in a Changing World: Politics, Participation and (Re)presentation*, Clevedon: Channel View Publications, 19–35.

Cohen, E. 1988. Authenticity and commoditization in tourism. *Annals of Tourism Research* 15(3), 371–86.

Council of Europe 2005. Framework Convention on the Value of Cultural Heritage for Society (Faro Convention). Council of Europe Treaty Series no. 199.

Fairclough, G. J. 2009. New heritage frontiers. In Council of Europe (ed.), *Heritage and Beyond*, Strasbourg: Council of Europe Publishing, 29–41.

Gordon, C. 2004. *European Programme of National Cultural Policy Reviews. Cultural Policy in Cyprus – European Experts' Report* [online]. Steering Committee for Culture. CDCULT(2004)07. Available at www.coe.int/t/dg4/cultureheritage/culture/reviews/cyprus_EN.asp (accessed 14 May 2013).

Hughes, H. and Allen, D. 2005. Cultural tourism in Central and Eastern Europe: the views of 'induced image formation agents'. *Tourism Management* 26(2), 173–83.

Kelly, C. 2005. Heritage tourism politics in Ireland. In M. Robinson and A. Phipps (eds), *Cultural Tourism in a Changing World: Politics, Participation and (Re)presentation*, Clevedon: Channel View Publications, 36–54.

Leriou, A. 2007. The Hellenisation of Cyprus: tracing its beginnings [un-updated version]. In S. Müller Celca and J.-C. David (eds), *Patrimoines culturels en Méditerranée orientale: recherché scientifique et enjeux identitaires*. 1er atelier (29 Nov. 2007): *Chypre, une stratigraphie de l'identité*. Lyon: Recontres Scientifiques en Ligne de la Maison de l'Orient et de la Mediterranée, 33pp. Available at www.mom.fr/sites/mom.fr/files/img/Ressources_numeriques_et_outils/Documents_numerises/Colloques_texte_integral/Patrimoines_culturels_en_Mediterranee_orientale/1er_atelier/Leriou_ed-2.pdf (accessed 25 January 2015).

Loizos, P. 1998. How might Turkish and Greek Cypriots see each other more clearly? In V. Calotychos (ed.), *Cyprus and Its People: Nation, Identity ad Experience in an Unimaginable Community*, Boulder, CO: Westview Press, 35–52.

MacCannell, D. 1973. Staged authenticity: arrangements of social space in tourist settings. *American Sociological Review* 79(3), 589–603.

Rizzo, I. and Throsby, D. 2006. Cultural heritage: economic analysis and public policy. In V. A. Ginsburgh and D. Throsby (eds), *Handbook of the Economics of Art and Culture, Vol. 1*, Amsterdam: North-Holland, 983–1016.

Sharpley, R. 1994. *Tourism, Tourists and Society*, Cambridgeshire: ELM Publications.

Shaw, G. and Williams, A. M. 2004. *Tourism and Tourism Spaces*, London: Sage.

Smith, M. K. 2003. *Issues in Cultural Tourism Studies*, London: Routledge.

Stylianou-Lambert, T. and Bounia, A. 2014. Resisting institutional power: the women of St Barnabas. *Visitor Studies* 17(1), 3–23.

Stylianou-Lambert, T., Boukas, N. and Christodoulou-Yerali, M. 2014. Museums and cultural sustainability: stakeholders, forces and cultural policies. *International Journal of Cultural Policy* 20(5), 566–87. DOI: 10.1080/10286632.2013.874420.

Taylor, J. 2001. Authenticity and sincerity in tourism. *Annals of Tourism Research* 28(1), 7–26.

Visual Sociology and Museum Studies Lab. 2013. Mapping of Cypriot museums: personnel and perceptions (PowerPoint presentation). Available at http://vsmslab.files.wordpress.com/2013/03/christodoulidou-lambert-powerpoint-presentation1.pdf (accessed 30 June 2014).

Waitt, G. 2000. Consuming heritage: perceived historical authenticity. *Annals of Tourism Research* 27(4), 835–62.

12 From dissonance to resilience

The heritage of Belgrade's Staro Sajmište

*Nevena Daković, Ljiljana Rogač Mijatović
and Mirjana Nikolić*

Introduction

This is a story of a place that has followed extremely turbulent paths, a place that has marked the fate of nearly 100,000 people, a place of many names and a place of 'dissonant voices' from the past. The first urbanised space on the left bank of the Sava River in Belgrade, the 'Old Fairground' – the Staro Sajmište – was originally built in 1937 as an international exhibition for the trade and industry of Serbia. But beginning in March 1942 with the arrival from Berlin of one of the notorious gas vans (*Gaswagen*), created for the mass killing of Jewish people during World War II, its trajectory changed and it became a death camp, a concentration camp and a place of torture and execution (but later a place of artistic life and creativity). It is this connection of Belgrade to Berlin, through the strong memories and symbols of the history of the Holocaust, that makes it particularly apposite to recall Karen Till's observation, in her book on memory and place in Berlin, that places 'are not only continuously interpreted, they are haunted by past structures of meaning and material presences from other times and lives' (Till 2005, 9). After seventy years of existence, the Fairground, this place of great historical significance, today exists as both a physical and a symbolic space, and one with strong dissonance at the core of its identity.

(Re)negotiating memory, history and place

The new ongoing concern for the past, the 'memory fever', is today being renegotiated between the forces of globalisation and the practices of local cultures. A new approach to framing history and memory is developing, which is in contrast to the dominant paradigms of modernity (Connerton 1991). This new perspective on the place of the past in the present addresses the changing nature of identities, especially national, in wider European and global contexts.

The relationship between collective memory and history is often treated as oppositional (Nora 1989). The term 'burden of history' most often refers to the uses and abuses of memory, whether manipulated blocked memory, commanded forgetting or the myriad abuses of historical appropriation (see Lowenthal 1998; Ricoeur 2009; Hall 2005; Assmann 2006).

> In all the debates over the relationship between memory and history, one constantly recurring theme is that although history is about the present, so too

is memory, and much more directly. Memory is still live and active, still charged with the weight of these contests, and it is to memory that one should turn in order to reveal 'what really happened'.

(Hodgkin and Radstone 2003, 1–2)

Memory is not a simple activation of stored data and information, but an active construction of identity, biography, and all the other elements that give us stability and continuity. Every moment we remember we also interpret; remembrances are always reinterpretations of and changes to our past. It is necessary to ask what the past actually means in the present, and for whom; and what people are to do with so many layered messages from the past. Thus selecting particular pasts to conserve is necessarily a matter of continuous negotiation among all interested parties (Mondale 1994, 15). Collective identities, as part of the imaginary field (Anderson 1991), are also being shaped in a constant battle of discourses, including memory battles. Identity reflects living processes in a society, the creation and change of social and cultural forms and contents, as well as the condition of absence of these changes. 'What to remember and what to forget' frames the cultural process of heritage that engages with acts of remembering to understand the present.

Drawing on the UNESCO definition of cultural heritage as the legacy inherited from past generations, maintained in the present and bestowed for the benefit of future generations, it is clear that heritage is an intergenerational phenomenon. On the other hand, heritage is valued in myriad ways and for myriad reasons, such as to bind communities together, but also to differentiate from others, or to construct identity and ensure continuity, as well as to manipulate the present and send political messages. The notion of universality in cultural heritage assumes that certain aspects of heritage are meaningful to all people, regardless of their cultural, social, political, and economic differences. But universality warrants closer critical attention. More and more, heritage has become distressing in character, shaming rather than laudatory, lamentable rather than lovable – what ancient Romans termed *heritas damnosa*, a damnable, crippling legacy with which the inheritors were stuck, like it or not. Heritage now is often laden with sorrow and guilt. The past still awakens pride in origins and precursors, but victimhood occupies centre-stage. It is often said that history belongs to the victors; heritage is now the special province of the victims (Lowenthal 2000, 17).

Within the field of 'critical heritage', special attention is given to the emerging concept of 'new heritage' (Fairclough 2008) and the opposing paradigms in reading heritage and history (Berkhofer 1997; Smith 2006). These questions of heritage as well as of history are conceptualised as a discourse mobilised for different social, political and cultural ends (O'Keeffe 2007). If heritage is the 'active processing' of the past, the cultural processes of the making and remaking of meaning and memory, it is related to the dialectical relation between material practices and the symbolic meanings that social agents attach to their environment. Discourses of heritage are entangled with the broader issue of the 'problematic past' with its conservation in terms of remembrance, inclusion and commemoration. The past is represented at heritage places that invoke often dissonant collective memories and create certain tensions within official accounts of heritage.

The dissonance of heritage

> The heritage creation process is controversial in a number of respects ... The idea of dissonance ... keeps at the forefront the ideas of discrepancy and incongruity. Dissonance in heritage involves a discordance or lack of agreement and consistency.
>
> (Ashworth and Tunbridge 1996, 20–2)

The concept of 'dissonant heritage' is located in the claim that heritage is a contemporary interpretation shaped by various narratives of history. Different meanings of the past create space for discordance and a lack of consensus over the heritage. Not only what is interpreted, but how it is interpreted and by whom, will create quite specific messages about the value and meaning of any given heritage place and the past it represents (ibid., 27). Dissonant or difficult heritage (Logan and Reeves 2008; Macdonald 2010), however, is part of the wider notion of the contested nature of heritage, because any heritage may be uncomfortable to someone, not only for the meanings or messages it carries, but also because of its particular power to legitimise someone's sense of place and identity. This collage of intersecting and overlapping meanings is not only a space where meaningful experiences occur, but is also where meanings are contested and negotiated.

> Heritage is dissonant – it is a constitutive social process that on the one hand is about regulating and legitimising, and on the other hand is about working out, contesting and challenging a range of cultural and social identities, sense of place, collective memories, values and meanings that prevail in the present and can be passed to the future.
>
> (Smith 2006, 82)

This contested nature of heritage implies that several different groups may claim, appropriate, use or exclude the cultural heritage of others as well as of themselves, or might seek to erase the markers and manifestations of such heritage. It is an exemplification of the dialogic narration and paradoxes of cultural heritage as prime battlegrounds for contested claims between different communities and groups (Silverman 2010, 2). Places of pain and trauma are far more than episodes in a single national or local community's history. Values and meanings of specific heritage places and the past they represent are at the core of the process of meaning-making and negotiation of history and memory.

If heritage were seen more as a process, it would not exclusively relate to protection, restoration or conservation, but it would call for understanding, changing and modifying, even replacing, and for sharing and using (Fairclough 2010, 30). This would further widen the scope of understanding heritage for sustainability, not only as a resource or outcome, but a process of negotiation, rethinking, resilience, innovation and creativity. This role of heritage means above all affirmation of certain values, as well as their becoming operative in order to enable sustainability of the place. Since sustainability has a strong normative component, this would mean building common goals and values of various social and political levels. Cultural sustainability itself could then be understood as a cultural evolution and a transformation of ways of life that will improve the life of communities and society in general.

The Old Fairground (Staro Sajmište)

Remembering and forgetting

The twentieth-century history of Southeast Europe is filled with many dichotomies, partly due to the particular ideologies of the time but also because of the peripheral position of this region that derives from deeper historical reasons (Kuljić 2010). These dichotomies are especially vivid in terms of types of heritage 'that bond and divide, places which remain neglected as the "heritage of others"' (Dragićević Šešić 2011) and are not used for community development.

The Old Fairground is a heritage place, a testimony of great importance for the identities of people and communities, which provides a living presence of the past. This historical place is a part of the everyday urban environment of present-day Belgrade and of Serbia more widely. With its multilayered identities and meanings, the Old Fairground marked the rise and fall of culture and society through several decades. It is a place that contains very many different messages and layers of memories intertwined as part of heritage. Over time it has received numerous meanings; today it exists as a multiple symbol-bearer.

The story of the Fairground was and still is marked by this 'dual symbolism', standing between the 'dark past' and a 'bright future'. The symbolism of the place within the identity of Belgrade is undoubtedly another important issue that is treated from the point of view of the institutionalised public memory. Through its institutions, a society or a nation produces shared sites, *lieux de mémoire* (Nora 1989), that are material, symbolic and functional. The timeline of the memory narrative of the Old Fairground is divided into several nodes that use the World War II period as the key point in relation to which all the others are identified, ethically, memorially and emotionally. Jovan Byford (Byford 2011) proposes a systematic recognition of several sometimes overlapping periods:

1937–1941	The Old Fairground
1941–1942	The *Judenlager*
1942–1944	The *Anhalterlager*
1948–1960	The headquarters of the Youth Brigades followed by the artists' colony
1957–1974	The first steps toward memorialisation
1984–1990	The Old Fairground as an anti-fascist monument
1990s	A symbol of martyrdom: the Serbian *Yad Vashem*.

Such a broad chronological order, however, can obscure details of high importance and interest for the re-profiling, in spontaneous and unexpected ways, of the *lieux de mémoire* into *lieux de culture*.

As Byford's periodisation (Byford n.d.) shows,the post-war era added a number of historical layers to the Holocaust site as the remaining original fairground pavilions were turned to new, and multiple, purposes. In the 1990s, the (hi)story of the Semlin *Judenlager* became a rediscovered or newly discovered object of attention when urban planners began to rethink their projects for the larger area of the Old Fairground, not knowing how to handle its complex history. Various solutions were offered, such as turning the site into an open air space for cultural events, using it for the new Belgrade opera (an idea dating to 1968), or preserving it in its original form as a Holocaust Memorial ground, a Serbian *Yad Vashem* (ultimately deriving from a 1965 concept of 'memorial bank'). The Old Fairground space became entangled in controversies over claims that the memories of the Holocaust were being erased; debates began about the 'final metastasis' of historical revisionism, shifting views and evaluations of World War II, and contemporary political instrumentations of a traumatic past (Daković and Uspenski 2014, 197).

The concentration camp

The most significant layer of memory in the historical significance of Belgrade's Old Fairground undoubtedly derives from the trauma of the Holocaust, initially the loss of about 7,000 Jewish lives in the *Judenlager* (the Jewish camp established on the fairground site), and subsequently from 1942 in the *Anhaltslager* (a temporary detention camp that replaced it) of about 33,000 citizens of Serbian and other nationalities and of people with different political orientations. Many prisoners died of hunger, cold, illness and inhumane treatment by the camp authorities, while others went to die a horrible death in the gas-trucks. This place is an important memory *topos*, both in the history of the annihilation of European Jews and as a crucial part of the history of the Holocaust in Serbia.

Unlike some other places of memory, traumatic places like this are multilayered, with many meanings, filled with memories and different interpretations, thus causing much confusion, conflict and irritation (Assmann 2006, 287).

The concentration camp at the Old Fairground was not only the biggest German concentration camp in Serbia but also in the European southeast and, as such, it bears strong testimony to this tragic period of twentieth-century Europe. The 'Semlin' *Judenlager* (named after the German version of Zemun, an adjacent town) is a specific case in the history of the Holocaust, because of how the community of interned Jews lived and how they were killed in the gas van in the spring of 1942 (Schelach 1987). This event is seen by Holocaust historians as an important landmark in the escalation of Nazi policy towards Jews and of the idea of the wholesale killing of European Jews that was later pursued in concentration camps such as Auschwitz (Browning 2010, 423). What happened in the *Judenlager* and the *Anhaltslager* on the Old Fairground site is therefore of particular significance to both Holocaust history and the history of Belgrade and Serbia. To borrow the description of Milan Koljanin, between December 1941 and March 1942

> in only four months ... more than 7,000 Jews were killed in the camp, and Serbia was the first country in Europe in which the 'Jewish question was solved'. After the Jews were executed, the concentration camp at the Old Fairground became a killing field of captured partisan and 'chetnik' fighters, as well as civilians captured in areas where fighting took place. By April 1944, around 90,000 people had passed through, and around 40,000 were killed in the 'Transitional Camp at Zemun'.
>
> (Koljanin 1992, 15, authors' translation)

Regardless of the fact that the *Anhaltslager* was located in the Independent State of Croatia within occupied Serbia, it was controlled by the German military police (Pavlowitch 2007, 69). Local authorities, police and individuals in this country, however, also played a significant role. It was because of the domestic support that 'solving the Jewish question' was achieved with such efficiency. Thus, in relation to the reduction of the role of local collaborators there has been an emphasis on the role of other collaborators (Manošek 2007). This represents part of the difficult heritage for Serbia – a part of the contested past that lives in the present.

Another difficult issue of this heritage place is that the camp was basically on the border, and just across the river from the Belgrade city centre, from where everyone could view the camp so clearly that it was even possible to identify people's faces. The gas vans were transporting Jews from the Old Fairground site to Jajinci on the outskirts of Belgrade, and their route passed through the city centre itself. The cries of the crammed passengers were heard until they were suffocated by toxic gas, for the sake of the efficient destruction of these people and their secret burials in mass graves (Browning 2010).

In the Allied bombing of Yugoslavia in 1944, a large part of the Old Fairground was destroyed and many lives were lost. The complex was never rebuilt as was the case with some other concentration camps, like Jasenovac, on the territory of the by then ex-Independent State of Croatia. This has remained a battlefield for endless debates on the bombing of concentration camps, and the attempts to hide genocide and the Holocaust in systematic and permanent oblivion. These uses of heritage as a powerful political resource served for the legitimisation of values and meanings by dominant groups which in turn produced a dissonance of the heritage place for many years to come.

Dissonance

The multilayered symbolism and dissonant identity of the Old Fairground is – to take a step backwards – related to the narrative of industrial progress and modernity of a city. That this was the location between 1937 and 1941 of the first industrial fair in the Kingdom of Yugoslavia bears witness to other aspects of the historical importance of this place. Construction of the Fairground began in 1937 when the central tower was built along with five Yugoslav pavilions, the Italian, Hungarian, Romanian and Czechoslovakian pavilions, and Spasic's Pavilion, named after a wealthy Serbian entrepreneur. Later in 1938 the Turkish and German pavilions were added. The Fairground was intended to put on show the ambitions of the young European kingdom and to display the technological advancement and industrial endeavours of Yugoslav society. Its internationalist, modernist architectural style was based on the idea of Yugoslavian-hood. It was also built as an important industrial and merchant complex, its construction not only advancing a modern image of Belgrade but also marking the beginning of Europeanisation on all levels of urbanity. It was a first urban 'oasis' across the river – a dream come true for the city of progress that opened the door to Europe. In 1938, the first television programme in the Balkans was broadcast in one of the pavilions. By a paradoxical turn of events, this gateway to Europe and to modern industrial progress became the gateway to torture, suffering and death.

In the post-war years the pavilions were put to new uses. The new authorities and their Youth Brigades used the Old Fairground to help build the new city, the beginning of the development of New Belgrade within Serbia's post-war recovery, giving rise to new uses for this heritage place. After the Youth Brigades that were in charge of these processes had left in 1951, artists from the Association of Fine Artists of Serbia moved into the pavilions, and created an avant-garde artists' colony. Their studios and vivid artistic life added another layer to the dissonance of the Old Fairground. The 'Belgrade Montmartre', as the Old Fairground was sometimes popularly known, provided a space for artists who had made significant achievements, some of them internationally, such as Olga Jevrić, Mladen Srbinović and Mića Popović, who had been elected to the Serbian Academy of Sciences and Arts. The atelier of Mića Popović in the Italian Pavilion served as the stage for the legendary event that was the performance of Samuel Beckett's play *Waiting for Godot* after it had been cancelled at the Belgrade Drama Theatre, probably because of political pressure. This performance of *Godot* in 1954 left a significant mark on the Serbian intelligentsia of that time (Miller 2007, 39–40).

In socialist Yugoslavia, within a broader political rhetoric of the heroism and suffering of all Yugoslav peoples, the Old Fairground was treated as a place where the tragic struggle of progressive mankind against fascism had left its mark. By 1972, however, there were discussions about completely demolishing all of the *sajmište* (fairground), and hence the *Judenlager* and *Anhaltslager* buildings, to make way for the construction of a new opera house, for which an international architectural competition was opened. Later, in the 1990s after the break-up of Yugoslavia, the Old Fairground became one of the main arenas for the Serbian and Croatian propaganda war and mutual accusations of fascist collaboration, yet another exemplification of imputed memory and political abuses at this heritage place.

These stories about the Old Fairground only tackle the surface of the past that shaped the dissonant 'destiny' of this heritage place. During the entire post-war period the site has been the subject of controversy, not only in terms of whether it should be (only) a place of remembrance, but also in terms of what should be remembered (Byford 2011, 15). In addition, commemorative practices in Serbia after the end of

World War II indicate that in spite of its importance as a Holocaust site, in post-war Yugoslav society the Old Fairground held a marginal place in the memorialisation of the destruction of Serbian Jews. The memory of the destruction of the Jews has almost been made invisible by emphasising other symbolic and ideological orders.

Although declared a monument of high architectural, artistic and cultural significance in Belgrade in 1987, the Old Fairground, one of the largest places of the suffering of the Jews in the Nazi Holocaust in Serbia, has not been adequately marked. While originally there were twelve buildings within the Fairground complex, only the central tower (Figure 12.1) and five former pavilions (the Czechoslovakian, Hungarian, German, Italian, Turkish and Spasic's) still stand, along with the barracks that were built after the war.

Figure 12.1 Central tower of the Staro Sajmište, Belgrade, in 2013
Photo: L. Rogač Mijatović.

Today the Old Fairground is almost unrecognisable in space. It has the appearance of a city slum, housing about 2,500 low-income residents of Belgrade, and it is suffering damage from neglected maintenance and illegal property usage. Although officially acclaimed as a memorial place, it nevertheless hosts catering, entertainment, fun and sports facilities and programmes, which many see as conflicting with the memorial significance and values of the place. There are almost no (only two) signs of remembrance: a commemorative board from the 1980s and a monument from the 1990s (Figure 12.2) as examples of previous, controversial, political interventions.

From dissonance to resilience

Belgrade's Old Fairground site is a memorial and a place of Holocaust; it is a symbol of suffering and trauma, but also a symbol of urban architectural modernity and of the artistic avant-garde, as well as a slum in the urban city matrix. The very different interpretations of the meaning of the Old Fairground, as well as the politics of oblivion, remain the main context in which its core purpose and future goals are being shaped. This place of trauma and memory is still tortured by the dissonant voices from the past, as well as from the present. The heritage cannot be escaped and the community plays an important role in determining, and thereby memorising its own cultural heritage. This is the question of both resilience to decay and sustainability of this place.

Figure 12.2 Monument to the Victims, on the Old Fairground site, Belgrade, erected in
          1995, the work of the sculptor Miodrag Popović

Photo: L. Rogač Mijatović.

Connecting different layers of time into one specific and historically relevant place as an important articulation of history and of memory, but also of forgetting, means addressing the episodes that were covered with the sediments of new concepts and meanings. It is a brave attempt to grasp dispersed elements of an untold history, as well as to organise these into one consistent narrative that sheds light on a traumatic episode, a 'chronotope' of the past which, due to its own undisclosed history, has become the 'forbidden area', a secret trauma, a part of the 'amputated geography' of Belgrade.

Even though the Old Fairground is characterised by extreme changes of purpose during a relatively short chronological period, the remaining structures do have potential for a sustainable reconfiguration. Buildings surviving from the period of the Fair are in bad condition, especially the central tower. Only a few hundred metres further down the river bank there are restaurants and night clubs that brought Belgrade the reputation of the 'New York of the Balkans' and of 'the city that never sleeps'. In contrast to this, there are semi-illegal slums, settlements of the poor and a large green area growing wild and unattended. It is underlined by the transformations that the compound has already lived through – from trade and exhibition space to concentration camp and then to residential neighbourhood. Contemporary ideas – becoming a museum space, a shopping mall or a cultural centre – vacillate among the remains of already lived-through stages, confirming that there is a need for a new 'heritage literacy' in and with the community, rather than about it.

The polarised concept of the area reflects the general disinterested and ignorant attitude of the city and government, confirmed by the dazzling project of the 'Belgrade Waterfront' planned for the opposite bank of the river and financed by multinational corporations. This Dubai-inspired project would be positioned between the dilapidated buildings of the old city behind it and the equally, or even more dilapidated pavilions of the Old Fairground. Thus, if nothing is done in the meantime, the left bank would be left as a kind of ghost with images of trauma and terror hovering above it, while the right bank would be a fast growing, exclusive, globalised and rich business and residential zone. Restoring the pre-war purpose of the Fairground by providing space for economic activities also implies more complex issues regarding its memorial purpose.

A deeper reconfiguration would be the sustainability of the cultural/historical heritage determined by the nature of the space through the decades and its sense of place. As the British forensic archaeologist Caroline Sturdy Colls suggests,

> [t]he role of the people who have been living here since the war should be duly acknowledged. Because in actual fact, the people who have lived in these buildings have played a role in preserving them. Many of these buildings wouldn't be here if people hadn't lived in them. Not only did the residents of the site prevent its structures from degenerating into rubble – as happens after the long-term inoccupation of a building – but their number and distribution over the entire site has successfully hindered the realisation of several redevelopment plans during the post-World War II period – which could have

meant the destruction of the historical buildings to make room for a denser or more profitable urban quarter. Based on these findings, our claim – which we publicly put forward on the occasion of the public forum – was the following: rather than evict the people living and working in Staro Sajmište, the City of Belgrade has a duty towards them, and surely must include them as an active party in any future plan for commemoration.

(www.forensic-architecture.org/case/living-death-camps/)

As a postscript to the story of the Old Fairground, it is worth asking what future there is for this place of multilayered, dissonant memory and identity, and whether cultural heritage such as this can be well managed and promoted while at the same time kept within parameters that would diminish contestation. After a number of mainly civil society initiatives, the City of Belgrade has adopted a formal project for the 'Memorial Complex of Staro Sajmište', including the reconstruction of the central tower, as well as the Italian and the Czechoslovakian pavilions which the City owns. The complex would also host a Memorial Centre for victims and a Research Documentation Centre. Until the Old Fairground comes out of the maze of jurisdiction in relation to issues of legal and financial status, it is important to revive the memory narratives that will encourage greater understanding of the common cultural heritage of Serbia, Europe and the world. Restoring the relevant values is at the core of ideas that lead to the sustainability of this place.

Conclusion

This chapter has examined the place of the Old Fairground in its various stages in the context of the value of incorporating building memory and *lieux de mémoire* into the plans for cultural sustainability of community and society. Facing the past, and facing the trauma on the national level of being both victim and perpetrator, is an important element in the construction of a functional state and its sustainable future (in all aspects). An escape into oblivion is a short-term solution that might bring relief to some but cannot be a sustainable foundation for the years to come.

People are constantly involved in the intertwining processes of remembering, forgetting, communication and appropriation of values. But although every local or national government of different periods had its own particular ideas for what to do with the space, the lack of real movement and solutions confirm the Old Fairground to be highly resistant to being hidden or pushed out of mind; it has resilience in the sense of being a location out of time and out of space – or conversely *of* all times and all space. Its (hi)story might be seen as a universal metaphor for all forms of individual and collective suffering and victimisation, and of the total absence of guilt and responsibility for that.

The reasons for the stalemate surrounding Staro Sajmište are enigmatic and complex. One might be the various nationally-biased interpretations of the multidirectional memory narrative that the Semlin *Judenlager* in particular has become. The monument, even though outside the territory of the camp, appropriately stands as the traditional method of memory preservation and an alibi for further passivity and the absence of acts or engagement regarding the space/time meanings. However, the cyclical initiatives for the revival of memory against forgetting, sustainability and development must not be left to some *deus ex machina*, but should be handled by and decided on by the community and the government.

Individual responsibility ranges from personal to national, from local to global: it is a part of many social segments. In terms of sustainability, this comes through a set of ecological, economic, ethical and aesthetic issues of memory. Sustainability through culture defines survival and maps out the future. The choice of forgetting and oblivion opens the door for the return of barbarism: an evasion of coming eye-to-eye with trauma annihilates the very possibility of memory rescue and healing through memory construction.

There are multiple challenges for cultural heritage on the path from dissonance to resilience. Understanding the value and meaning of heritage requires interaction between people and between communities – the sense of belonging and continuity for generations to come. Focus must be placed on multiple voices rather than singular ones, in order to make room for the previously excluded and the silenced and to show concern for future 'ways to live together'.

References

Anderson, B. 1991. *Imagined Communities*, London: Verso.

Ashworth, G. and Tunbridge, J. 1996. *Dissonant Heritage: The Management of the Past as a Resource in Conflict*, Chichester: Wiley.

Assmann, A. 2006. *Der lange Schatten der Vergangenheit. Erinnerungskultur und Geschichtspolitik*, Munich: C. H. Beck.

Berkhofer, R. F. 1997. *Beyond the Great Story: History as Text and Discourse*, Cambridge, MA: Harvard University Press.

Browning, C. 2010. *The Origins of the Final Solution. The Evolution of Nazi Jewish Policy, September 1939–March 1942*, London: William Heinemann.

Byford, J. 2011. *Staro Sajmište: mesto sećanja, zaborava i sporenja*, Belgrade: Beogradski Centarzal Judska Prava.

Byford, J. n.d. *Semlin Judenlager in Serbian Public Memory*. www.open.ac.uk/socialsciences/semlin/en/ (accessed 19/11/2014).

Connerton, P. 1991. *How Societies Remember*, Cambridge: Cambridge University Press.

Daković, N. and Uspenski, I. 2014. The Memory of the Holocaust and the New Hyper/Cyber-Textuality. In M. Cornis-Pope (ed.), *New Literary Hybrids in the Age of Multimedia Expression. Crossing Borders, Crossing Genres*, Amsterdam: John Benjamin, 193–206.

Dragićević Šešić, M. 2011. Cultural Policies, Identities and Monument Building in Southeastern Europe. In A. Milohnić and N. Švob-Đokić (eds), *Cultural Identity Politics in the (Post-) transitional Societies: Cultural Transitions in Southeastern Europe*, Zagreb: Institute for International Relations, 31–46.

Fairclough, G. 2008. New Heritage, an Introductory Essay: People, Landscape and Change. In G. Fairclough, R. Harrison, J. Schofield and J. H. Jameson Jr (eds), *The Heritage Reader*, London: Routledge, 297–312.

Fairclough, G. 2010. Community and Culture, Society and Sustainability: The Faro Convention on the Value of Cultural Heritage for Society. In Heritage Council Ireland, *Heritage Outlook*, Summer 2010, 29–31. www.heritagecouncil.ie/fileadmin/user_upload/heritageoutlook/Outlook_Summer_2010.pdf (accessed 25 January 2015).

Forensic Architecture Research Project. www.forensic-architecture.org/case/living-death-camps

Hall, S. 2005. Whose Heritage? Un-settling 'The Heritage', Re-imagining the Post-nation. In J. Littler and R. Naidoo (eds), *The Politics of Heritage: The Legacies of 'Race'*, London: Routledge, 21–31.

Hodgkin, K. and Radstone, S. 2003. Introduction: Contested Pasts. In K. Hodgkin and S. Radstone (eds), *Contested Pasts: The Politics of Memory*, London: Routledge, 1–22.

Koljanin, M. 1992. *Nemački Logorna Beogradskom Sajmištu: 1941–1944*, Belgrade: Institut za Savremenu Istoriju.

Kuljić, T. 2010. *Umkämpfte Vergangenheiten: Die Kultur der Erinnerung im post-jugoslawischen Raum*, Berlin: Verbrecher Verlag.

Logan, W. and Reeves, K. 2008. *Places of Pain and Shame: Dealing with 'Difficult Heritage'*, London: Routledge.

Lowenthal, D. 1998. *The Heritage Crusade and the Spoils of History*, Cambridge: Cambridge University Press.

Lowenthal, D. 2000. Stewarding the Past in a Perplexing Present. In E. Avrami, R. Mason and M. de la Torre (eds), *Values and Heritage Conservation Research Report*, Los Angeles: The Getty Conservation Institute, 18–25.

Macdonald, S. 2010. *Difficult Heritage: Negotiating the Nazi Past in Nuremberg and Beyond*, London: Routledge.

Manošek, V. 2007. *Holokaust u Srbiji: Vojnao Kupaciona Politika i Uništavanje Jevreja 1941–1942*, Belgrade: Službeni list SRJ.

Miller, N. 2007. *The Nonconformists: Culture, Politics, and Nationalism in a Serbian Intellectual Circle, 1944–1991*, Budapest: Central European University Press.

Mondale, C. 1994. Conserving a Problematic Past. In M. Hufford (ed.), *Conserving Culture: A New Discourse on Heritage*, Urbana: University of Illinois Press, 15–23.

Nora, P. 1989. Between Memory and History: Les Lieux de Mémoire. *Representations* 26(Spring), 7–24.

O'Keeffe, T. 2007. Landscape and Memory: Historiography, Theory, Methodology. In N. Moore and Y. Whelan (eds), *Heritage, Memory and the Politics of Identity: New Perspectives on the Cultural Landscape*, London: Ashgate, 3–18.

Pavlowitch, S. K. 2007. *Hitler's New Disorder: The Second World War in Yugoslavia*, New York: Columbia University Press.

Ricoeur, P. 2009. *Memory, History, Forgetting*, Chicago: University of Chicago Press.

Schelach, M. 1987. Sajmište: An Extermination Camp in Serbia. *Holocaust and Genocide Studies* II(2), 243–60.

Silverman, H. 2010. *Contested Cultural Heritage: Religion, Nationalism, Erasure, and Exclusion in a Global World*, Berlin: Springer.

Smith, L. 2006. *Uses of Heritage*, London: Routledge.

Till, K. 2005. *The New Berlin: Memory, Politics, Place*, Minneapolis: University of Minnesota Press.

Aftermath or futures
Concluding thoughts

Elizabeth Auclair and Graham Fairclough

Transferability, transmission and transition

The contributors came to this book from many different disciplinary or national contexts, bringing disparate experiences and cultural memories of both the past few decades and of events in earlier European history that have shaped present-day culture and social life. This book thus displays something of the shared problems and challenges that exist across Europe, and the similarities of changing approaches to them over the past century. Because the book was produced as part of a COST Action, most of the contributors were able to meet during the Action's workshops to co-design the book, exchange views and compare their emerging case studies. This is not always the case with edited collections of papers, and we think the additional coherence and interconnectivity of the collection is visible.

The principal cross-cutting themes that were used to frame the writing of the book's chapters were outlined in our Introduction, as were the book's main threads that we recognised during the editing process. In this conclusion we now try to draw out some common ideas, focusing on both the similarities and the contrasts contained in the various chapters. Beginning with their general transferability as well as specificity, we believe that the case studies in this book contain a basic level of transferability – of theory, analysis, conclusions and perhaps lessons – from one side of Europe to the other, from post-Soviet Estonia to divided Cyprus, with their very different histories and heritage, or from Bristol to Belgrade. If this is true, these essentially European narratives will have relevance to other continents, just as, for example, heritage and sustainability ideas from indigenous, colonial or 'simply' divided contexts in Australia, Africa, Asia or the Americas have relevance in Europe. In other words, our case studies transcend their origins to touch on issues of cultural sustainability common to all humankind.

In this conclusion we also look back to the book's subtitle, specifically the transmission of heritage and culture from past to future. This is a transfer that needs to be made in the light of a culturally-centred sustainable development. Some lines of future investigation and research arise from the case studies that might help to make the heritage/culture/sustainability relationship more utilitarian and embedded in policy. Our conclusions, therefore, are poised between past and future, just as are the societies and cultures, and the communities and places, studied in the book.

We see two opposing ways of understanding the present; both appear to have resonances for sustainability. In one view, the present day is simply the narrow threshold between past and future, and the process of transition is more important than the present day per se, just as the starting and end points of a journey are generally regarded as more important than the journey itself. The 'present' is such a fleeting moment that perhaps it can only be appreciated and used as an interface, a transition. When sustainability discourse speaks of inter-generational transfer, or inter-community equity transfer, we should recall that our theories, plans and policy to achieve these things are made in what very rapidly becomes the past. The alternate (*sic*) view is about learning to live with and in the present, as the increasingly international 'slow' movement suggests. This way of seeing the present places much greater emphasis on the journey itself, recognising that whole lives can be lived 'between' past and future. It could be argued that sustainability, especially perhaps culturally focused sustainability, is partly created by not necessarily having goals, especially those connected to ever-continuing growth towards an imagined future, but instead by going along in life, relaxing, and enjoying the journey without knowing where it will lead, without always fixing goals, that may often actually never be reached.

Aftermath anxiety

It is striking how many chapters and case studies in this book have narratives built round some concept of aftermath, of being post- something. Post-industrial landscapes are discussed (and for that matter, post-agricultural in areas with high levels of land abandonment or of peri-urban sprawl), post-colonial contexts, post-crash problems, post-Soviet and post-war periods, and of course the spread everywhere of urban or urbanised lifestyles, which might well be termed post-rural. It is true that every town or society can consider that the present situation comes after something else, but today's apparently heightened concern for the past and for aftermaths that is evidenced here seems to go beyond that truism, beyond the mere fact that every historical period, every landscape, every society is built on its predecessors. In this book the 'after' seems to be portrayed as almost always worse and less sustainable than what came before.

In Britain, the term 'post-war' for identifying the years after 1945 was stretched in use until long after it became necessary to ask 'which war'. Only in the last decade or two has it begun to be qualified, and replaced by other formulations, notably 'post-Thatcher', and most recently 'post-crash', although the latter example denotes an ongoing crisis, rather than something safely in the past. In France, there is a feeling of living *après les Trente Glorieuses*, after the fortunate and prosperous thirty-year period of growth between 1945 and 1975. The passing of this wealthy period is regretted (even though it did a lot of harm to the planet), rather as in Ireland the demise in the crash of 2008 of the so-called 'Celtic Tiger' (a label denoting the few years of hectic 'boom', of rapid impetuous growth, since 1995) is regretted even whilst being severely criticised for having 'wrecked' the nation's countryside.

Everywhere, it seems, there is a 'post' period, a 'post'-event feeling. It may of course be a good thing to be 'post' some things (e.g. post-war). Often it is nostalgia, which seems normal and understandable, because changes are not always positive for people and communities. An example is in the case of major regeneration and housing renewal projects conducted in Paris suburbs (and in many other cities across Europe and indeed the rest of the metropolitan world) when inhabitants are worried or sad because their houses or towers are torn down and their neighbourhood completely transformed, because the familiar place where they have lived – their landscape, their heritage – is being 'disappeared'. They are in a situation on the verge of becoming 'post'. But sometimes the 'aftermath anxiety' seems to go deeper than nostalgia. The French philosopher Edgar Morin, in his books *Où va le monde?* ('Where's the world going?') and *Vers l'abîme?* ('Towards the abyss?') has raised crucial questions. In an ostensibly pessimistic voice, he in fact points to where changes in our ways of considering the world and civilisation (for example, promoting culture or even cultural sustainability through civil society movements) can improve the world or change its direction. This profound interlinking of cultural attitudes and sentiments with socio-economic change, which we see in all our case studies, and which adds to the complexities of finding sustainable ways forward that are ethically based, does, however, seem to us to argue against culture being merely a fourth pillar of sustainable development. Culture, rather than being freestanding, impinges on and shapes all aspects of sustainability and dictates the form and response to many challenges, such as growth, social equity and environmental damage.

The phenomenon that our Serbian contributors termed 'memory fever' is presumably related to this set of cultural attitudes about aftermaths, but whether as cause or effect is not entirely clear. This 'fever' refers to the apparently growing public interest in history, in the past, in re-enactment, in the appropriation of others' heritage. It is, in these current years, most clearly shown in the many ceremonies of remembrance and commemoration, almost 'in real time', day by day in some cases, of the 100th anniversary of the First World War, although that is just the latest, if perhaps the most extreme and widespread, example.

Cities, places and other scales

The book as a whole is mainly urban in its preoccupations and interests. Almost every chapter is directly concerned with cities and towns; where they are not it can be argued that rural heritage is being seen and reconstructed from urban perspectives. Is this where cultural sustainability mostly resides, in the urban frame? The city has always been a crucible for culture and creativity. The word 'culture' etymologically links itself to agriculture, to farming, to the shaping of nature, but at the same time, if a person is said to be 'cultured' (or cultivated) she or he is also likely to be thought to be 'civilised', that is, a dweller in a city, so the connection between city and culture has been long-made. Our reasons for choosing to include so many urban/civic case studies were given in the Introduction, but the fact that half the world's population, and much more of Europe's, is now urban or lives urban lifestyles, was a major reason. We are aware, however, that the relationship between culture and sustainable development raises issues in many other spheres, many of which will be examined in other books in this Culture and Sustainable Development series, such as the nature/culture interface, sustainable regional and rural planning, and the place of arts and culture in sustainable cities. Yet this book leaves us thinking that it would be interesting to see a similar range of case studies from rural contexts, or perhaps from the standpoint of different scales other than place, whether urban or rural.

As we have said previously, most of the chapters in this book focus to one degree or another on 'place', which on the whole is predisposed to a particular scale that is mainly if not exclusively local. Heritage and culture are not, however, confined to place. Aspects of both can exist within, that is below, the level of place. They can also transcend place in the sense that a particular type of heritage or cultural activity or memory can occur in many places and perhaps in different contexts at the same time; outcropping is perhaps a good metaphor here. For example, a varied and diverse range of heritage sites might be united by a single label (World Heritage for example) or by journeys (cultural pathways). Then, also, there is the question of 'national heritage' – easy to dismiss as imposed and undemocratic, but nonetheless a powerful force and not always, perhaps, one that causes problems, as long as distinctions are drawn between 'national' and 'nationalistic'. Both culture and heritage can be 'carried' within landscape, which is a scaleable concept functioning from the ultra-local to the supra-national.

Looking higher up the scale, what are we to make within cultural sustainability discourse of the frequently summoned ambitions of a common 'European heritage', a European identity, the 'European landscape', a shared European culture? All continents might well reach out for similar overarching unities. What of the truly global view: surely there is a more representative and democratic notion to be constructed of global heritage or culture than the World Heritage 'list of the best'? Risks can be seen in such ideas, risks of homogenisation, globalisation or the subordination of other scales of identity and being. Yet the ability to hold on to multiple scales of identity (in other words for a person to 'have' more than one place or landscape, to have multiple identities as a member of a household, a family, a tribe, a community of interest, a city, region, country and more global communities) might be argued, as have thinkers like Amartya Sen, for example in his book *Identity and Violence*, to be a part of human culture and a goal of sustainability in its own right.

Similarity and difference, specificity and generality

The similarities between our case studies are sometimes obscured by manifesting themselves in different vocabularies and ideologies. All places and histories are exceptional but they can offer exemplars of wider currency than their own city or even nation. The stories they tell are present-day situations, but they are rooted in history, although from different historic periods, and it is thus necessary to be aware of historical specificity as well as place-specifics. Different regions of

Europe have followed different trajectories (not always linear) through time, even within the short duration of the twentieth century but even more so in the *longue durée*, for instance (to keep things in bounds) of the past ten centuries, the second millennium CE. Behind the superficial and obvious place-specific details of individual case studies, there are similarities in terms of management and of cultural and social sustainability, and throughout this book important comparisons can be dug out. Common problems and challenges, and common reactions to them, can be seen; perhaps more to the point, relevant parallels, analogues and even solutions can be found in other places. One of the virtues of a book like this is that it encourages a glance over the horizon that reveals another world, one that might or might not be similar, but one from which useful perceptions and perhaps lessons can be brought home. Further, because we are dealing here with culture and heritage, those horizons are not only geographic but chronological; the view over some horizons can be to another time as well as another place. The sort of comparative research that this book offers is needed on a much wider scale, as are international research networks that bring people together – physically not virtually – to help us know what is happening elsewhere.

Nonetheless, we cannot ignore the strong element of place-specificity in heritage and perhaps almost as much in culture more generally, which means that global solutions for moving towards sustainability can be difficult to impose. These specificities are very often cultural in character, the product of particular histories and of adaptations to particular geographical contexts. Solutions and ways forward therefore need to be culturally based, and this again argues for culture being a fundamental framework of sustainability. Human beings have always been aware of their past and of their predecessors' legacy, but the particular shape that modern ideas of heritage take is only a couple of centuries old, and has changed significantly even in that brief period of time; the conservation, 'rescue'-type approach is even younger, and a 'new' heritage philosophy seems to be arising, if slowly and intermittently. It is worth reminding ourselves of this, because what we might take if we are not careful as being a wholly and commendable 'natural' (and thus irreversible) evolution of heritage practice, or an improved paradigm to replace outmoded or even 'wrong' views, is also 'merely' contingent on current ideological, economic and social assumptions, all of which are culturally determined, or shaped by environmental pressures, which themselves change rapidly. There are already some signs that a future society – or some section of it: neoliberal politicians come to mind – might start to wonder if there is any room for heritage in (for example) post-crash or post-peak oil worlds if (as) they reach the 'limits to growth'. Except of course that heritage is a cultural phenomenon, and human beings, or at least human society, seem not to be able to live without a past. The past, or its traces and memories, shape all dimensions of sustainability, although usually (through lack of academic research and absence of political awareness) its role goes largely unnoticed or is thought to be nature's voice. Perhaps a bigger cause for worry is that some politicians re-attach heritage to nationalistic perspectives.

The relentless contingency of heritage and culture leads also to dynamism, however. Heritage cannot be static, and attempts to preserve buildings and places 'forever' – to 'save them' – will not be more than transient in the longer span of time that sustainability demands as its frame. Contingency creates continual renewal as the surrounding cultural circumstances change. Even generational change in attributing meaning and deciding what is valuable, and why, is not a long-term corrective to old 'errors', but merely a new temporary contingency. Little is ever permanently resolved, but instead there is a continual remaking and shifting-around of social meaning.

Narrative, and new modes of heritage

The important issue is perhaps the methods by which new and changing meanings are constructed and passed on or replaced. The case studies in this book repeatedly return to the idea of narratives (or equivalents, such as museum displays) and the important role they have in defining heritage and in driving changes in attitude and perception. Some of the narratives look *towards* heritage, to establish a particular building or place in public consciousness as something valuable and significant; other narratives emerge *from* heritage and contribute to broader stories that are valuable to society for understanding and consensus on issues such as identity, ideology, history and social cohesion. We mentioned this in the Introduction as well, because it seems a crucial result of the book, showing that in all these European countries, actors are shifting away (or trying to move away) from official and authorised, institutional and legitimated, and fixed but partial representations of heritage and national (or local) narratives. There is no longer agreement that a single heritage exists, or that heritage should last forever.

These new ideas are buttressed by an increasingly large academic literature and by the Council of Europe's Faro Convention and its associated documents, for example on conflict reconciliation, and by the recent UNESCO HUL recommendation. They have been developing since at least the 1980s but have not taken root everywhere or strongly. They have not yet in many places found full support at governmental levels (and perhaps if they did they would begin to become over-legitimated). Nor do they have broad agreement across the more conservative parts of the heritage sector or in academia, which can sometimes see within these ideas a challenge to conventional fundamental principles such as the primacy of the physical fabric of heritage or of authenticity. When taken up in civil society, and by NGOs, for example, it seems all too easy for the self-definition of heritage to become a form of local particularism, or a 'Not-In-My-BackYard-ism' (the so-called 'NIMBY' tendency) that resists change or protects vested interests (a 'pulling-up of the "ladder"'). On the other hand, experts exhibit anxiety about what might be overlooked by such generally-local self-determination and fall back on the 'safe' and tested traditional policies of specialist-led selection and protection or musealisation, instead of using the full spectrum of heritage responses which these ideas advocate as part of greater flexibility.

The need for this greater flexibility can be seen to arise from the collision of four new paradigms within heritage theory and practice. First, there is the culturally sustainable viewpoint that heritage is the framework of everyday life, and that in order for it to play its part in society it must have room to change when necessary. Added to this is the increased scope of heritage, caused partly through increased participation, which means that heritage can now be 'everything'. But resources exist only to 'protect' the 'best': what do we do with the rest? Third, there has been a relocation of the value of a heritage object (artefact, building, city centre) from the object itself (i.e. as an intrinsic, inherent value) to the person/community who is seeing or valuing the thing (i.e. values are attributed, thus all heritage is intangible at some level); this leads, fourthly, to a revised interpretation of heritage as not merely bricks and mortar, but also (because the range of values attributed to heritage has expanded) as memory, symbolism and economic reuse, thus enabling forms of transmission other than the merely physical.

This flexibility is based on a wide spectrum of ways of 'doing' heritage, that begins (or finishes) with traditional heritage preservation, but includes the passing on of cultural skills and knowledge, the preservation and creation of identity, or the recognition of other 'audiences' as well as other heritage. This palette of options helps to achieve greater inclusion, better representation of cultural diversity and a broader fostering of intercultural dialogue. It uses creativity, innovation and artistic vitality both to pass on inherited heritage and to create modified and new forms of heritage for the future. This approach is close to seeing heritage as a social 'commons', something used sustainably and shared by everyone, a concept more usually associated with landscape discourse but equally valid with heritage. The converse, privileging the preservation of the fabric of monuments, can lead to a loss of use, neglect, vandalism, resentment, and to indifference among civil society. In such matters, we move into the realm of the relationship between culture and the economy. This has been examined only partly in our case studies and it still seems to be an ambiguous and complicated area that requires further research and thought. What are the risks of the instrumentalisation of culture and heritage? Why do so many people think it is bad?

'Mending its ways': culture and society

Several chapters raise unresolved issues, usually surrounding the inability or failure of policy makers (or the public) to resolve heritage issues. It could be said that this is because heritage can never be permanently resolved, being a process that is ever-changing and contingent upon cultural social context. But that avoids the issue, and at the same time, and especially in the context of the emergence and adoption of the new approaches to heritage outlined above, there are questions to ask about why governments, policy makers, the heritage sector and academia so often 'continue to follow the preservation paradigm' and 'give priority to ... top-down, object-oriented approaches and predetermined ... narratives'. Those words come from our chapter on Cyprus, in relation to a nation that is 'relatively newly-formed ... with an unstable and contested national identity', a circumstance in which a nation 'usually tries to avoid polyphony and instead uses heritage to construct a solid common past that will, it is imagined, unite its people'. Other case studies in the book come from similar contexts, and the difficulties described in the Cypriot situation probably apply much more widely; few nations now can claim to have fully stable narratives, given climate change, economic stress, demographic change or urbanisation (for example). Older countries have their identity and memory issues as well. Countries with a well-founded sense of nationhood and identity may suddenly find heritage-led narratives are turned upside down. It is not only countries that are so affected. These issues can apply to communities within countries, where (as several case studies show) groups by virtue of social status, lack of wealth or power, or marginalised positions are excluded both physically and symbolically from much of what society claims to offer to its members.

There are deep ideologies and political cultures to take into account when asking why heritage and cultural policies (and ultimately the place of culture within sustainable development) grow, improve or change only slowly or imperfectly. To take just the editors' own countries as examples (two countries separated by only a few kilometres of water but by several centuries of culture), we see two very different cultural approaches to governance, ideology, democracy, and policy making. One is a highly centralised, top-down, 'rational' state, but paradoxically with an ideal of the active citizen, the other is a neoliberal, semi-privatised, almost non-state, but paradoxically also centralised and top-down. Such differences affect approaches to everything, not least heritage, culture and sustainability, and are highly influential in how we approach the goal of a greater sustainability. They are all also born of cultural attitudes and cultural relationships acting through the medium of society. This is perhaps where the distinction between 'social sustainability' and 'cultural sustainability' becomes difficult to draw. It does not help that the 'social' in sustainable development is very often taken to mean not 'society' in the round, by which we mean, the framework for life, an actor in its own (collective) right and of course a product of cultural processes and decisions. Rather, the 'social pillar' normally in practice is confined to social problems and challenges, such as exclusion, inequality, deprivation or poverty. Even as a whole, sustainability development discourse does not really talk of the big concepts of society (or even civilisation), but relates mainly to very technical, practical solutions.

From their fundamentally cultural perspectives, the authors of our case studies do, however, touch on that wider and more intrinsic understanding of 'society'. In doing so, some speak of social sustainability, others of cultural sustainability. How to separate the cultural and the social in sustainability? Can they be separated? Where do they differ? Are cultural issues, as many actors consider, a part of the realm of social issues, or (as implied above) does culture act *through* societal frameworks and mechanisms? Probably it is to some degree an iterative and reciprocal relationship, in which culture constructs society but society shapes culture. To make an analogy, people have for thousands of years designed their architecture to contain their specific, culturally constructed lifestyles and economic activities; yet once built, the architecture in its turn shapes and changes how people live, so that their future 'ways of living', their culture, fit into the (by then) pre-existing structure. It seems that an inescapable conclusion of this book is that the term and the concept of 'cultural sustainability' remains under construction, and is still evolving. There is a lot more research and thinking to be done, and the new series of which this book is a volume has much territory to cover and much to achieve.

Index